Palgrave Studies in Languages at War

Series Editors
Hilary Footitt
Department of Modern Languages and
European Studies
University of Reading
Reading, UK

Michael Kelly
Department of Modern Languages
University of Southampton
Southampton, Hampshire, UK

Languages play a crucial role in conflict. They enable or disrupt communication between the people involved. They express the identities of the participants. They convey representations and interpretations of what is happening. And sometimes language differences are a key part of what the conflict is about.

This series brings together books which deal with the role of languages in many different kinds of conflict, including international war, civil war, occupation, peace operations, humanitarian action, the preludes to conflict and its aftermath. The series embraces interdisciplinary approaches, drawing on applied linguistics, sociolinguistics, translation studies, intercultural communication, history, politics, international relations, peace studies and cultural studies. Books in the series explore conflicts across a range of times and places and analyse the language-related roles and activities involved. The Editors welcome proposals for new contributions, including monographs and edited volumes.

Alamin Mazrui • Kimani Njogu

Swahili in Spaces of War

A Sociolinguistic Odyssey

palgrave
macmillan

Alamin Mazrui
Academic Building, West Wing
Rutgers, The State University of New Jersey
New Brunswick, NJ, USA

Kimani Njogu
Twaweza House, Muthithi Road
Mpesi Lane
Twaweza Communications
Nairobi, Kenya

ISSN 2947-5902 ISSN 2947-5910 (electronic)
Palgrave Studies in Languages at War
ISBN 978-3-031-27337-7 ISBN 978-3-031-27338-4 (eBook)
https://doi.org/10.1007/978-3-031-27338-4

© The Editor(s) (if applicable) and The Author(s), under exclusive licence to Springer Nature Switzerland AG 2023
This work is subject to copyright. All rights are solely and exclusively licensed by the Publisher, whether the whole or part of the material is concerned, specifically the rights of translation, reprinting, reuse of illustrations, recitation, broadcasting, reproduction on microfilms or in any other physical way, and transmission or information storage and retrieval, electronic adaptation, computer software, or by similar or dissimilar methodology now known or hereafter developed.
The use of general descriptive names, registered names, trademarks, service marks, etc. in this publication does not imply, even in the absence of a specific statement, that such names are exempt from the relevant protective laws and regulations and therefore free for general use.
The publisher, the authors, and the editors are safe to assume that the advice and information in this book are believed to be true and accurate at the date of publication. Neither the publisher nor the authors or the editors give a warranty, expressed or implied, with respect to the material contained herein or for any errors or omissions that may have been made. The publisher remains neutral with regard to jurisdictional claims in published maps and institutional affiliations.

Cover illustration: Arterra Picture Library / Alamy Stock Photo

This Palgrave Macmillan imprint is published by the registered company Springer Nature Switzerland AG.
The registered company address is: Gewerbestrasse 11, 6330 Cham, Switzerland

Acknowledgments

On the recommendation of Professor Kobus Marais of the Department of Linguistics and Language Practice at South Africa's University of the Free State, Professor Hilary Footitt, acquisitions and series editor for Palgrave Studies in Languages at War, contacted us on January 28, 2021, soliciting a book proposal on the theme of the series but focused specifically on an African experience. Two months later we had submitted a proposal on the subject of this book, "Swahili in Spaces of War," to which Hilary and the publishing editor, Cathy Scott, responded with great enthusiasm. And so the book project was born.

The speed with which we accepted the invitation had much to do with the fact that the kernels of the topic of this monograph were already present here and there in several of our earlier publications. These include:

Chapter 2 of Ali A. Mazrui and Alamin M. Mazrui's *Swahili, Society and the State: The Political Economy of an African Language*. Oxford: James Currey, 1995

Chapter 9 of Ali A. Mazrui and Alamin M. Mazrui's *The Power of Babel: Language and Governance in the African Experience*. Oxford: James Currey, 1998

Chapter 4 of Alamin Mazrui's *Cultural Politics of Translation: East Africa in a Global Context*. New York and London: Routledge, 2016

Chapter 6 of Alamin Mazrui and Kimani Njogu's *Mikondo ya Kiswahili: Siasa, Jamii na Utandawazi*. Nairobi: Twaweza Communications and Trento; Red Sea Press, 2022

For some of the chapters of this book, then, our efforts were directed at developing many of these seeds of ideas into a full-scale monograph.

The first draft of the manuscript for this book benefited immensely from comments and recommendations from two highly respected colleagues in the field of Swahili Studies: Dr Peter Githinji, Associate Professor and Chair of the Department of Kiswahili at Kenyatta University in Kenya, and Dr Aldin Mutembei, Julius Nyerere Professor of Kiswahili Studies at the University of Dar es Salaam, Tanzania. To both, we owe an immense debt of gratitude! Asanteni sana!

Contents

1 Introduction   1
  Alamin Mazrui

2 Swahili and the Maji Maji Resistance Against German Rule   29
  Kimani Njogu

3 Swahili in Military Context: Between World War I and World War II   57
  Alamin Mazrui

4 Swahili and Imperial Britain: Colonial Creation/African Appropriation   89
  Alamin Mazrui

5 Swahili and the Wars of the Great Lakes Region   117
  Alamin Mazrui and Kimani Njogu

6 Swahili in the Context of Cold Wars   147
  Alamin Mazrui

7 Swahili and the War on Terrorism 179
   Alamin Mazrui

8 Conclusion 215
   Alamin Mazrui

Index 225

List of Figures

Fig. 1.1 Swahili language usage (Rutgers Geography 2019)   4
Fig. 3.1 Sample page from *"First Aid" to the Swahili Language*   69

1

Introduction

Alamin Mazrui

This monograph examines the location and the role of Swahili in situations of violent conflict/wars and shows how the language is integral to our understanding of the conflicts discussed. Covering a period of over a century, the monograph traces some important dimensions of the Swahili language experience in conditions of conflict and their aftermath, beginning with the Maji Maji Resistance against German rule in what was then German East Africa and culminating in the ongoing experience of how the language continues to be deployed in the so-called war against terrorism. In geographical focus, some of the war situations explored here are "local," others are "transnational," and others still rather "global" in scope and ramifications. In the final analysis, this monograph, the first of its kind, provides crucial snapshots of the conflict-based history of the Swahili language in East Africa, demonstrating once again that language is a malleable tool that can be appropriated and galvanized to serve the interests of either party in a conflict and, through translation and interpretation, a means of creating hegemonic, anti-hegemonic, and counter-hegemonic meanings.

We realize, of course, that clashes of ideology underpin many of the wars discussed here, though ideological differences do not necessarily lead to violent conflict. African wars of resistance, from Maji Maji to Mau Mau, pitted particular forms of nationalism against imperialism. Militant Nazism exploded into the two world wars, just as the competition between communism and capitalism later came to frame the Cold War. In the aftermath of the Cold War, Westernism versus Islamism became the new fault line, at times articulated in the language of terrorism and anti-terrorism. In this monograph, however, we shall avoid discussion of the ideological foundations of the various wars, as this would only lead us away from our primary sociolinguistic focus on Swahili in spaces of war.

It is a universal fact of war that it can influence language change in various ways and in different directions. Among these is the influence of war in the creation of new words and expressions. With almost every major war discussed, Swahili experienced some growth in its lexicon related to the military and military technology, with its greatest expansion coinciding with the European colonial period and the participation of East Africans in the two world wars. Indeed, a study of Swahili's military terminology is also a study of the different layers of its war history.

Because it tends to bring different languages in contact with each other, the arena of war may impact a region in ways that can disturb and change the language ecology of a community. Such contact situations can lead to new linguistic formations. Kinubi, for example, the language of the Nubi people who settled in Kenya and Uganda especially during the British colonial period, is a creole of Arabic that evolved from a long history of military service of the people of south Sudan, first in independent Sudanese kingdoms like Darfur, then in Muhammad Ali's Egypt, and finally as conscripts in the King's African Rifles during World War I. Arguably, and as we shall see later in Chap. 3, the evolution of the variety known as Standard Swahili in the interwar period is also a product of the condition of war.

Wars are also known to have led to the endangerment and even extinction of languages or dialects. With regard to Swahili, however, its location in the military and war situations has often resulted in its expansion and consolidation rather than its decline. On the whole, the record seems to indicate that, combined with other factors, the conditions of war discussed in this book have broadened Swahili's geographic and demographic horizons.

Expansion of Swahili

Swahili is arguably the most widely spoken "indigenous" language on the African continent after Arabic. In its various forms, it is used to varying degrees as a first or additional language by millions of speakers in several countries in Eastern Africa, including Kenya, Tanzania, Uganda, the Democratic Republic of the Congo (DRC), Mozambique, Somalia, Burundi, Rwanda, and the Union of the Comoros. It is also spoken in some concentrations of East African Diaspora communities in England, Canada, and Oman and the Emirates. Described by Schadeberg (2009, 78) as a "contact language *par excellence*," Swahili is the national language of Kenya, Uganda, Tanzania, the Democratic Republic of the Congo, Rwanda, Burundi, and the Comoros, and has official or co-official status in Tanzania, Kenya, the Comoros, and Uganda (Fig. 1.1). How did the language acquire such a phenomenal geographic and demographic scope, and what have been the forces behind its expansion?

The bulk of the evidence would seem to suggest that the language remained overwhelmingly an East African coastal phenomenon until about 200 years ago. Its original native-speaking location is the East African coastal strip stretching from Kismayo in present-day Somalia, in the north, to the central part of the coast of Mozambique, in the south, and the adjacent islands of Zanzibar–Unguja and Pemba–Mafia, the Comoros, and the Lamu archipelago. How the language evolved over time, and how it spread to other parts of Eastern Africa and became the region's lingua franca, can be attributed in part to four primary forces: economics (especially commerce and mining), education and missionary activity, urbanization, and war. Let us look at the impact of each of these contact situations on the destiny of Swahili, bearing in mind that even those conditions underlying Swahili expansion that were not directly war-related were often underpinned by coercion and violence.

As a maritime society, the Swahili had a long, sustained history of interaction with peoples of the Orient. They are said to have "controlled most of the intercontinental commerce between the interior of Eastern and Southern Africa and the Eurasian world" for over 1000 years (Horton and Middleton 2000, 5). Particularly productive and strong in this trade

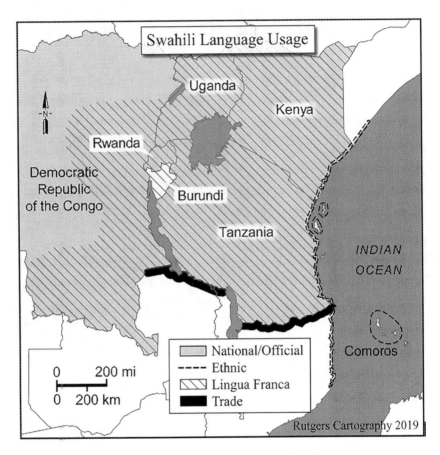

Fig. 1.1 Swahili language usage (Rutgers Geography 2019)

nexus was the relationship between the Swahili coast and the Arabian Peninsula. The earliest evidence of this Afro–Arab interaction appears in a 100 AD anonymous trader's manual in Greek which, among other things, records how well Arab seafarers knew the coast of East Africa and their familiarity with the language of the area due to continual interaction and intermarriage (Horton and Middleton 2000, 33).

Part of the impact of this history of Afro–Asian interaction was the Swahili adoption of a wide range of vocabulary items from a number of Asian languages. The most comprehensive study of these adopted words so far is that of Abdulaziz Y. Lodhi, *Oriental Influences in Swahili* (2000). Of all the Oriental languages that have influenced Swahili over the years, however, none has been more pronounced than Arabic. In a sense, Arabic is to Swahili what Latin has been to English – a major source of "loanwords" and the original donor of its earliest alphabet. And because Islam was such an important catalyst in its early formation, Swahili has long been associated with an Afro-Islamic identity. As discussed in Chap. 5, this Arabo-Islamic stimulus to and impact on the Swahili language became an issue of great concern in the European "civilizational war" to reconfigure and control the "native."

In addition to Oriental influences, of course, there was the impact of Portuguese, German, and English on the Swahili language. The two centuries of Portuguese presence in East Africa, from about 1498 to 1699, had a major effect of limiting Swahili contact with other Indian Ocean civilizations, because Portugal was bent on exercising complete control and monopoly of the Indian Ocean trade. The ultimate aim of the Portuguese "was nothing less than to suppress completely the previous ways of trade. They tried quite openly to prevent any direct traffic" between Indian Ocean ports (Strandes 1961, 49). Therefore, while the contact with the Portuguese did introduce some Portuguese terms into Swahili, this was a period of immensely reduced commercial and language contact between the Swahili coast and its Asian partners. At the same time, the persistent state of hostility between the Portuguese and some of the Swahili city-states like Mombasa mitigated against Portuguese influences on the Swahili language.

Commerce with the outside world (of Eurasia) was linked to trade with the interior of Africa. Swahili made tremendous gains through trade between the coast of East Africa and its hinterland. The beginnings of trade with the interior have been traced to the last quarter of the eighteenth century. But it was not until Seyyid Said bin Sultan, the Sultan of Oman, established full residence in Zanzibar in 1832 and consolidated the al-Busaidy sultanate on the East African coast – all arising indirectly from the Swahili-Portuguese wars (Strandes 1961) – that trade with the interior of the continent developed more substantially. The momentum of this trade was also a momentum of linguistic spread, extending the language further into the interior of what is today mainland Tanzania.

This trade also took Swahili all the way to the eastern region of the DRC, in the Katanga area. Swahili-speaking traders and porters interacted with local people in trading towns like Bukenya, in time making Swahili the primary language of trade and interethnic communication. Some of these traders and their porters settled in the DRC, giving Swahili a foothold and presence that would endure over time. At this time the Swahili of the area had not been influenced by the local Bantu languages and was most probably not too different from the Swahili of Tanganyika and its approximations.

Almost two centuries after the Portuguese, the East African coast came into contact with other European nations – Germany, Belgium, and Britain – all arriving on the scene in the 1880s. Germany took control of what came to be known as German East Africa, encompassing the area currently covered by mainland Tanzania, Rwanda, and Burundi, then called Tanganyika, Ruanda, and Urundi, respectively. In spite of initial opposition to Swahili from certain sections of the German colonial establishment, German colonialism gave a major boost to the consolidation of the language in the region, adopting it as the official language of communication through a system of indirect rule, education, and missionary activity. German plantations in East Africa, employing a multiethnic African labor force, became important sites for the continued rise of Swahili. However, the influence of the German language itself on Swahili was limited, perhaps partly because German rule in East Africa was short-lived, having come to an end by the conclusion of World War I.

Across the border from German East Africa was the British colony of Kenya. This was partly a British settler colony, and many of the settlers in the so-called White Highlands established commercial plantations of cash crops, especially tea, coffee, and pyrethrum. While their settlement was a colonial project of Britain in East Africa, many of the settlers themselves were motivated by the prospects of establishing cash crop plantations for commercial interests. Between the colonial administration, the missionaries, and the settlers, it was the latter that were the most ardent advocates of Swahili as the language that would better link settler capital and African labor. Many of these Englishmen in the colonial days insisted on speaking Swahili to their employees partly as a way of maintaining social distance even if neither spoke Swahili well enough while both spoke English fluently.

Education, combined with its interplay with missionary work, was yet another important factor in the spread of Swahili in Eastern Africa. Of course, the entry of Swahili into the mainstream of formal education in East Africa on any significant scale did not come until European countries colonized the region and missionaries infiltrated African societies. The great debate then got under way about the medium of instruction for Africans. This debate, especially when it touched upon the fundamental issues of educational policy, quite often became an issue between the Church and the State, between the missionary imperative of converting the soul and the administrative imperative of training the mind.

Swahili became part of this debate between the spiritually oriented missionary activist and the modernizing colonial administrator. Because Swahili developed within an Islamic culture and borrowed many Arabo-Islamic words, the language initially carried considerable Islamic associations. Some of the earliest evidence of colonial hostility toward Swahili on account of these associations came from Tanganyika under German rule (Wright 1971, 113). This was in the initial stages of colonial rule, when matters pertaining to education were often left in the hands of missionary societies.

Increasingly, however, the German administration became concerned that the mission schools were too narrowly focused on the spiritual at the expense of the intellectual and the cultural. And, as we show in Chap. 2, after the Maji Maji war, the German colonial administration amplified its efforts to promote the language in education and other domains of its dominion. Swahili was thus found to be an adequate medium to cater to the interests of missionaries, administrators, and German civilization at large. This realization was accompanied by increasing German interest in the idea of a standard Swahili.

Equally important as a sociolinguistic factor in the educational system in German East Africa was the rivalry between the English language and German. The presence of the English almost next door (in the Kenya Colony) became an additional impetus to German efforts to promote Swahili. English was seen as a direct threat to the establishment of German colonial control over its colonies (Pike 1986, 22). Interimperialist rivalry, then, led to a rather ironic position in German colonial circles with regard to the language of African education. A Germanic language, English, was a threat to the promotion of a sister culture of the Germans, but a Bantu language, Swahili, could be transformed to play precisely that role.

In the Belgian Congo (now DRC), the issue of Swahili's Islamic association does not seem to have concerned Belgian authorities at all. This might be explained in part by the possibility that the DRC's Swahili had already begun to assume a life of its own through adaptation of certain linguistic features of local Bantu languages and was somewhat different from the Swahili of the East African coast and, in part, by the absence of an Islamic population that was large enough to challenge the ascendancy of Christianity in the region.

More paramount in the Belgian mind – whenever there was some concern with the education of the Native – was the question of the medium of education most suitable for African education. A group of missionaries and colonial administrators felt that the educational interests of the African child would be served best by using French as the medium of instruction. Using perspectives on what was seemingly most practical in the situation, others argued for the use of one or more of the DRC's lingua francas. Others still favored the use of the mother tongue of the child. In the end, however, Belgian Congo settled for a solution that was deemed most pragmatic. It adopted Congo's four lingua francas – namely, Lingala, Swahili, Kikongo (-Kituba), and Tshiluba – for early primary education and retained French for the higher levels.

Where the linguistic debate between the soul and the mind came to feature even more prominently in East Africa was in the region of British rule. In the earliest days of European colonization and evangelism, the association of Swahili with Islam was not held against Swahili by the Christian missionaries. On the contrary, quite a number felt that since both Islam and Christianity were monotheistic religions drawn from the same Middle Eastern ancestry and shared a considerable number of spiritual concepts and values, Swahili would serve well as a language of Christianity precisely because Swahili could already cope with the conceptual universe of Islam. As in German East Africa, there was a quest for a standard Swahili that would serve missionary and educational needs in British colonies, a quest that did not materialize until after World War I.

Within a few years, however, there was a swing of opinion, and the principle began to hold sway among many missionaries that in the final analysis each African community could be consolidated in its Christianity by the efforts of its own indigenous members and by using the conceptual tools of its own indigenous cultures. Swahili became suspect precisely because it had developed into a lingua franca. A lingua franca was deemed unsuitable to reach the innermost thoughts of those undergoing conversion to Christianity. This principle received further support from the argument that was gaining international currency that a child should in any case be educated initially in their own language.

On the eve of Independence, then, English was already on an irreversible course to replace Swahili and other East African languages as the medium of instruction at all levels of education throughout the region. Nonetheless, different developments in East African countries during various periods in their postcolonial history eventually ensured that Swahili would continue to have a place in education. Ujamaa philosophy in Tanzania, a sense of African nationalism in Kenya, the rise to power of the National Resistance Movement in Uganda, and the conflicts in Rwanda and Burundi all opened up new spaces for the advancement of Swahili in East African schools.

The European colonial experience in East Africa also induced a momentum toward urbanization that had linguistic implications. As East Africa approached Independence, opportunities for the educated and semi-educated were disproportionately located in the urban areas. Many rural boys who were not so well educated and wanted to go to the city to look for employment as porters or domestic workers proceeded to acquire some competence in Swahili in order to facilitate their own individual urbanization. In other words, the educated went to the city because they had already acquired the English language; the less educated strove to acquire Swahili because they wanted to move to the city. At the same time, there must have been many from the rural areas who discovered the need to learn Swahili after they had migrated to the cities and, stimulated by the urban immersion environment, quickly proceeded to gain some proficiency in the language.

As East African cities grew and became home to a rapidly growing multiethnic and multilingual population, Swahili became increasingly central in horizontal interactions between Africans of the lower socioeconomic classes, as well as in vertical interactions between members of the African upper class and those in the lower ranks. During the colonial period, English served vertically as the medium of communication between British colonial administrators and the emergent educated African intelligentsia. Now it became the prominent medium of communication at the upper horizontal level of interethnic interaction between members of the African upper classes. In Kenya specifically, this coming together of urban populations speaking different languages sometimes also belonging to different language families gave rise to a simplified form of Swahili, which Bernd Heine (1979) described as "Kenyan Pidgin Swahili" and which is more commonly known as *Kiswahili cha Bara* (Upcountry Swahili). It is fair to say that Kenya Upcountry Swahili consists of a wide range of regionally and ethnically marked varieties across the country.

The growth of trade unionism in East Africa added a new and important organizational role of Swahili. The wage sector of each East African economy was expanding, and the workers after World War II began to experiment with collective bargaining. In Uganda, a significant proportion of the workforce came from Kenya, and trade unionism was for a while partially led and controlled by Kenyan immigrants as well. The importance of Swahili was enhanced in a situation where the labor force was not only multiethnic but also international. So closely was Swahili associated with workers and proletarian organizations in Uganda that the social prestige of the language among the more aristocratic Baganda declined substantially. It was deemed to be a language for "lower social classes" and of the migrant proletariat.

The pattern of urbanization and urban settlement in Kenya varied substantially from other Swahili-speaking areas of Eastern Africa. As partly a European settler colony, Kenya experienced a segregationist and quasi-apartheid system that, in urban areas like Nairobi, translated into some degree of residential zoning. Eastlands, the eastern side of Nairobi, became the primary area where African migrant workers were permitted to settle, while different parts of Westlands were populated by Europeans and Asians. After Independence, members of the African elite gradually moved into the hitherto exclusive European and Asian neighborhoods, while the postcolonial stream of African migrant laborers continued to settle in Eastlands. In other words, racial zoning during the colonial period now translated into social class zoning. While this residential division has become more complex over time, it is nonetheless true that sharp socioeconomic disparities is one of the most glaring factors in Nairobi's settlement and residential patterns. This residential partition may have stimulated the emergence of two youth languages in Nairobi, Sheng and Engsh (Nzunga 2002), which later spread to other urban areas of the country.

In addition to the impact of trade, education, and urbanization on the spread of Swahili, there has been the condition of war, the main subject of this book. War not only contributed to the expansion of Swahili, but also shaped the language in certain ways and served a variety of roles in the service of war combatants. And at times it precipitated new conditions that set the ground for new kinds of war.

In the final analysis, Swahili grew to become a preponderant language without being hegemonic. A preponderant language is triumphant itself, but its native speakers are not necessarily so; a hegemonic language in the African context, on the other hand, is one with a large and powerful constituency of native speakers. Swahili today is used as an additional language by hundreds of millions of East Africans who outnumber the native speakers of the language by a very large margin indeed. Swahili became accepted as a national language in both Kenya and Tanzania, without opposition from any of the other ethnic languages, partly because the Swahili people are not numerous enough as an ethnic unit to be a significant factor in the ethnic power politics in either of these two countries.

In spite of its geographic and demographic spread, and its functional expansion into domains of religion and politics, however, Swahili is yet to pose a serious threat to English in key areas of society like education, law, and governance. Even in a country like Tanzania where Swahili has made important strides, there is evidence that English continues to have a tremendous hold on the popular imagination of "modernity." In fact, one of the most remarkable linguistic features of many African societies south of the Sahara is the prevalence of European languages that are part of the legacy of European colonialism. Their presence is so predominant, and Africa's dependence on them so pervasive, that we have come to have this gross linguistic anomaly where whole classes of African countries are named after the imperial languages they have adopted as their official languages. We constantly refer to Anglophone Africa, Francophone Africa, Lusophone Africa, and so on. How does one explain this pervasive linguistic state of affairs in postcolonial Africa?

Language and Nationalism: Between Internal and External Wars

From the very beginning of European incursions into African societies, there were forms of armed African uprising and resistance. Because these "primary resistance" movements were founded on local structures and forms of authority, they were met with strong colonial military might as part of wars of imperial conquest bent on the subjugation of African populations not only politically, but also culturally. The European response aimed not only at defeating the African resisters militarily, but also at destroying the very cultural foundations that had inspired and consolidated those movements in the first place. It is in these wars that we can locate the root of the linguistic imposition and ascendency of European languages in Africa whose maintenance thrived on a continued state of cultural war against local institutions and traditions.

But colonial military and political conquest of Africa offers only part of the explanation for the dominance of European languages in Africa. After all, Asia too was colonized, yet nobody refers to Anglophone Asia or Francophone Asia. What then is the difference between Africa and Asia? It lies in the scale of nationalism. Statewide nationalism in Africa is made more difficult partly because of the relative weakness of loyalty to local languages – a factor that in turn facilitated Euro-linguistic penetration. The less nationalistic a society is, the more vulnerable it becomes to penetration from outside. The fact that most African languages south of the Sahara were unwritten before European colonization could be one of the reasons for Africa's diluted commitment to their preservation. The national boundaries of most African states, themselves a product of competition and wars between European states, lack the underpinning of any national linguistic identity.

Linguistic nationalism is that version of nationalism that is concerned about the value of its own languages, seeks to defend them against other languages, and encourages their use and enrichment. Africans south of the Sahara have been nationalistic about their race, and often about their land; and, of course, many have been nationalistic about their particular ethnic groups. But nationalism about African languages has been relatively weak as compared with India, the Middle East, or France, for example.

It is indeed relevant, but not adequate, to point out that most boundaries of African nations south of the Sahara have created multilingual countries. Deciding which local language to promote as a national language within those boundaries carries the danger of ethnic rivalry and the possibility of conflicts and wars arising from perceived ethnolinguistic hegemony. This is a point of view that has been expressed repeatedly by African politicians and policy makers in favor of continued use of European languages. Any move to make Hausa the national language of Nigeria, it is said, could precipitate a national crisis in Yorubaland and Igboland. After all, though Hausa is a transnational lingua franca spoken by tens of millions of West Africans, it is considered potentially hegemonic because those to whom Hausa is a native tongue constitute a large proportion of the Nigerian population.

On the other hand, we need to bear in mind that India too is a multilingual country. Its language policies in favor of Hindi have at times provoked riots. The original constitutional ambition to make Hindi (a northern language) the language of all India met stiff resistance in the South. The Tamil Nadu region, for example, has experienced several anti-Hindi agitations and riots that go back to the 1930s. In Chennai, there is even a structure constructed to memorialize those who died in the anti-Hindi riots. Compromises have had to be made. In spite of the presence of so many languages in India – and sometimes because of it – linguistic nationalism is one of the continuing political forces in the land.

One of the reasons for this relatively low linguistic nationalism in most African countries may have to do with the non-expansionist history of much of the continent. It is one of Africa's glories that in spite of the artificial borders that have split ethnic and linguistic groups, there have been very few border clashes or military confrontations between African countries. But it is also a terrible fact to acknowledge that one of the tragedies of the African state is that there has not been enough tension and conflicts between states. The balance between external conflicts and internal conflicts has tilted too far on the side of the internal. The external borders have often remained friendly. And as human history has revealed time and again, civil wars often leave deeper scars, are more often indiscriminate and more ruthless, than are interstate conflicts short of a world war or a nuclear war (Licklider 1993). The USA, for example, lost more people in its own civil war in the 1860s than in any other single war in its history so far, including Vietnam and the two world wars.

Moreover, the history of the nation-state in Europe reveals a persistent tendency of the European state to externalize conflict and thus help promote greater unity at home. A sense of nationhood within each European country was partly fostered by a sense of rivalry and occasional conflict with its neighbors. And the consolidation of the sovereignty of European states, too, was forged partly in the fire of inter-European conflicts. The Peace of Westphalia of 1684, often credited with the formal launching of the nation-state system, was signed after thirty years of European interstate conflict and wars (Lee 1991).

What ought to be remembered, therefore, is that the state system that Africa has inherited from Europe was nurtured in the bosom of conflict and war. It can even be argued that, just as one cannot make an omelet without breaking eggs, one cannot build and strengthen statehood and nationhood without the stimulus of calculation and conflict. The only question is whether the conflict is with outsiders or with the state's own citizens. Postcolonial Africa is burdened disproportionately with internalized conflict. At least in the short run, internalized conflicts are detrimental to the consolidation of statehood and to the promotion of a shared sense of nationhood in the population, without which strong linguistic nationalism that could militate against linguistic domination by others is unlikely to emerge.

Ironically, when it comes to language as a source of conflict and war, Africans south of the Sahara have been inspired more by the imperial languages than by their own local languages. In Apartheid South Africa, the tension was between Afrikaans and English rather than between either of these two languages and the local languages. Until the 1990s, the great divide between Black and White South Africa was indeed racial. But the great divide between White and White was, in fact, linguistic. The White communities of South Africa were the Afrikaans-speaking Afrikaners, on the one hand, and the English-speaking Europeans, on the other. Language had ethnicized the White population of South Africa.

In time, however, this linguistic division between the White communities of South Africa also came to have its own impact on the Black population of the country. More and more Black South Africans felt that if they had to choose between English and Afrikaans, the former was of greater pan-African relevance. Two languages of Germanic origin had widely differing implications. Afrikaans was a language of racial claustrophobia; English was a language of pan-African interaction. The bloody Soweto uprising of 1976, precipitated in part by the forced use of Afrikaans as a medium of education in African schools, was part of that linguistic dialectic and tension.

An African country that is in a category of its own perhaps is Cameroon. It is the only African country that has two ex-colonial languages, English and French, as official languages. This policy has essentially framed much of the linguistic debate in the Cameroons along the lines of English-speaking and French-speaking regions, relegating the role of local languages to a subsidiary position. The two languages have become preeminent even in the question of Cameroonian identity. In the process several "sociolinguistic problems have emerged between the Anglophones and the Francophones because each of them prioritises their colonially-inherited identity and language even over the locally-based indigenous language identity" (Anchimbe 2011, 8). Claiming increasing marginalization by Francophones, Anglophones launched their own political parties, some with their own military wings like the Ambazonia Defense Forces and the Southern Cameroon Defense Forces, inspired by separatist objectives.

Functions of Language in War and War's Impact on Language

In the rest of the region of Africa south of the Sahara, what has been more prevalent is not language as a cause of war, but language as a tool of war employed for organizational, inspirational, and propaganda purposes. The Swahili people, for example, have been involved in several wars in the course of their long history. These have included wars with the Portuguese, with Arabs of Oman, and with each other in inter-city-state conflicts. They also participated in wars of resistance to more modern forms of colonialism, especially against Germany and Britain. In all these instances, Swahili served as a language of command for both organizational and strategic purposes.

Equally important has been the use of language to inspire the fighters. In many African societies, this role of language in war was often entrusted to griots and poets. Sundiata, the legendary king of Mali, for example, had a griot, Balla Fasséké, who regularly delivered passionate speeches before the beginning of every war to inspire Sundiata's forces. Giving such a speech before the Battle of Krina, Balla concluded by saying:

> Griots are men of the spoken word, and by the spoken word we give life to the gestures of kings. But words are nothing but words; power lies in deeds. Be a man of action; do not answer me any more with your mouth, but tomorrow, on the plain of Krina, show me what you would have me recount to coming generations. Tomorrow allow me to sing the 'Song of Vultures' over the bodies of thousands of Sosso whom your sword will have laid before evening. (Niane 1965, 63)

In spite of Balla's claim that "words are nothing but words," it is precisely his words that inspired the heroic action that was to feed the words of griots with stories of their gallantry in later years.

The role played by Sundiata's Balla Fasséké was evident in the lives of leading poets of the East African coast. Almost every city-state had its own poets who were expected to galvanize the power of their words in the service of the state in times of war. The city-state of Mombasa, for example, had its Muyaka wa Mwinyi Haji and Lamu had Zahidi Mgumi. Some of Muyaka's poems, in particular, "are those that refer to the historical incidents that took place in Mombasa and the rest of the Swahili Coast in the first four decades of the nineteenth century. The poems seem to express the patriotic spirit of the people of Mombasa in their long, drawn-out struggles against repeated attempts by Seyyid Said, the Imam of Muscat, to colonize them" (Abdulaziz 1979, 114).

In one of his well-known verses, for example, Muyaka urges his compatriots from the Kenyan Coast, especially Mombasa, Lamu, and Pate, to unite in resistance against colonial attempts of the Omani Arabs and scoffs at the Omanis' military ability:

Jifungetoni masombo mshike msu na ngao
Zile ndizo zao sambo, zijile zatoka kwao
Na tuwakulie kombo tuwapige hario
Wakija tuteze nao, wayawiwiapo ngomani

Fasten your belts and arm yourselves with spears and shields
Yonder are the ships coming from their far lands;
Take your war positions and let us cry out to them: Ahoy, here we are!
When they alight let's fight them, if it is to the battle-field that they have come.

Perhaps inspired by Mombasa's other name, Mvita (the War City), the poem depicts the natives as warriors by nature, with war itself "likened to a dance to give the impression that war to the Mombasans was so much part and parcel of their everyday life" (Abdulaziz 1979, 128).

Many of the poetic compositions of the early nineteenth century, however, are related to conflicts and wars between Swahili city-states themselves. Many of the verses are inspirational in nature, with each poet seeking to arouse the patriotism and courage of fighters from his own community. As Abdulaziz (1979, 114–155) and Shariff (1988, 121–130) demonstrate, however, many of the poems also had a propaganda value, often intended to instill fear in the forces of the enemy. As a result, threats and provocations became a recurring part of the poetic discourse in the form of wars of words on the eve of military engagements on the battlefield. This state of affairs explains, at least in part, why Swahili works of poetry of the precolonial period have been such "indelible records of military terms" (Adika Kevogo and Kevogo 2014, 177).

As much as language plays different roles and has different functions in different war situations, war and its aftermath can also have an impact on language. One of the impacts of war on Swahili has to do with the expansion of the language demographically, on the one hand, and lexically, on the other. World War I, World War II, the First Congo War (1996–1997) that ousted Mobutu Sese Seko, and the war of the National Resistance Army that brought an end to the reign of Milton Obote are examples of wars that may have stimulated the spread of Swahili among sections of East Africans. In the process, as Adika Kevogo and Kevogo (2014) show, with every war the Swahili language acquired new sets of vocabulary items related to the military.

But the end of war, too, can have implications for language. It is easy to see how the end of a war that was triggered in part by a language conflict of one kind or another – as was the case with the 1971 Bangladesh Liberation War – could affect the fate of language(s) depending on who is the winner and who the loser. But even when language is not one of the causes of war, the outcome of a war can have a significant impact on the linguistic landscape of a country or region. The fate of the Igbo language of Nigeria today might have been quite different if the Biafrans in the Nigerian civil war (1967–1970) had succeeded in their secessionist ambition. As we argue in Chap. 3, if Germany had not been defeated decisively in World War I, and continued to hold onto its East African colony, Swahili might have been consolidated much faster in Tanzania, though the situation might have weakened the language's integrative potential on the wider regional plane. In Uganda, Swahili was long associated negatively with the army, especially because the army was an arm of an unpopular state, first under Milton Obote and later under Idi Amin. But as we show in Chap. 5, the victory of the National Resistance Army that had taken Swahili as its organizational language against the Ugandan army of Milton Obote had an immediate positive effect on the fortunes of Swahili in Uganda.

War and the Swahili Literary Imagination

Poetry was crucial not only at the very moment of war, but also later as a reflection and record of war events. Wars have repeatedly tended to inspire Swahili poets over the centuries, many narrating the heroic deeds of combatants from the community that the poets support and identify with. Some of the wars that have been a subject of Swahili poetry go back to the earliest years of the founding of Islam. The latter include *Utenzi wa Vita vya Uhud* (The narrative poem of the Battle of Uhud) with verses of unknown authorship that were collected and compiled by Haji Cham, in which Muslims, heavily outnumbered, fought courageously to gain the upper hand initially, but were eventually vanquished by their non-Muslim Arab compatriots in 625 AD. The period immediately following the ascendancy of Islam witnessed a series of Muslim-Byzantine wars that inspired *Utenzi wa Tambuka* (The narrative poem of Tabuk) – sometimes known as *Chuo cha Herekali* (The book of Heraclius) – that was composed by Mwengo wa Athumani in 1728. In this category we can include some of the *tenzi* (narrative poems) mentioned by Jan Knappert (1983, 52–57), including *Utenzi wa Katirifu* (Narrative poem of Katirifu) by Abu Bakari Mwengo, *Utenzi wa Rasi'l Ghuli* (Narrative poem of Rasi l'Ghuli) by Mgeni bin Faqihi, and *Utenzi wa Vita vya Badiri* (Narrative poem of the Battle of Badr) of unknown authorship.

If Islamic nationalism inspired poems like *Utenzi wa Vita vya Uhud* and *Utenzi wa Tambuka*, African nationalism in the twentieth century came to inspire literary works of another category of wars, wars of resistance against European colonial rule. With regard to Tanzania, such writings in poetry have included *Utenzi wa Vita vya Wadachi Kutamalaki Mrima* (Narrative poem of the German war to conquer the Mrima/Swahili coast) by Sheikh Hemed bin Abdallah Al-Buhry and *Utenzi wa Vita vya Maji Maji* (Narrative poem of the Maji Maji War) by Abdul Karim Jamaliddin on Tanzania's earliest nationalist war of resistance (1905–1907) to German rule. Before the Maji Maji war, of course, there was the ethnic-based war of resistance led by Chief Mkwawa of the Hehe people of south-central Tanzania that, at least in its guerilla form, continued until Mkwawa's death in 1898. The Hehe war inspired Mwengo Shomari to produce his *Utenzi wa Mkwawa* (Narrative poem of Mkwawa).

Both these wars of resistance in what was to become Tanzania, the Hehe and the Maji Maji wars, also inspired the production of dramatic works. Most popular among these has been Ebrahim Hussein's *Kinjeketile*, focused on Kinjeketile Ngwale, purported to have been the leader and spirit medium of the Maji Maji uprising. Since its publication in 1969, the play has been read and performed in numerous schools in East Africa, especially in Kenya and Tanzania. An important but less known play (at least in Kenya) is *Mukwava wa Uhehe* by Mugyabuso Mulokozi. Though both these plays are deemed to be fictional by their authors, they draw primarily on available historical records and community memory about the leaders of the two East African resistance movements.

In Kenya, the most widely known anti-colonial war has been the Mau Mau against British colonialism. Ironically, however, apart from its relatively brief mention in Salim Kibao's *Utenzi wa Uhuru wa Kenya* (Narrative poem of the independence of Kenya), the Mau Mau war has not been a source of poetic celebration in the *utenzi* tradition as the Maji Maji war has been in Tanzania. Part of the reason for this poetic "erasure" may have to do with the fact that until recently, successive Kenyan political regimes have been hostile to the memorialization of Mau Mau, almost maintaining a silent policy of erasure of the history and memory of Mau Mau. Nonetheless, the Mau Mau has inspired at least one Swahili novelette, *Kaburi bila Msalaba* (A grave without a cross) by Peter Kareithi, and the less known Swahili play *Mkuki wa Moto* (Spear of fire) by Farouk Muslim and Said Mzee.

The East African region, of course, has experienced other kinds of wars that have also been the subject of literary attention. These have included wars between states in the greater East African region, with the war between Tanzania and Uganda in particular inspiring Henry Muhanika's *Utenzi wa Vita vya Kagera* (Narrative poem of the War of Kagera), and World War II that went on to inspire Shaaban Robert to compose his *Utenzi wa Vita ya Uhuru* (Narrative poem of the war of freedom/liberty). On the other hand, country-internal wars, like the Shifta War in Kenya, the war of the National Resistance Army that toppled the second Milton Obote regime in Uganda, or the civil wars in the Congo, are yet to arouse the artistic impulse of East African poets and writers.

One observation that emerges from our discussion so far is that the composers of all the Swahili war-related *tenzi*, plays, and prose texts have been male. In the West African Hausa society, Nana Asma'u, the celebrated daughter of Sheikh Usman Dan Fodio, and other Hausa women who had acquired literacy in Arabic and the Ajami scripts are known to have been important contributors to what came to be known as "jihad literature" (Alidou 2002, 141). There is nothing comparable to these Hausa women's experiences in the Swahili-speaking world. This gendered literary space is reminiscent of Nwoye, the son of Okonkwo in Chinua Achebe's *Things Fall Apart* who was always drawn to his mother's stories rather than to the masculine stories of violence and bloodshed that his father loved to narrate. This narrative situation also seems akin to the distinction that Alidou draws in Hausa oral literature between *tatsuniya*, the type of stories crafted and transmitted by women, and *tarihi*, "epic narratives about historical heroes" that tend to be in the male domain of transmission (Alidou 2002, 139). The absence of women authors in the Swahili language so far in the area of war-related imaginative works begs the question as to whether Swahili war literature, if one can construct such a category, will develop as a primarily male genre.

Finally, let us conclude this section by mentioning a particular category of Swahili "war" poetry. If Swahili poetry has been used to inspire war combatants and as a means of recalling and recording war events, it has also served as a weapon of war. There is an entire genre of Swahili poetry, *mashairi ya kulumbana* (*malumbano*) – dueling poetry – in which words, poetically framed, rather than guns, swords, and spears, serve as the arms of war. Like the Lebanese *zajal* and other poetry duels and contests in parts of Africa, Asia, the Middle East, and other areas of the world, poets from different sides engage in a war of poetic words, often in the presence of a public audience, where the act of composition is often spontaneous and improvisational. This poetic tradition is amply exemplified in Yunus Rafiq's 2012 documentary film *Swahili Fighting Words*, in which two "youth gangs," Zula Moyo and Macho Tumbo, repeatedly engage in public poetic battles, especially over the issue of local identities and citizenship rights, in colonial Tanzania of the 1940s.

Outline of the Book

The body of this book is divided roughly into two parts, each consisting of three chapters, excluding the introduction and the conclusion. The first part (Chaps. 2, 3, and 4) focuses on wars that took place during the European colonial period in which Africans were players or played a part as a direct result of the colonial condition. Part two, comprising Chaps. 5, 6, and 7, deals with wars in the postcolonial period, even though these conflicts too are directly or indirectly part of East Africa's imperial history and connections.

In Chap. 2, we begin with the observation that before the Maji Maji war of resistance against German rule (1905–1907), no extensive efforts were made by the German colonial government to promote either German or Swahili in what was then German East Africa. But the Maji Maji war confirmed some of the worst fears of sections of the German colonial establishment about the unifying role of the presumed intersection between the Swahili language and the Islamic religion. The Maji Maji war led to a decisive shift in German colonial language policy, for the resistance demonstrated clearly the power of Swahili and its Arabic-derived script, in polemics as in poetry, to unify and mobilize the African subjects against German colonial rule. The "minimalist" approach to German colonial administration with regard to the utility of the language now gave way to purposeful colonial policy that included deliberate interventions to (re)configure and control Swahili and (re)direct its (socio)linguistic development.

Chapter 3 turns to the effects of World War I and World War II and their aftermath on the destiny of Swahili in East Africa, including the emergence of a Swahili variety used almost exclusively by conscripts of the King's African Rifles (KAR). A distinction is drawn between British East Africa, German East Africa, and the Belgian Congo in terms of how World War I influenced the fortunes of Swahili. More important than the actual war itself for the future of Swahili was its *outcome*. The interwar period raised the important question of coordinating, if not integrating, the armed forces of the King's African Rifles regionally. In the meantime, the imminence of World War II and the possibility of wider recruitment, as well as the problem of a suitable language of command, effective enough for a multilinguistic unit of East African forces, assumed a new prominence, with Swahili taking center stage and Swahili periodicals and media featuring as significant instruments of war.

Outside the context of the world wars, we see in Chap. 4 how British engagement with linguistic diversity was part and parcel of its colonial project in East Africa. In time this led to the "discovery" of Swahili as a potential tool of regional control. As Joseph Errington points out in his book *Linguistics in a Colonial World* (2008), colonial agents turned "alien ways of speaking into objects of knowledge, so that their speakers could be made subjects of colonial power" (2008, vii). We also examine how British colonial functionaries sought to reconfigure, even reinvent, Swahili, to better serve the colonial project, with the colonial education system as an important crucible. But as the chapter demonstrates, far from rejecting it as a linguistic product of colonialism, sections of the East African community appropriated it and transformed it into an instrument of resistance through political organizing, trade union mobilization, and publication of both colonial and anti-colonial periodicals.

The Great Lakes region, the subject of Chap. 5, has experienced multifarious conflicts in recent times. These have included the Tanzania-Uganda War or Kagera War of 1979 that led to the ouster of General Idi Amin Dada in Uganda, and the Luwero War of 1989 that was launched by the National Resistance Army (NRA) of Yoweri Museveni against the government of Milton Obote and, later, Tito Okello. It is significant that a large proportion of the NRA combatants were Banyarwanda in ethnic compositions. Sections of this Banyarwanda constituency in the NRA were later to form the core of the Rwandan Patriotic Front, which subsequently, with its base in Uganda, engaged in a prolonged war (1990–1994) with the Rwandan Armed Forces. Other wars of the region included the two Congo wars (1996–1997 and 1998–2003), the series of civil wars in Somalia, and the Sudan civil wars that eventually led to the creation of the Republic of Southern Sudan, though these are not the subject of this book. All these wars had a direct impact on the fortunes of Swahili partly because of the important role played by the Swahili-speaking nations of Tanzania and Kenya in the service of one or the other of the warring parties.

In the meantime, as we discuss in Chap. 6, the Cold War propelled Swahili to a new position in the international relations policies of both the USA and the Soviet Union. In the USA in particular, Swahili (among other languages) became linked to the vision and mission of "Area Studies," itself a direct response to the Cold War. This war coincided with a cultural cold war that was best expressed by the Black Power movement that, in part, demanded greater visibility of Africa and the African Diaspora in the corridors of the American academy. In the process, Swahili gained new visibility not only in the American and Russian academies, but also in broadcasts of Voice of America and Radio Russia for propaganda purposes. There were also competing Swahili translation projects by the two superpowers, all intended to influence the ideological direction of "Swahiliphone" Africa. In addition to an analysis of all of these Cold War developments in the Swahili experience, this chapter demonstrates how East Africans responded to these superpower designs in Swahili by creating alternative readings of the translations to lend support, not to one or the other of the superpowers, but to their own struggles against internal tyranny. With the end of the ideological Cold War, there arose another cold war, an economic war between the USA and China that, as the chapter shows, also has had implications for Swahili.

Finally, in Chap. 7, we look at Swahili in the context of the war on terrorism. As Emily Apter shows in *The Translation Zone* (2006), it became clear in the tragic wake of 9/11 how linguistically unprepared the USA was in interpreting the intercepts, documents, and intentions of "the enemy." As a result, the study of "foreign" languages moved to the fore as an issue of major political significance, taking on special relevance as a matter of war and peace. This development led to the creation of the National Security Education Program and its African Flagship Languages project to promote the study of "critical" languages, Swahili among them, to support America's war against terrorism (in the East African region). In the process, as the chapter shows, the US government engaged in (Swahili) translation projects involving selections of texts and visuals that enacted particular significations that answered to the condition of war (on terrorism), and that took for granted the idea that mistranslation is part of a legitimate strategy in a time of war. This centrality of Swahili in America's war on terrorism in East Africa can be traced to the perceived role of

Swahili-speaking Muslims in anti-American violent extremism and their suspected links with the Al-Shabaab organization in neighboring Somalia. In the conclusion (Chap. 8), in addition to providing a summary of the main points emanating from the different chapters, we offer a reading of how the experiences of "Swahili in spaces of war" contribute to our wider understanding of language in conflict/war situations and the kinds of new questions it raises for future research on the subject.

Terminology: Between Swahili and Kiswahili

In closing, a word about terminology used in the book should be added. Writing about the Swahili language in English poses a problem of choice between a terminology of authenticity and a terminology of intelligibility. With regard to Swahili Studies, in particular, the tradition of terminological authenticity has sought to maintain a distinction between the following derivatives as used by the Swahili people themselves:

Kiswahili =	Name of the language
Mswahili =	Single member of the Swahili community
Uswahili =	Swahili culture and ways of life
Uswahilini =	Land inhabited by the Swahili
Waswahili =	Swahili people

The tradition of terminological intelligibility, on the other hand, shows greater sensitivity to the linguistic rules of the medium of discourse itself, in this case the English language. The French people refer to their language as *français*, but in English it is known as French. Intelligibility would likely be affected if we were to retain the French term in an English sentence as in "*Le français* is spoken in over twenty African countries." The same logic applies to "Swahili." Observing the different derivations of the term "Swahili" when writing in English would not be in accord with the morphological rules of the language. To do so, therefore, would be to maintain authenticity at the expense of intelligibility. Many "Swahilists" are strong adherents of terminological authenticity and may consider a departure from this tradition as a kind of "terminological betrayal." In our opinion, however, both these traditions are equally valid. But because our readers may include those who are not familiar with the Swahili language, we have opted not to follow the common Swahilist terminological practice, in the interest of terminological intelligibility. Throughout this text, therefore, "Swahili" will appear independently without the usual prefixes and suffixes that distinguish between the language, the culture, the people, and their homeland.

References

Abdulaziz, Mohamed H. 1979. *Muyaka:19th Century Swahili Popular Poetry*. Nairobi: Kenya Literature Bureau.

Adika Kevogo, Stanley, and Alex Umbima Kevogo. 2014. Swahili Military Terminology: A Case of an Evolving Non-Institutionalized Language Standard. *Research on Humanities and Social Sciences* 14 (21): 176–193.

Alidou, Ousseina. 2002. Gender, Narrative Space, and Modern Hausa Literature. *Research in African Literatures* 33 (2): 137–153.

Anchimbe, Eric A. 2011. The English Language and the Construction of a Cameroonian Anglophone Identity. In *Postcolonial Linguistic Voices: Identity Choices and Representations*, ed. Eric A. Anchimbe and Stephen A. Mforteh, 77-96l. Berlin: Walter de Gruyter.

Apter, Emily. 2006. *The Translation Zone: A New Comparative Literature*. Princeton, NJ: Princeton University Press.

Errington, Joseph. 2008. *Linguistics in a Colonial World: A Story of Language, Meaning and Power*. Oxford: Blackwell.

Heine, Bernd. 1979. Some Linguistic Characteristics of African based Pidgins. In *Readings in Creole Studies*, ed. I.F. Hancock, E. Polomé, M. Goodman, and B. Heine, 89–98. Ghent: E. Story-Scientia.

Horton, Mark, and John Middleton. 2000. *The Swahili. The Social Landscape of a Mercantile Society*. Oxford-Malden, MA: Blackwell Publishers.

Knappert, Jan. 1983. *Epic Poetry in Swahili and Other African Languages*. Leiden: E. J. Brill.

Lee, Stephen J. 1991. *The Thirty Years War*. London: Routledge.

Licklider, Roy, ed. 1993. *Stop the Killing: How Civil Wars End*. New York: New York University Press.

Lodhi Abdulaziz Y. 2000. *Oriental Influences in Swahili: A Study in Language and Culture Contacts*. Ph.D Dissertation. Göteborg University.

Niane, D.T. 1965. *Sundiata: An Epic of Old Mali*. Trans. G.D. Pickett. Essex: Longman.

Nzunga, Kibande Michael Peter. 2002. Sheng and English: The Booming Offspring of Linguistic Intermarriage. In *Language in Contrast*, ed. Ingrid Rissom, 87–94. Bayreuth: African Studies 51.

Pike, Charles. 1986. History and Imagination: Swahili Literature and Resistance to German Language Imperialism in Tanzania 1885–1910. *International Journal of African Historical Studies* 19 (2): 201–234.

Schadeberg, Thilo C. 2009. Loanwords in Swahili. In *Loanwords in the World's Languages: A Comparative Handbook*, ed. Martin Haspelmath and Uri Tadmor, 76–102. Berlin: Mouton de Gruyter.

Shariff, Ibrahim Noor. 1988. *Tungo Zetu: Msingi wa Mashairi na Tungo Nyinginezo*. Trenton, NJ: The Red Sea Press.

Strandes, Justus. 1961. *The Portuguese Period in East Africa*. Nairobi: East African Literature Bureau.

Wright, Marcia. 1971. *German Missions in Tanganyika: 1891–1941*. Oxford: Clarendon Press.

2

Swahili and the Maji Maji Resistance Against German Rule

Kimani Njogu

The Maji Maji war (1905–1907) against German rule in what was then called German East Africa is widely regarded to have been one of the most formative and transformative periods in the history of Tanzania. In the realm of Swahili language studies, it is recognized that German colonialism itself was quite consequential in the demographic and geographic spread of the language. The Maji Maji war and its aftermath had additional implications for the fortunes of Swahili, especially in the nation that became known as Tanzania. It also went on to inspire Swahili creative writers to produce quasi-imaginative works that have been read and performed widely and that continue to inscribe a particular reading of that moment in the minds of subsequent generations of East Africans.

As we have seen in Chap. 1, by the nineteenth century, Swahili had spread from the coastal region to the hinterland through exploration, trade, and missionary activities. Trading centers had emerged due to demands especially for ivory and slaves. Upcountry communities, such as the Nyamwezi, Yao, and Sukuma, engaged in business with Swahili and Arab traders who sought to meet global commercial demands and had easy access to the Indian Ocean markets through trading centers along the coast such as Bagamoyo, Pangani, and Zanzibar. During these trading ventures, Swahili and Islam spread further afield, inserting themselves alongside and competing with upcountry languages and religious beliefs. As a foreign way of life with relative power and prestige on account of its trade associations across borders, coastal Swahili culture was viewed as relatively prestigious and sophisticated.

Christian missionaries entered Tanganyika in the early 1800s and embarked on learning Swahili as well as other African languages to advance their mission. Johann Ludwig Krapf (1810–1881) translated the New Testament, wrote a simple Swahili grammar, and developed a list of Swahili lexical items. On their part, Johannes Rebmann (1820–1876) translated the Bible into Swahili, Bishop Edward Steere (1828–1882) translated a book of hymns and basic grammar, and Reverend C. Buttner of the German Evangelical Mission Society (Lutherans) wrote a Swahili grammar book. These missionaries had learnt that their evangelization would only succeed if they paid attention to Swahili, which was already popular, having established itself as a lingua franca and a language of interethnic communication along the trade routes. Generally, while away from the trade routes where other languages were in use, conversion into Christianity was often accompanied by acquisition of literacy skills and the use of Swahili in religious activities. The new converts preached in Swahili and spread the language in communities as they evangelized.

The language was also an inter-European facility and was used among European missionaries who did not have a common language. According to Michelle Moyd: "In a situation where Europeans of many different backgrounds were likely to encounter each other in a foreign environment, Kiswahili provided them a common language through which they could communicate to conduct business and personal affairs" (1997, 21). Even as the missionaries used Swahili in their work, there were those who considered the language to be a carrier of the Islamic faith and ill equipped as the language of Christianity. Moreover, they argued, it was written in the Arabic script and was therefore a tool for advancing Arabic beliefs and worldview through its orthography. In matters of spirituality, Islam was considered the "ultimate religious other and its linguistic conveyor, Swahili, as an anathema to the very spirit of Christianity" (Mazrui 2017, 58).

The Quiet Entry of German Rule in East Africa

During the formative stages of colonial occupation, German colonial presence in East Africa was principally a private affair. It is in this context that the German colonial explorer Carl Peters (1856–1918) had founded the Society for German colonization (later renamed *Deutsch Ostafrikanische Gesellschaft* [German East Africa Society], DOAG), before the 1885 Berlin Conference in which European nations determined their spheres of influence in Africa. In making inroads into Africa, Carl Peters was driven by the urge to identify and procure colonies for Germany, enhancing the status of the German Reich, and benefiting personally from his activities in East Africa. Through a number of expeditions, he signed "treaties" with local leaders in which the latter ceded their land to the DOAG. Soon after the Berlin Conference, Chancellor Otto von Bismarck (1815–1898) granted the DOAG a protectionist charter and thus the opportunity to enter into mainland German East Africa with a feeling of support from the German government.

This quiet but significant entry into East African communities by Germany was disrupted in September 1888 by the Abushiri revolt against the DOAG. At the time, the East African coastal areas were generally autonomous political entities, albeit subject to the sovereignty of the Sultan of Zanzibar based on the military and administrative resources available to the Omani Arab regime (Akinola 1975, 614). The relationship between the coastal leaders and the Sultanate enabled the former to freely trade and undertake agricultural activities along the coast and the hinterland without hindrance. But these interests would be jeopardized under German rule. When Sultan Sayyid Khalifa granted the DOAG a concession agreement in April 1888, there was bound to be resistance. Two components were problematic for the local leaders: first, the decision to transfer to the DOAG the administration of coastal parts previously under the Sultanate of Zanzibar and, second, the assumption by the German company of the control of collection of various taxes imposed on the local population at the coastal ports on the mainland of Tanganyika. Furthermore, the onset of German rule was a threat to the economic and social power and prestige held by the local leadership. The assumption of power by the DOAG evoked latent resentment—in the Swahili population in general—of the Germans. As Akinola states:

> The decrees and ordinances promulgated by the DOAG went a long way towards giving substance to the coastal people's apprehensions. These new regulations were as burdensome as they were comprehensive—they affected landowners and cultivators as well as merchants, shipowners and seamen. Admittedly the concession provided for the administration of these institutions by the DOAG. But the company officials went about this in a spirit of contempt for the people's culture and way of life. (1975, 616)

Numerous taxes—poll tax, burial tax, pass tax for dhows, and so on—were introduced, as were district courts. The DOAG also ventured into land governance by requiring registration of all land and buildings within six months, failure of which they would be declared public and taken over. The local leaders organized their communities to resist these excesses.

In particular, Abushiri bin Salim (c.1833–1889), a wealthy Swahili merchant and plantation owner, mobilized Swahili, Arab, and African traders, and from September 20, 1888, led attacks against German trading centers and towns. Meanwhile, Bwana Heri bin Juma, the powerful local Swahili leader of Saadani town with strong political ties with the Zigua community, had been running a thriving trade with the upcountry Nyamwezi and with Zanzibar. To stop the German infiltration, Bwana Heri joined forces with Abushiri to secure the coastal territory. The Swahili language was at hand as a tool of the coastal uprising.

The DOAG was overwhelmed by the guerilla attacks. Chancellor Otto von Bismarck stepped in and dispatched Hermann Wissman to support the DOAG. The resistance was pacified with the hanging of Abushiri on December 15, 1889, in Pangani, after a failed attempt to defend his stronghold in Jahazi, near Bagamoyo, and being betrayed as he sought refuge at the Imperial British East Africa in Mombasa. To consolidate the pacification, administrative functions previously handled by the DOAG were taken over by the imperial Government (Iliffe 1979) to allow for better extraction of resources to develop the German economy. Germany began to establish a formal administration and military presence in East Africa, including setting up an Imperial Governor based in Dar es Salaam.

2 Swahili and the Maji Maji Resistance Against German Rule

Swahili literary works often capture significant historical experiences and provide another way of interpreting them. In this case, the resistance to the DOAG in Tanga, Bagamoyo, and Pangani settlements in the coastal region of German East Africa bequeathed Swahili literature with the epic *Utenzi wa Vita vya Wadachi Kutamalaki Mrima* (Narrative poem of German rule of Mrima, 1891) by Hemed Abdallah Al-Buhry. The epic functions as a culturally situated historical document about German colonial experience and a work of art rich in stylistic devices: character, imagery, symbolism, rhythm, and rhyme.

After the introductory stanzas, as is usual with Swahili *tenzi* (epics), the narrator provides the purpose of his work of art:

> 46. Na mimi kusudi yangu
> iliyo moyoni mwangu
> kisa cha hawa wazungu
> takachowahadithia
> (Al-Buhry 1960, 14)

> And my purpose
> that is in my heart
> the story of these Europeans
> I am going to tell you.

The narrator then provides a context of the war and how the German colonial power agreed with the Sultan of Zanzibar, Sayyid Khalifa bin Said, to the concession of the Mrima coast, and the violent oppression by the Germans in Pangani, Bweni, and Tanga, among other coastal settlements. The narrator introduces Abushiri bin Salim and tells how he led the war of resistance. After Abushiri loses the war and retreats from Bagamoyo to Pangani, he is advised to seek support from a traditional healer and astrologer. The poet, then, in a creative twist, assumes the role of the said healer's identity:

> 384. Jinale etwa Hemedi
> Huyo mganga kazidi
> Falaki na mfuradi

> His name is Hemedi
> An expert healer
> Astrologer and poet

> 489. Wazungu tawapumbaza
> Na mimi tangia kwanza
> Wala pasiwe kuwaza
> Wauawe wote pia

> I will confuse the Europeans
> And I will be the first to enter
> And before they can think
> All of them shall be killed

The healer is shown as having powers to confuse the Germans and render them weak in the face of his magical abilities. As it progresses, the epic portrays the invasion of coastal towns by the Germans, the local resistance to domination, and the eventual victory of the Germans, who had superior arms. In terms of perspective, Al-Buhry suggests that the resistance was religiously motivated. But as Mbogoni (2004) observes, it was in fact politically motivated. The religious element of community anger toward some Germans accompanied by their dogs provoking worshippers by entering mosques during the month of Ramadhan was a trigger for the violence. But at the core of Abushiri resistance was German ruthlessness, the imposition of head tax, burial tax, and inheritance tax.

The Germans were also being challenged to the south by Chief Mkwaniyika Munyigumba Mwamuyinga, commonly known as Chief Mukwava (c.1855–1898), a leader of the Wahehe in Kalenga, Iringa region, who in 1885 declared war against German rule. After three years of guerilla warfare, he shot himself on July 19, 1898, rather than be captured. Sergeant Major Merki ordered that his head be cut off. The head was dried, and the skull shipped off to Germany. After numerous attempts at locating it, the skull was eventually returned to Tanganyika on February 15, 1954. The resistance led by Mukwava is captured in the play *Mukwava wa Uhehe* by Mugyabuso Mulokozi (1979). In writing the play, Mulokozi not only engages with a historically significant period in colonial history but also artistically dignifies the resistance movement and contributes to the body of Swahili historical plays. The play contributes to the understanding of the intersection between the colonial government, missionary activities, community leadership, and commitment to freedom in Tanzania by drawing on a particular historical period to address the past, present, and future.

Following the resistance wars of the 1890s sketched above, the German administration beefed up its administrative capacity by incorporating the existing largely Islamic and Swahili- speaking political structures and institutions. The colonial government employed the *wajumbe* (headmen), *maliwali* (governors), *askari* (police officers), and *maakida* (subordinate administrators) to advance German interests in the hinterland. In addition to their administrative work, the *maakida* also served as tax collectors and judges. In other cases, non-Islamic local leaders were co-opted as *maakida*. During this period, the focus was on territorial control and resource extraction, and the German administration did not have a well-formed position on Swahili as a language of administration or education. Nonetheless, there were Swahili people who had attended Qur'anic schools in the coastal region and were literate in Arabic script who could be recruited to serve German administration.

The Rise of Maji Maji

The Maji Maji war of resistance took place in German East Africa with a concentration to the east and south of this expansive and ethnically diverse country. The initial battleground was Nandete among the Matumbi people after two persons, 'Ngulumbalyo Mandai and Lindimyo Machela, uprooted three cotton plants from the German colonial plantation three years after the introduction of cotton farming in the area (Rushohora 2015). The aggression associated with extractive pursuits of the colonial enterprise had invariably led to resistance that was expressed through grievances around emergent oppressive practices, social dislocations, and the new economic obligations such as paying taxes. In the words of archeologist Nancy Rushohora:

> Although the war was initiated by one ethnic group, more than twenty tribes joined the resistance with the interest to fight the Germans. The Maji Maji war spread from the Matumbi to Luguru, Mahenge, Lukuledi, Kilombero valley, Songea and Jombe. The warriors were bounded together by rituals and traditions. (2015, 3)

The social restlessness and grievances related to German rule had created an opportunity for the mobilization of the masses. The region had not, prior to this resistance, shown signs of intense interethnic unity or consciousness. Mazrui and Mazrui (1995) have correctly observed that the Maji Maji war was a transethnic movement, and most likely the first one in Tanganyika. It was widespread in scope and underpinned by an ideological positioning. How, then, were the people organized and mobilized for action against German rule?

In delineating how this development could have happened, Iliffe (1967) identifies three key organizational principles. In his view, the first principle relates to the possibility of a marshaling of "prior political and cultural groupings," or what he refers to as "the tribal [ethnic] principle." Ethnolinguistic groupings tend to have shared histories, values, and experiences and can coalesce to address a common challenge. They might also have familial solidarities and alliances. The second organizational principle, in his view, relates to shared pressures and excesses of German rule on smallholder farmers, or "the peasant principle." German rule had imposed taxation, forced labor on construction, and European plantation and replaced local leaders with intermediary agents drawn from the coastal region. The new administrative framework was unpopular, and smallholder farmers in German East Africa had expressed their grievances against the foreign authority prior to the Maji Maji rebellion. The grievances were further amplified when in 1902 Governor Count Adolf von Götzen (1866–1910) began a large-scale cotton-growing enterprise that had failed in the northern coast region. The governor ordered smallholder farmers to set up a cotton plot in each neighborhood under the supervision of the local headman (*jumbe*), with the peasants taking turns to work for a fixed number of days on the communal cotton farms. As Iliffe (1967, 499) observes:

> [A]lthough the cotton scheme was not in operation throughout the rebel area, the uprising began where the scheme did operate. Second, it is surely significant that the revolt began early in the cotton-picking season. Third, R.M. Bell's evidence suggests that the first outbreaks in Matumbi and Madaba were directly connected with orders to begin cotton picking. Fourth, several rebel leaders had suffered from the scheme ...Fifth, cotton was everywhere on object of attack. In Kilosa, the rebels burned the crop in the fields.

The scheme was also an attack on the sociocultural life of the smallholder farmers. Men, women, and children were forced to work together in the cotton plantations—under very harsh conditions—without regard for the sociocultural norms of interaction and the indignity of forced labor. Communal labor, in which groups of workers were assigned portions of land to cultivate, was a factor in the Maji Maji war, especially in the earlier stages of the rebellion, which were characterized by sporadic tactics of agitation among certain ethnic groups, such as the Wamatumbi and Wakichi, discussed in the poem *Utenzi wa Vita vya Maji Maji* by Karim bin Jamahddini (2006) to which we return later in the chapter.

Another factor worth serious consideration relates to the organization and mobilization of those aggrieved around ideological and religious beliefs and allegiance. This principle was encapsulated in the Swahili word "Maji,"water. Maji became the medicine and glue that united the smallholder farmers and workers and formed the ideological magnet for a collective vision and courage to confront German administrators and their politico-commercial agents. Women were involved in many contexts of the Maji Maji resistance. Sometimes the maji medicine was even "administered by women who were a substantial, integrated element in ritual activities and in war" (Rushohora 2015, 20).

Among the Germans, however, the "maji" was interpreted as a form of "witchcraft," under the leadership of Kinjeketile Ngwale of Ngarambe and his brother-in-law, Ngameya of Uporogo (Mbogoni 2004). The spiritual leaders were also seen by missionaries as enemies of Christianity needing to be stopped. This spiritual direction, in their interpretation, went hand in glove with a revival (*Wiederaufleben*) of the snake-god Kolelo among the Wazaramo and Walugulu, leading to action (*Wechselwirkung*) against German administrators (Iliffe 1967). The Kolelo belief system was activated in a manner that linked German colonialism to threats on land that, as heritage and site of production, sustained community life.

Maji was distributed among most communities before violence broke out. Maji, as a concept of resistance, spread rapidly by word of mouth, in popular rumors and whispers, capturing the imagination of potential warriors and supporters throughout the process. Moreover, the Swahili word *maji*, used in its reduplicative form to refer to the war, inspired action buttressed by a spirituality rooted in local religious and spiritual beliefs about the power of the supernatural beings that are eternal, active, and creative. This belief system is part of the African worldview. In the words of philosopher and theologian John Mbiti:

It is to be remembered that for many African people, God's active part in human history is seen in terms of His supplying them with rain, good harvest, health, cattle and children; in healing, delivering and helping them; and in terms of making His presence felt through natural phenomena and objects. The people constantly turn to God in various acts of worship which in effect constitute man's response to God's interest and active part in human affairs. They do not sever man from his total environment, so that in effect human history is cosmic history seen anthropocentrically or microcosmically. God is not divorced from this concept of history; it is His universe. He is active in it and apparent silent may be a feature of His divine activity. (2002, 47)

This spirituality was evident in the Maji Maji war. In the case of the resistance movement, it drew from the Islamic faith and local indigenous religions. In the latter case, creeping animals such as snakes may feature and carry attributes of sacredness, human spirits, or the living dead. The sun, moon, stars, mountains, and rivers feature in African religions. Swahili was therefore more than a tool for exchange of information. It was a carrier of a philosophy about the world. It is also significant that although some Muslim traders, teachers, *akidas* (district administrators), *liwalis* (governors), and plantation owners cooperated with the Germans during the war, there were many other Swahili-speaking Muslims who supported the Maji Maji war. In fact, Muslim presence may have been so pronounced in the resistance movement that in the aftermath of the war, memories of "the savage repression of the Maji Maji revolt in 1905–1907 induced the Ngindo and other people in the south-east to espouse Islam as a modern belief system which owed nothing to Europeans" (Curtin 1978, 198).

In discussing the unity manifested in the war, John Iliffe (1969, 25) says:

> Maji Maji was quite different from the early resistance which the Germans had faced when occupying Tanganyika, for that had been local and professional–soldiers against soldiers–whereas Maji Maji affected almost everyone in the colony.... In the long term, the movement may have provided an experience of united mass action to which later political leaders could

appeal .... Maji Maji became a mass movement because it acquired an ideological content which persuaded people to join and fight.

Once the war started, it spread fast and encompassed diverse communities. The religious symbolism and the calls for interethnic unity marshaled the affected communities to rebel and face German colonialism. Iliffe (1969, 19–20) further describes the situation as follows:

> Within a fortnight, nearly all the peoples surrounding the Rufiji valley, from Kilosa to Liwale, were in revolt ... [In another two months] most of the peoples south of the line from Dar es Salaam to Kilosa and thence to the northern top of Lake Malawi were in revolt.

The war was an early manifestation of a mass movement in the struggle against colonial rule. It was the first nationalist war against German colonialism. The others, including the Abushiri resistance along the coast and the war led by Mukwava in Iringa to the south, were mainly local.

Disentangling Language Choices

Prior to the Maji Maji war, the German government was conflicted on the language policy that best suited its interests in East Africa. Recognizing that multilingualism was dominant, it had reached the conclusion that a lingua franca was required to advance German administration. There were two choices: German or Swahili. German could have been selected, introduced, and promoted as the language of interethnic communication. But there was general hesitation because it would have been the key to European knowledge and philosophies—liberty, freedom, equality, and democracy. Acquired knowledge would then have been used to advance radical arguments against colonialism and imperialism. The other alternative was Swahili, a Bantu language that had been used in trade, education, and the spread of Islamic values and beliefs in East Africa. Among certain German leaders and scholars, Swahili was a carrier of Islamic beliefs that posed a major challenge to Christianity and

European values and was "the unrepentant enemy of colonial politics" (quoted by Charles Pike 1986, 231).

While recognizing this opportunity, there had been no systematic way of promoting either German or Swahili as the language of education or German administration in East Africa before 1905. The German government encouraged the teaching of Swahili and to a certain extent German in secular schools to give the requisite linguistic and literacy skills to personnel who would then join its administration. In Germany, the Oriental Seminar at Berlin University was offering Swahili classes for those interested in traveling to German East Africa and linguists were developing teaching materials, giving the language and its culture prestige and status as a potential tool of administration. But Swahili was also viewed, among certain missionaries, as providing the most pragmatic route as the language of education, Christian evangelizing, and German administration, if it was shed of its Arabic lexicon and Islamic role. They saw education as linked to the perpetuation of Christianity and therefore sought the most efficient route to achieving the goal of conversion. Consequently, local languages, Swahili, and German were used as the languages of instruction in schools. Furthermore, Swahili newspapers were published mainly by missionaries, and *Msimulizi* was established in 1888, while *Habari za Mwezi* (Monthly News) was rolled out in 1894. Other papers included *Pwani na Bara* (Coast and Upcountry) and *Rafiki Yangu* (My Friend) published by the German protestant mission. The newspapers were part of information sharing about Christianity in Swahili. The ambivalence regarding the colonial language was further manifested through the colonial administration's 1897 ban on the use of indigenous languages in schools and the instruction that the German language be used for teaching and learning. Soon after, in 1900, the *Schutzgebietgesetz* (protectorate) law gave missionaries the right to carry out their evangelization mission only in local languages. Michelle Moyd notes:

> Not only was there disagreement between missions and colonial government on what language(s) should be used for instruction, but there was also disagreement among the various missions themselves on this issue. Some mission societies, like UMCA and Holy Ghost Fathers, were in agreement with colonial government policy regarding the use of Kiswahili

2 Swahili and the Maji Maji Resistance Against German Rule 41

as the language of instruction, and in fact were pioneers of sorts in this area. Others, however, such as Lutherans and Moravians, were steadfastly against it. As if this situation were not complex enough, the German government in Berlin began to request that the study of German become a standard part of the curriculum in German East African schools. (1997, 48)

To help build consensus and get additional government funding, mission schools undertook to provide an education that would serve German administration. This meant incorporating the teaching of Swahili and German in their curricula as standard practice to prepare future junior administrators.

But the use of the Arabic script and concerns about an Arabic lexicon in Swahili as a carrier of Islam persisted among some missions. Some colonial administrators also regarded the language as a potential site of interethnic solidarity against German rule. The existence of Swahili anti-colonial literature in Arabic script and the *El-Najah* Swahili periodical were cited as evidence of this subversive potential. In the words of Pike (1986, 224), to the European mind,

> the Arabic script symbolized Islam, and so the rationale for changing scripts became much grander. It was also a simple solution to an increasingly untenable situation. By symbolically exorcising Swahili of its 'Islamic character,' European administrators, clergy, and profiteers could continue to support its use (which they both needed and were in no position to change). It was a strange deception given the continued widespread use of the Arabic script in Koranic schools, the fact that Swahili was largely a spoken lingua franca, and that the real danger to German rule was Swahili as a unifying language which would not be changed, but could even be enhanced, by introducing the Roman script.

The German linguist Carl Meinhof agreed with the view that adopting Swahili for the advancement of German administration was the most pragmatic and practical path but need not advance the Arabic worldview. It could be "purged of its Islamicity" (Mazrui 2017, 55). Therefore, in 1905 during the Colonial Congress he proposed that Swahili be de-Islamized and de-Arabized by replacing the Arabic script—which had been creatively adjusted into the Ajami script and used for centuries in

Swahili writings—with the Roman script. He also proposed that Arabic loanwords be replaced with terms from German. But Meinhof was also aware of the relationship between language and power and warned: "We have to be clear about the consequences that with German magazines and conversation open to the African, he can use this knowledge of German political intentions to inform his people" (cited in Pike 1986, 224). Once Swahili could be "filtered" of Arabic and Islam, it could be used in the advancement of European values. As can be gleaned from the above context, by the time the Maji Maji war broke out, the language policy in German East Africa was eclectic.

Gearing toward the war, Swahili became not only a medium of interethnic communication but also a carrier of competing worldviews and philosophical content about German rule. On one hand, it enabled communication across ethnicities, and on the other provided a Swahili counter-narrative about German rule. The war was enabled through a secret whispering campaign popularly referred to as *nywinywila*. The code depended on Swahili to reach communities speaking other languages for intraethnic communication. The term *whispering campaign* inspired the term *nywila* (without the duplication) currently employed as the word for "password" in information technology.

Kenyan linguist Mohamed Abdulaziz (1971) has argued that the Maji Maji war was the genesis of the interethnic and worker peasant movement in Tanganyika. He has affirmed the place of Swahili in this process. He notes:

> Swahili has played a very significant role in the development of political values and attitudes in Tanzania. Its integrative qualities have influenced the style of Tanzania politics, especially its non-tribal and egalitarian characteristics. All movements of national focus have used Swahili as an instrument for achieving inter-tribal unity and integration. The Maji Maji war of 1905–1907 against German colonial rule drew its support from the different mother-tongue speakers who already possessed a rallying force in Kiswahili. (1971, 164)

In a sense, then, traders, German administrators, and European missionaries had inadvertently contributed to the promotion of the very linguistic tool that Maji Maji combatants needed in their war of liberation.

Swahili became the language of nationalism and mass mobilization. It was utilized as a transethnic medium of communication during the war and served as a tool for mobilizing, organizing communities, and sharing an ideological direction. When TANU, on July 7, 1954, declared Swahili the language of mobilization for independence, the nationalist party was building on the foundation established by the Maji Maji war. Julius Kambarage Nyerere, when addressing the Fourth Committee of the United Nations in 1956, paid tribute to the Maji Maji war as a mass movement against German rule in Tanganyika. He told the committee:

> [F]or fifteen years, 1885 and 1900, my people, with bows and arrows, with spears and clubs, with knives or rusty muskets, fought desperately to keep the Germans out. But the odds were against them. In 1905, in the famous Maji Maji rebellion, they tried again for the last time to drive the Germans out. Once again the odds were against them. The Germans, with characteristic ruthlessness, crushed the rebellion, slaughtering an estimated number of 120,000 people. (1966, 40–41)

This foundational basis was inspirational to the Arusha Declaration of 1967 and can be felt today with the UNESCO declaration of July 7 as World Swahili Day (UNESCO 2021).

German Reaction to the Maji Maji War

The Maji Maji war was a turning point in German colonialism and missionary work. Soon after war broke out, Governor Count von Götzen appointed a Commission of enquiry into the causes of the resistance and what could have prompted the local *jumbe* to participate. He did not want a situation where his leadership could be accused of abuse or bad governance, especially within the context of the Herero-Nama uprising in German South West Africa. There was also change of policy in Berlin. More accommodating policies were introduced in German East Africa and economic activities were intensified with the cultivation of cash crops. The German government decided to be purposefully more involved politically than was the case before 1905. Political penetration was no longer an option but an imperative to enable the German administration to be felt in the interior of Tanganyika. Iliffe (1969, 180) argues as follows:

> In colonial history, the normal European response to widespread rebellion was to decentralize, to encourage 'strong and isolated tribal nationalism.' It was of great importance to Tanganyika that the German administration did not do this after Maji Maji. Instead, it tended to reinforce centralization and bureaucracy....

The government strengthened its presence by building more schools and through co-optation and employment of literate Swahili-speaking people in the hinterland. While some employees took up the positions of *akida*, others worked with the *jumbe* or as tax clerks. These individuals were expected to "improve" and advance German interests in a sustained manner (Iliffe 1969, 166). But many were, in fact, "organic intellectuals" in the Gramcian sense who occupied an in-between position in the community as they interrogated the practices of German rule and mediated with colonialism within their particular contexts. Part of that context was the utilization of Swahili as the community's linguistic arsenal. Swahili was a language through which power was expressed and challenged in discourse.

The German colonial government, meanwhile, was not willing to open up the learning of German, though in Germany itself there were voices in favor of teaching German to the colonized as part of the civilizing agenda. In articulating the colonial positioning of European languages, Ali Mazrui avers:

> The French tried to create a mystique of France by popularizing the French language; the Germans were tempted to create a mystique of Germany by isolating their language from the squalor of popular comprehension and making it mysteriously and powerfully distant.... It was therefore, basically presumptuous for an African to aspire to Germanhood in culture. (1975, 135)

Language is more than a vehicle for passing on information. It can mark status, prestige, and power (Fairclough 1989). By opening East Africa to the German language, the power of the colonial regime could be demystified. The limited access to German led to the mushrooming of Swahili within the educational system and in communities. It was used for socioeconomic and political activities. The German government continued to teach German to a small population, but devoted more resources to the teaching of Swahili.

Following the recommendations of Carl Meinhof discussed above, the process of de-Islamizing Swahili and the use of the Roman script had begun slowly, but after the Maji Maji war it was accelerated. Missionary schools started using Swahili more deliberately as the language of instruction and churches embarked on de-Islamizing the language to cater for Christian values within the colonial administration system and in the communities. A new translation of the Bible was initiated in 1914 to "purify Swahili as a Bantu language, by eliminating the majority of the Zanzibar Arabic words" (Mojola 2000).

Winfred Whiteley (1969) captures this post-Maji Maji spread of Swahili in the following words:

> By 1914, the Administration was able to conduct much of its correspondence with village headmen in Swahili: indeed, letters not written to the administration either in Swahili or German were liable to be ignored. This was one feature of German administration which proved to be of great value to their successors, the British, and evoked a good deal of approval in later years. The Report on the territory for 1921, for example, stated [that] the later German system has made it possible to communicate in writing with every Akida leader and village headman, and in turn, to receive information from him reports written in Swahili. (Whiteley 1969, 60–61)

While prior to the Maji Maji war the German colonial government had an ambivalent attitude toward Swahili, after 1907, it sought to promote it deliberately. The teaching of German remained minimal, while the war also provided a context for artistic imagination in Swahili.

Swahili Words in Action

Just as in the previous wars against German rule in East Africa, the Maji Maji war provided vital context and content for Swahili literature. One of the most celebrated works in this corpus of Swahili war literature is *Kinjeketile* (1969a), the Swahili play by Ebrahim Hussein that reconstructs the Maji Maji war by drawing on community memory and oral stories of the war and juxtaposes them with available historical records to reconstruct imaginatively a past that has relevance to the present. Hussein (1969b, vi–vii) says:

> In my play, I have tried to demonstrate three things. First, I have tried to show how the Wamatumbi felt about the cruel invasion by the Germans, especially to show the master-servant relationship then pertaining. Secondly, I have tried to show briefly the political climate of that period (1890–1904). Thirdly, I have touched on the theme of economic exploitation of the Africans by the Germans, when Tanzania was being deprived of her produce and manpower, and yet her people were being made to pay taxes, without being given any change of earning an income.

The playwright draws on these problems as background to the play. The German invasion was extractive, brutal, disruptive of community life, and based on a relation of subservience to the alien rule. Politically, it was enabled through German structures, institutions, and agents derived from coastal German East Africa, namely, the *akida, jumbe,* and *liwali.* The introduction of cash crops, forced labor, and taxation undermined food security in the communities. The exchange between Bibi Kinjeketile and Bibi Kitunda brings to the fore the vivid memories of German rule. These memories of the historical period are a contextualization and a foreshadowing of the violent resistance to be presented later in the play. To demonstrate these tensions in this historical reenactment of the resistance, Hussein depends on multiple sources that enrich his epic dramaturgy. He recasts the grievances of community members, which included forced labor on the cotton plantations, taxation, whipping, and public humiliation. In the words of the character Mkichi:

> ... It is better to die than to live like this. We are made to work like beasts in the cotton plantation. We are forced to pay tax. We die of hunger because we cannot work on our shambas. I say death is better than this life. (1969b, 8)

The sociolinguistic thrust is made evident through at least two approaches: the instrumentalization of the language by Kinjeketile and the varieties of Swahili used by the characters in the play. The protagonist of the play, Kinjeketile Ngwale, is a historical figure who lived in Ngarambe and was a diviner who possessed magical powers (Mwaifuge 2014). He uses Swahili as a site for articulating ethnic divisions and the revolutionary potential of the language for interethnic unity. On the basis of his legitimacy among the Matumbi people, Kinjeketile was able to inspire and organize people and foster resistance against the Germans and their agents. Kinjeketile uses Swahili to communicate his vision of a united people wielding power against German colonialism. He articulates that he had communicated with Bokelo, the Supreme deity of the Matumbi people, who urged him to unite his people against German colonialism by administering the magical *maji*, which would, in turn, protect them against German bullets. He organized the people on the basis of their various belief systems.

In the introduction to the play, Hussein (1969b, v) says:

> Kinjeketile, the man, is a historical reality: he lived. His name was Kinjeketile Ngware, and he lived at Ngarambe in what is now southern Tanzania. He is mentioned in the *Records of Maji Maji* rising. However, Kinjeketile of the play is not a historical evocation of the real man. Kinjeketile here is a creature of the imagination, and although the 'two men' closely resemble one another in their actions, they are not identical.

The historical figure was charged with treason and hanged by the Germans on August 4, 1905, a month after the breakout of the war.

The war is driven by the Swahili word *maji*. Uttered in a community setting, the word gains a life of its own and leads to unrelenting action. Kinjeketile tells Kitunda in a Matumbi variety of Swahili:

> Kinjeketile: (*sauti ya kwa mbali*) Binadamu huzaa neno—neno hushika nguvu—likawa kubwa—kubwa, kubwa likamshinda binadamu kwa ukubwa na nguvu. Likamuangusha. Neno ambalo limezaliwa na ntu likaja kuntawala ntu yule yule aliyelizaa. (*kwa Kitunda*) Mutanipa siku moja zaidi. (1969a, 33)

Kinjeketile: (*To himself*) A Man gives birth to a word ... the word grows bigger and bigger ... and destroys the man who let it loose. A word born of man grows strong, and ends up enslaving him. (*To Kitunda*) You will give me one more day.

By speaking in the Matumbi-laden Swahili, Kinjeketile is negotiating an identity distinct from that of coastal Swahili that would mark the coastal region. Here he is using Swahili to signal his proximity to his Matumbi community and connecting with local indigenous wisdom to articulate the power of the word, once uttered. At that moment, he is rooted in the Matumbi community as he pleads for more time to make sure that his prediction is reliable. In a desperate tone of voice, he tells Kitunda, "[M]aelfu kwa maelfu wanaweza kufa kama hatuna hakika, watu wale wote sisi itakuwa tumewaua. Mimi nimewaua. Hongo amewaua" (Thousands of people might die if we are not sure, we will have killed them. I will have killed them. Hongo will have killed them) (1969a: 33). But the word, once unleashed, cannot be contained. It becomes its own master and takes control of the utterer. The people believed in maji and there was no turning back.

The historical facts about interethnic tensions and conflicts are presented in the play through characters with differentiated varieties of Swahili to mark their ethnic backgrounds. The varieties are used to unify the Matumbi and to simultaneously differentiate them. For example, the Wamatumbi in their variety of Swahili pronounce the sound [r] like the sound [l] and thus say "nzuli" instead of "nzuri." Moreover, the nasal [m] is replaced with the nasal [n] in their variety. But these differences marked by Swahili varieties are suppressed in the mobilization of communities to face a common enemy. According to Alain Ricard:

> The man who dreams about a Tanganyika become Swahililand in the future only dreams the dream when in a trance. His dream is first of all that of an end to tribalism–the central theme of his vaticinations. The differences and conflicts are a reality in the play and the author indicates the different Swahili accents between the ethnic groups. (2008, 81)

In his trance, Kinjeketile gets a glimpse of tomorrow. He predicts the departure of the Germans and the arrival of Seyyid Said, the Sultan of Zanzibar, who embraced the British and ceded parts of the coast to the Germans. He is shocked at his words, but they have left his mouth. His words are in coastal Swahili, foreshadowing the tomorrow of Swahili in postcolonial Tanzania.

The instrumentalization of Swahili as a tool for mobilization against German rule is artistically presented in *Utenzi wa Jamhuri ya Tanzania* (Narrative poem about the Republic of Tanzania) by Ramadhani Mwaruka (1968). This poem captures the history of Tanzania from the period of Arab slavery to independence, the poet devoting stanzas 252–93 to the depiction of the Maji Maji war. In these stanzas the poet shows how widespread the resistance was on account of maji.

But was the maji that Kinjeketile pronounced inspired by African indigenous knowledge systems or the Islamic spiritual realm? In which sociolinguistic terrain does this particular word reside? In *Jihadi Kuu ya Maji Maji* (The powerful jihad of Maji Maji), Mwalimu Hussein Bashir Abdallah presents this war as part of the Islamic Jihad, a Holy War waged by Muslims against German colonialism. His main argument is that the majority of the fighters were Muslim and referred to themselves in Swahili as "Askari wa Mungu" (Soldiers of God) and that Kinjeketile would have used the "maji ya Zam Zam" (Zamzam water), believed by Muslims to be blessed and sourced from the Zamzam well at the Masjid-al-Haram in Mecca:

Al Haj Ali Abdallah Kinjeketile Ngwale na wenzake waliamua kutumia maji haya ya Zam Zam ikiwa ni sehemu ya kiapo maalum kinachofahamika kama Baia (kiapo cha siri cha kutorudi nyuma katika mapambano).

Al Haj Ali Abdalla Kinjeketile Ngwale and his colleagues decided to use the water of Zam Zam as part of the special oath known as Baia (oath of no return in a struggle).

In making this claim, Hussein Bashir amplifies Kinjeketile's identity as a Swahili who lived in the Matumbi area. The view that there were many Muslims in the war is also shared by others. In fact, according to Mbogoni (2004), Islam may have been the moving spirit of the war in the Matumbi area, at least in the initial stages. In any case, it would appear that although the fighters saw themselves as "Askari wa Mungu," their God was not a Christian one. It is evident that they targeted mission stations and European missionaries. Moreover, there were many Muslim fighters in the war mentioned in Jamalidinni's narrative poem. Notwithstanding the lingua-religious basis of the *maji*, Kinjeketile called his community to war against German rule, as no bullet would penetrate the body of those who had partaken of it, even as he encouraged them to train, as shown in the Ebrahim Hussein play. The fighters are linked to their ancestors as sources of spiritual protection. Each community located its belief system and contextualized Kinjeketile's prophesy in its unique spiritual circumstances.

In the play by Hussein, the fighters—under the leadership of Kitunda— believe in the ability of the maji mixed with castor oil and millet seeds to protect them against bullets fired by German soldiers. The fighters drink the maji, which is also sprinkled on their heads. The maji ritual emboldens them and they gain courage and a sense of unity. At a time when he is overwhelmed by the fighters' eagerness to go to war, Kinjeketile cautions against the unchecked faith in the water, but it is too late. The Swahili word *maji* has taken over. It has been released to the community as a powerful tool of liberation, of interethnic solidarity, unity, consciousness, and collective confidence. Before he gave them the word, they were divided ethnically. Swahili gives them the unity they needed as a country.

As the plot develops, Kinjeketile has more doubts about the wisdom of going to war, especially when Kitunda tells him that while in a trance he had prophesied that Seyyid Said (the Sultan of Zanzibar) would take over once the Germans (the Red Earth) leave. The suggestion that power would be transferred from the Germans to Seyyid Said is problematic for Kinjeketile and shakes his spirituality and faith in Hongo as a reliable and sufficient basis for the war. Kinjeketile is spiritually conflicted because the words he uttered while possessed betray his beliefs about the meaning of freedom. He therefore resorts to his faith in the power of his people uttered earlier through Swahili in the pursuit of community dignity. The fictional Kinjeketile in the play articulates a position about the past and the future. He uses language to call for political unity and caution against a neocolonial relationship in Tanzania.

2 Swahili and the Maji Maji Resistance Against German Rule 51

Another important literary work that captures the Maji Maji war is *Utenzi wa vita vya Maji Maji* by Abdul Karim Jamaliddin. The poet, a Sufi religious teacher in Lindi, was actively involved in resisting German colonialism. He was arrested in 1910 and died in prison before 1912. His poem was translated into German in 1912 and published in 1933 by A. Lorenz. Later it was republished in 1957 by the Inter-Territorial Language Committee and again in 2000 by the Institute of Kiswahili Studies, Dar es Salaam. In writing the *Utenzi*, Abdul Karim Jamaliddin was following the Swahili tradition of capturing historical events through poetry (Mulokozi 2006, v). The poet provides an elucidation of the violence meted on individuals and property by the "rebels," the weaknesses of the "magical water," and the violent actions that rendered maji impotent in the face of bullets.

In this latter situation, the poet captures the voice of Hongo, who rebukes the fighters over their violence and looting that neutralized the power of maji. Written in a multiplicity of narrative voices—the fighters, the Germans, and the local Swahili elite—the *Utenzi* carries a perspective that can be read, on the one hand, as suggesting that the Swahili people were opposed to the rebellion, while on the other hand rationalizing the resistance by pointing to the factors that led to the war. According to Casco (2007):

> [C]ompared to previous poetry, it shows a high degree of impartiality and contains information that can be confirmed by academic research and oral testimonies as well. A careful reading of the whole contents of the poem demonstrates that, more than supporting any of the contending parts, the *Utenzi wa Vita vya Maji Maji* is an open condemnation of the violence and the terrible outcome wrought by the uprising. (2007, 244)

The balance that Casco refers to relates to the violence on both sides. But there is a sense in which by condemning the resistance against colonialism, the poet does perpetuate a German interpretation of the Maji Maji war. He elucidates the brutality of the colonial experience, but is simultaneously disgusted by the people's violent act of resistance and the disruption of the "peaceful" life before the war. He says:

(7) Twalikaa tukilala We were sleeping
    na ndisha njema tukila And eating well
    mara ikaja ghafula And then suddenly
    tukasikia habari We heard the news

(8) Ya washenzi wamehuni Of revolting
    na hivi waja bomani And heading to the fortress
    na silaha mkononi With weapons in their hands
    na miji kuihasiri And destroying the towns

(9) Na sote tukadharau And we all scorned at them
    Kwa habari ni kuu The important news
    Huwaje hata na wao How could even they
    Kufanya mno jeuri? Act insolently?

Unlike the poem *Utenzi wa Vita vya Wadachi Kutamalaki Mrima* by Hemed bin Abdallah El-Buhriy (1891), which depicts the Abushiri war as a heroic struggle for liberation, *Utenzi wa Vita vya Maji Maji* is presented by "an observer" position (Mulokozi 2006, v), but in that narrative posture appears more aligned with the German interpretation of that historical event, notwithstanding the oppressive practices of domination and resource extraction that set it in motion. In describing the German colonial practices and the community grievances the poet says:

(25) Bwana wetu, tumechoka Master, we are tired
     Kila siku kutumika Working each day
     Tufe, yatoke mashaka! Let's die and leave this disgrace
     Naam tumekhitari! Yes, we've made this choice

(26) Mara kulima mashamba At times, we work in the fields
     Jioni tuvune pamba In the evening, we pick cotton
     Tena tujenge majumba Then we construct houses
     Na kodi tukidabiri And pay taxes

(27) Mazito tukayaona We've seen this burden
     Tukaucha na kunena We've discussed this matter
     Tukaizua fitina We planned the resistance
     La kufa kumekhitari And we chose to die

(28) Sisi umetukamata   You have arrested us
    Wengine hutawapata;   But others you will not get
    Hapana budi na vita   War is inevitable
    Ndio yetu mashauri   This is our decision

The verses point to the context and determination of the communities to resist German rule due to its excesses and concur with the historical records about the factors that contributed to the war. Casco (2007, 242) indicates that the poet "had friendly relations with German authorities" even though he ended up in jail. His father, Jamaliddin bin Ahmedi, was a Kadhi, an Islamic magistrate. His children occupied privileged positions in Lindi and were well "integrated into German oligarchy in last office. The Jamaliddin family had close relations with German members of the local administrators" (Casco 2007, 249).

When the resistance is suppressed and its leaders executed, the poet captures that moment in these terms:

(325) Killa mkuu wa vita   Every leader in the war
    Wote aliwakamata   All were arrested
    Wengine walijileta   And some surrendered
    Bila mtu kudabiri   Any none running away

(326) Washenzi hawana akili   Non-believers are not intelligent
    Fukara hana rijali   Poor people are not real men
    Wote wakamkubali   They all agreed with him
    Kila alilo dhukuri   In everything he said

(328) Na kila mwenye jina   And each of high rank
    Abadan hakupona   Was not spared at all
    Kitanzi alikiona   He faced the gallows
    Sasa amani sururi   All is peace and happiness now

There is no remorse in the words used here; instead, there is a strong sense of contempt and an aura of cultural superiority. The poet uses the term *washenzi* (the uncultured), notwithstanding the fact that many of the people who participated in the war were Muslim. In using the word, the poet introduces a binarity between the cultured and uncultured, ignoring the complex relationship between ethnicities, faiths, and social status during the war.

As we have seen, leaders and fighters in the Maji Maji war utilized Swahili as the language of mobilization and popularized its usage during the war. Through its whispering campaign referred to as *nywinywila*, the war has offered the lexical term for "password" (*nywila*) used in the arena of information technology. On their part, German administrators saw the role that Swahili had played in the war and decided to review their language policy. While, prior to the war, the language policy was ambivalent, lukewarm, and indecisive with regard to promoting German and Swahili, the war called for more direct political engagement with communities through Swahili. The government employed literate Swahili speakers to serve it in administration and other functions. Missionary schools also purposefully introduced the teaching of Swahili and integrated the language in its evangelizing, albeit within a de-Islamizing agenda of reducing Arabic and Islamic terms in the language. Swahili creative writers have also been inspired by the war, and as we have seen in the case of Kinjeketile and Vita vya Maji Maji, the experiences of the war have enriched Swahili literature, which has in turn contributed to our understanding of the feelings that might have been experienced in 1905–1907. The fact that Julius Nyerere invoked the war and its use of Swahili in his 1954 declaration that the Tanganyika National Union (TANU) would use Swahili as the language of political mobilization speaks to the centrality of the war in the sociocultural imagining of the time.

References

Abdulaziz, Mohamed H. 1971. Tanzani'a National Language Policy and the Rise of Swahili Political Culture. In *Language Use and Social Change: Problems of Mulrilingualism with Special Reference to Eastern Africa*, W. H. Whiteley, 160–178. London: Oxford University Press.

Akinola, G.A. 1975. The East African Coastal Rising, 1888–1890. *Journal of the Historical Society of Nigeria* 17 (4): 609–630.

Al-Buhry, Hemed bin Abdallah. 1960. *Utenzi wa vita vya Wadachi kutamalaki Mrima, 1307 A.H. The German Conquest of the Swahili Coast, 1891 A.D.* Dar es Salaam: East African Literature Bureau.
Casco, José Arturo Saavedra. 2007. *Utenzi, War Poems, and the German Conquest of East Africa: Swahili Poetry as a Historical Source.* Trenton, NJ: Africa World Press.
Curtin, Philip. 1978. *African History from Earliest Times to Independence.* 2nd ed. Nairobi: Longman.
Fairclough, Norman. 1989. *Language and Power.* London: Longman.
Hussein, E.N. 1969a. *Kinjeketile (Swahili Version).* Dar es Salaam: Oxford University Press.
———. 1969b. *Kinjeketile (English Version).* Nairobi: Oxford University Press.
Iliffe, J. 1967. The Organization of the Maji Maji Rebellion. *The Journal of African History* 8 (3): 495–512.
———. 1969. *Tanganyika Under German Rule, 1905–1912.* Nairobi: East African Publishing House.
Mazrui, Alamin. 2017. The Arabic Stimulus to the Swahili Language: A Postcolonial Balance Sheet. *JULACE: Journal of the University of Namibia Language Centre* 2 (2): 51–67. https://journals.unam.edu.na/index.php/JULACE/article/view/136 Accessed?
Mazrui, Ali. 1975. *The Political Sociology of the English Language: An African Perspective.* The Hague: Mouton.
Mazrui, Ali A., and Alamin Mazrui. 1995. *Swahili, State and Society: The Political Economy of an African Language.* Nairobi: East African Educational Publishers.
Mbiti, John. 2002. *African Religions and Philosophy.* 2nd ed. Nairobi: East African Educational Publishers.
Mbogoni, Lawrence E.Y. 2004. *The Cross Versus the Crescent, Religion and Politics in Tanzania from the 1880s to the 1990s.* Dar es Salaam: Mkuki na Nyota Publishers.
Mojola, Aloo Osotsi. 2018. *Bible Translation and Culture: Critical Intersections and Conversations.* Nairobi: Bible Society of Kenya.
Moyd, M.R. 1997. Language and Power: Africans, Europeans, and Language Policy in German Colonial Tanganyika. M.A. Thesis. University of Florida.
Mulokozi, Mugyabuso. 1979. *Mukwava wa Uhehe.* Nairobi: East African Publishing House.
Mwaifuge, E.S. 2014. German Colonialism, Memory and Ebrahim Hussein's *Kinjetketile. Research on Humanities and Social Sciences* 4 (28): 37–48.

Mwaruka, R. 1968. *Utenzi wa Jamhuri ya Tanzania*. Nairobi: East African Literature Bureau.
Nyerere, J. 1966. *Freedom and Unity: A Selection of Writings and Speeches, 1952–1965*. Dar es Salaam: Oxford University Press.
Pike, Charles. 1986. History and Imagination: Swahili Literature and Resistance to German Language Imperialism in Tanzania 1885–1910. *International Journal of African Historical Studies* 19 (2): 201–234.
Ricard, Alain. 2008. *Ebrahim Hussein: Swahili Theatre and Individualism*. Translated from the French by Dr. Naomi Morgan. Dar es Salaam: Mkuki na Nyota.
Rushohora, Nancy A. 2015. An Archaeological Identity of the Maji Maji: Toward an Historical Archaeology of Resistance to German Colonization in Southern Tanzania. *Arch* 11: 246–271.
UNESCO. 2021. A Proclamation of a World Swahili Language Day. https://unesdoc.unesco.org/ark:/48223/pf0000379076.
Whiteley, Wilfred H. 1969. *Swahili: The Rise of a National Language*. London: Methuen.

3

Swahili in Military Context: Between World War I and World War II

Alamin Mazrui

In the previous chapter we saw how the fortunes of Swahili were greatly facilitated by the Maji Maji war of resistance both as a pioneer in mass organization and in terms of its impact on German colonial policy in Tanganyika for the subsequent decade. Equally important for the fortunes of Swahili, however, were the *Vita Vikuu*, the two world wars and their aftermath, as well as the interwar period that separated them. Let us look at the dynamics of each of these wars in terms of their implication for Swahili. As we shall see in the following pages, in addition to Swahili's multiple roles in the course of the wars, the wars themselves were a "mother of invention" for the Swahili language just as they were for the English language (Gooden and Lewis 2014). In the process, we see how the use of Swahili both directed and reflected the relationship between different constituencies in the context of the wars and their aftermath.

World War I and Its Aftermath

During the war itself, Swahili helped to emphasize fratricidal aspects of the violence between local peoples. After all, during World War I soldiers from Kenya, Tanzania, and Uganda were deployed primarily within the

East African region. African men were subjected to compulsory recruitment in the hundreds of thousands to serve as soldiers in European military campaigns on East African soil. In addition, "even more men, as well as women and children were recruited, often forcibly, as carriers to support armies whose supplies could not be moved by conventional methods such as road, rail or pack-animal" (Crowder 1985, 283).

The East African coast especially, where the majority of native speakers of Swahili are located, was torn by the simple fact that the Germans, occupying the southern part of the coast—a portion of German East Africa that roughly encompassed Tanganyika, Rwanda, and Burundi—were fighting the British, occupying the northern part of the coast (as part of Kenya Colony), and Swahili was the language of cultural and economic interaction down the seaboard as a whole. Both the Germans and the British recruited into their armed forces local people who would not otherwise have been at war with each other and who, in the case of the East African coast, were culturally and linguistically related to each other.

Of course, wars between the Swahili themselves preceded European colonial rule by centuries. Some Swahili city-states, connected to both the interior and the Indian Ocean, were locked in repeated warfare as a result of competition for commercial control and other reasons, sometimes in collaboration with external forces like the Portuguese and the Omani Arabs. In an earlier century (1586–1589), the Swahili were engaged in proxy wars between the Ottomans and the Portuguese as they competed for control of the East African coast. Being the native language of the region, Swahili naturally served as the language of military command in these conflicts along the Swahili coast. But the language was also known to have served an important inspirational role. Some of the poems of the celebrated Muyaka wa Mwinyi Haji (1776–1840), for example, are best known for precisely this function of inspiring his Mombasa compatriots in the warfront against their enemies.

Between World War I and World War II, however, Swahili's major role in the East African region as a whole was primarily functional and organizational. Of course, there were many languages at play in East Africa as a theater of war. Most of these were African "ethnic" languages. However, there were also the European languages of the different

3 Swahili in Military Context: Between World War I and World... 59

colonizing powers locked in conflict: English, German, Belgian, Italian, and Portuguese. Indentured workers and immigrants from India had added several South Asian languages to the mix. Under these circumstances, who spoke which language to whom would often be determined by the context of interlocution. There was little doubt, however, that Swahili was rapidly becoming the main language of communication at the lower horizontal level—between African *askaris* (soldiers) and porters themselves—and in the vertical dimension between senior officers, primarily European, and African military personnel under their command and authority.

A particularly significant section of Britain's East African colonial military force, the King's African Rifles (KAR), was composed of South Sudanese recruits whose reputed loyalty and experience "ensured that they dominated the ranks of the KAR's 'Native Officers' and senior African non-commissioned officers (NCOs) until the beginning of the Second World War. Many Sudanese made KAR their career, and served lengthy terms, some lasting as long as thirty years" (Parsons 1997, 88). Trained and serving side-by-side with East Africans in a colonial military setup where Swahili served important official functions, these Sudanese soldiers ended up acquiring Swahili as an additional language. Later many of these military veterans and their families settled in East Africa and developed a special affinity to Swahili partly because of their Muslim background.

In both German East Africa (Tanganyika and Ruanda-Urundi) and British East Africa (Kenya and Uganda), European officers were encouraged to learn Swahili even when they were on board naval ships traveling from one point to another. The British Colonial Office communicated the "great importance that British ranks should be acquainted with Swahili as early as possible and [given the] length of time occupied in voyage, should continue learning on board supported by administrative officers returning from leave" (Samson 2021, 34). The British government even established a training program in London partly designed to teach Swahili to military officers who would be dispatched to East Africa.

There was also extensive colonial use of Swahili for propaganda purposes throughout the World War I period intended to galvanize local moral, political, and material backing for the British cause. In what was then the Sultanate of Zanzibar, for example, the British "colonial administration began publishing a weekly newspaper in both Arabic and Swahili called *El Usbueyah* (The weekly), with Swahili in both Roman and Arabic characters, for propaganda work and to enable the mass of the population to be acquainted with the latest telegrams concerning the war. Further, the administration issued updates on the war on broadsheets in 1916 in Swahili written in Arabic characters, which they called Kiswahili Arabic" (Bolton 2016, 68). The circulation of both *El Esbueyah* and the broadsheets was restricted to the Muslim, native Swahili-speaking population along the East African coast for it was this constituency alone that was then regarded as literate in Swahili and Arabic.

World War I may have affected the destiny of Swahili in what was then the Belgian Congo (or what is today the Democratic Republic of the Congo, or DRC for short) in a different direction altogether. Trade relations between the coast and the interior of Eastern Africa had taken Swahili all the way to the eastern region of the DRC, in the Katanga area, sometime prior to the inception of European colonialism. Swahili-speaking traders and porters interacted with local people in trading towns like Bukenya, in time making Swahili the primary language of trade and interethnic communication. Some of these traders and their porters settled in the DRC, giving Swahili a foothold and presence that would endure over time. During these early stages of penetration, the Swahili of the area was most probably not too different from the Swahili of Tanganyika and its approximations, not having adopted the morphosyntactic features of local Bantu languages.

Later the DRC fell under the colonial control of Belgium as a possession of the Belgian King Leopold II at just about the time when rich reserves of minerals in the southern area of Katanga had been discovered. Mining now rose to the fore as a lucrative domain of colonial economic activity, resulting in the development of Lubumbashi, then known as Elisabethville, as the new center of economic life. The rapid expansion of the mining industry led to the recruitment of mine workers not only from DRC regions outside Katanga, but also from the neighboring countries of Burundi, Rwanda, Zambia, and Zimbabwe. In the southeast on the Katangese plateau, in particular, an area

3 Swahili in Military Context: Between World War I and World...

which was practically devoid of population before the arrival of European colonists, the development of the copper industry, creating a constant appeal for more immigrant labor, gave rise to a situation where the multiracial inhabitants of booming towns could resort to no other language than the trade language as a means of communication. This 'lingua franca' was Swahili, which had been introduced from the east by a group of former members of Arab trade caravans–well-armed adventurers of Sumbwa origin–who seized power in poorly defended territory …. (Polome 1967, 7)

The Belgian labor recruitment pattern then had a direct bearing on the multiethnic composition that emerged gradually in Katanga. An additional colonial incentive for preferring immigrant labor is that workers "could be gotten cheaper and more readily in distant lands" and could be "more easily controlled" (Fabian 1986, 95). And because demand for production increased dramatically during World War I, the Belgian authorities doubled their efforts at "long distance recruitment" of African labor (Fabian 1986, 97).

This large interethnic and multilingual pool of African laborers favored the continued use of Swahili in the mining region, a linguistic continuity that was both in line with the wishes of and promoted by the Belgian administration (A. Kapanga 2001). Fabian is of the opinion that the choice of Swahili as the language of mining work in Katanga cannot be explained merely by "its actual preponderance in preindustrial southeastern Katanga, or by the arrival of important numbers of Swahili-speaking workers from some other area, but as part of a political strategy" (1986, 97). A significant aspect of this strategy of the Belgian administration in developing a policy of aggressive promotion of Swahili was partly to counter British colonial and linguistic influences in the mining belt (Fabian 1986, 136). Yet, it is fair to say that the Belgian authorities succeeded in imposing a form of Swahili in the mining area partly because the diversity of the labor pool itself provided a fertile environment for the success of the strategy. Whatever the case, what emerged out of this mining context is what has come to be known as "Shaba Swahili," a variety of Swahili that evolved not from simplification of the Swahili originally introduced from Tanganyika but from its adaptation to the morphosyntactic patterns of local Bantu languages (M. T. Kapanga 1991). The world war appears to have posed no threat to this lingua franca status of Swahili in the mining region.

Where the war may have influenced the fortunes of Swahili in the Belgian Congo was in the military. The Belgian colonial administration relied heavily on mercenary soldiers from other regions of Africa during the early phase of colonialism. The Belgians "kept up the usage of Swahili in the area by recruiting their police force in the Zanzibar area and preserving Swahili as the language of the army until the First World War" (Polome 1967, 8). Later, however, there was a change of policy and the recruitment for the army began to rely on the more local (Congolese) pool that was not Swahili-speaking. World War I may have been one of the factors that led to this change in recruitment policy. Because of the war and the events leading to it, each imperial power now had to depend more exclusively on the population under its direct colonial control for its military recruitment.

Long before Swahili became the language of the mines, "it was used by the armed forces and was the medium of instruction in a school for non-commissioned officers" (Fabian 1986, 178). The change in recruitment pattern in the Belgian Congo, however, had the effect of de-Swahilizing the army. Lingala now gradually moved in, in time creating a lingua-economic divide, with Lingala now serving "the military and much of the administration in the capital of the lower Congo" and Swahili becoming "the language of the workers in the mines of Katanga" (Fabian 1986, 42). By then, Lingala, a Bantu-based creole, had developed into a lingua franca in much of the northwestern part of the Congo. Though Swahili was probably spoken by as many Congolese nationals as was Lingala, the latter had established itself over a wider geographical area in the country. Lingala then had an edge over Swahili in an army that recruited widely throughout the Belgian colonial territory of the Congo.

More important than the actual war itself for the future of Swahili in Eastern Africa, however, was the outcome of World War I. The defeat of Germany and the assumption of administrative authority in Tanganyika by Great Britain had long-term repercussions not only for Tanganyika, but for East Africa as a whole. From a linguistic point of view, the triumph of the British over the Germans was a mixed blessing for Swahili. The British as a colonial power were, in their language policy, different

3 Swahili in Military Context: Between World War I and World... 63

from both the French and the Germans. The French were tied to a missionary vision to disseminate their culture and spread their language. Language was in fact central to the French colonial policy of "assimilation." Because of that vision, the French were among the least tolerant of colonial powers in their attitude to local African languages and cultures.

With the Germans, on the other hand, language remained a controversial issue in terms of its colonial policy that continued to be debated until the end of German colonial rule in East Africa: "The authorities in Berlin favoured German, arguing that Swahili was the linguistic base for spreading Islam while the German language was more suited to inscribing *Deutschtum* (Germanness) in the East African colony" (Bromber 2004, 39–40). According to Marcia Wright, for example:

> In Germany, Director Buchner proved to be an unrelenting foe of Swahili, going so far in a speech before the Kolonialrat in 1905 as to declare that it was irredeemably mixed with Islam that every expedient ought to be employed to obstruct their joint penetration …. Buchner's opposition to Swahili was adopted and expanded by Julius Richter, a member of the Berlin Committee. Richter delivered a diatribe during the Kolonial Kongress in 1905 against the pernicious influence of Islam everywhere in Africa. Isolating East Africa as the scene of the worst danger, he envisaged a mosque alongside every coastman's hut, and took the official support for Swahili to be blatantly pro-Islamic. (1971, 113)

Within German East Africa itself, however, it was Swahili that continued to hold sway. As the language they first encountered on the coast of East Africa, the Germans took Swahili with them as they spread their rule inward, making it the medium of local administration in various districts as well as of military posts (Bromber 2004, 39).

In addition, German administration regarded it as inefficient to have to deal in too many different languages all over the colonial territory. There was, therefore, a case for singling out one medium or a few major media to be used for administrative purposes and letting some of the others become imperiled or die by administrative disuse. This policy held even in other regions of Africa that had a German presence, favoring the promotion of Herero in Southern Africa, for example, and Hausa in

Western Africa (Pugach 2012, 68). In East Africa, it was Swahili that became especially privileged. The use of East African languages other than Swahili was generally regarded as impractical and unnecessary. In time, then,

> … Swahili became the primary colonial language in the region. German officials wanted to use the language, which had been spreading from inland as a vehicle of trade well before their arrival, to consolidate German rule. They also saw it as a bulwark against English, which was in use throughout the colony and which they wanted to 'drive' out of it. Eventually, German became so enamored with Swahili that they even envisioned transplanting it to Cameroon [their colony in West Africa] and also making it the Verkehrsprache [lingua franca] in West Africa. Research into other vernaculars or study of them…could only hamper the German objective of making Swahili their main colonial language, and so it was actively discouraged. (Pugach 2012, 69)

For all practical purposes, then, "the use of Swahili by Germans may well be seen as pre-determined from the very beginning" (Brumfit 1980, 242), and the fate of other East African languages was of least concern to the German colonial administration.

The British were in an intermediate position between the Germans and the French. They believed in the ideology of indirect rule and its cultural appendages. They conceded a certain right of survival to local cultural ways and local languages in their colonies. They even set up committees to coordinate the growth of key languages in their colonial territories. But the British also believed, with some ambivalence, in bestowing the gift of the English language on the elites of the colonial territories. As a generalization, then, we might say that the British colonial administration favored a native acquisition of English a little more than the German colonial administration had once favored a native acquisition of German; and the British were more tolerant of smaller African languages and more prepared to put up with linguistic plurality than either the Germans or the French (Mazrui 1970, 19–21).

The fortunes of Swahili within Tanganyika suffered a little, though by no means fatally, when the country shifted from German control to British control. The British toleration of smaller languages, to the extent

3 Swahili in Military Context: Between World War I and World... 65

that it was greater than the German, slowed down the spread of Swahili as a lingua franca. The British colonial administration, leaning toward promoting the English language to the extent that it was greater than the German colonial administration in Tanganyika leaning toward promoting the German language, again affected adversely the fortunes of Swahili within Tanganyika. Indeed, the spread of the English language under British rule had the effect of relegating Swahili to the status of second-class language among Africans themselves. In the words of Wilfred Whiteley:

> Whereas in German times the acquisition of Swahili represented a first stage toward participating in Government through membership of junior Civil Service, no further stage in this participation could be achieved through the language. The next stage involved the acquisition of English and for this reason, Swahili was seen increasingly by Tanganyikans as a 'second-class language.' (1969, 61–62)

Educational policy was framed under the British on the basis of a declining utilization of Swahili. The language was used as a medium of primary school education but became only one subject among several at secondary school and disappeared completely even as a required subject in higher education:

> As time went on, the difference in the quality and quantity of secondary school materials and teachers was clear evidence to pupils, if to no one else, of the inferior status of the language. Institutions designed primarily for East Africans made no prevision for the study of Swahili while their use of English simply confirmed East Africans in their belief that it was on this language that they should concentrate their sights. While Swahili newspapers were plentiful, the glossy magazines were in English. (Whiteley 1969, 62)

Of course, if Tanganyika had been entrusted as a League of Nations mandate to the administration of France, the fortunes of Swahili would have suffered even more drastically. French culture would have made Swahili an even more second-class language than it became under British rule. What is likely to be overlooked is that within Tanganyika the language would probably have fared better, and developed faster, as a national language enforced by the colonial power had the Germans remained in control after World War I.

Not least significant of the consequences of World War I was the fact that Zanzibar and Tanganyika now shared the same imperial power, Great Britain. Zanzibar, as the heartland of what later became Standard Swahili, maintained its ease of communication with Dar es Salaam as the capital of Tanganyika. The dissemination of Swahili throughout East Africa as a whole received additional boosting by the very fact that the Sultanate, then still relatively powerful, shared the same metropolitan "protecting" power as what later became mainland Tanzania. Indeed, the very union of Tanganyika and Zanzibar in 1964 might well have been inconceivable if the island and the mainland had reached the 1960s under the impact of two entirely different colonial powers.

But while the fortunes of Swahili as a language of Tanganyika might thus have suffered when the country fell under German rule, the fortunes of Swahili as a language of East Africa probably improved. With the outcome of World War I being what it was, it was now conceivable for Kenya, Uganda, Zanzibar, and Tanganyika to develop on the basis of increasing regional integration. Among the most unifying factors in modern Africa has been that of being ruled by the same colonial power. Tanganyikans are much closer today to Kenyans and Ugandans than they would have been had Tanganyikans been German-speaking, while Kenyans and Ugandans were English-speaking. Regional organizations, like the East African High Commission, and its successors right up to the once defunct and now revived East African Community, would not have been conceivable if there had continued to be a German East Africa in that part of the continent. The very concept of an East African Federation, hotly debated as it once was for decades, would not have featured realistically if Tanganyika had been the colony of a European power other than Britain, which had colonized Kenya and Uganda.

World War II and Its Aftermath

In the interwar period, between World War I and World War II, the question of coordinating and integrating the armed forces and the police of British East Africa also became important. The colonial King's African

Rifles (KAR) had sought to recruit across ethnic boundaries within the region. The issue was not absent even during World War I, when East Africa was the scene of battle between Britain and Germany over the possession of German East Africa, Tanganyika, and Ruanda-Urundi, and British military recruiters often looked "outside East Africa for the bulk of their rank-and file askaris" (Parsons 1999, 61). But with the imminence of World War II, the question of wider recruitment in the region arose once again. In their efforts to recruit soldiers, the British were particularly guided by the notion of "martial tribes," though which ethnic group qualified for this designation had much more to do with British politico-economic interests than the martial traditions of the various ethnic groups (Parsons 1999, 54–56). Less selective was recruitment of military carriers. Whatever the case, here the problem of a suitable language of command, effective enough for a multiethnic unit of the armed forces, came back to the fore. And Swahili tended to be the language of choice.

In the end, both the fortunes of Swahili and the spirit of regionalism became part of the history of the armed forces. In the case of East Africa, the promotion of Swahili enabled the emergence of regional consciousness. This was facilitated partly by the method of recruitment into the King's African Rifles. Recruitment was conducted all over East Africa, but it did not follow that Ugandan soldiers would serve only in Uganda, Tanganyikans in Tanganyika, and Kenyans in Kenya. On the contrary, an important aspect of British colonial policy was its trans-territorial dimension. There was a persistent attempt to minimize the significance of the territorial origins of new recruits in determining where they were to serve. Swahili then played a critical role in making this interterritorial command feasible, especially in functioning as the language of the armed forces.

Of course, the recruits had different levels of competence in this language, which was not native to the majority of them, ranging from rudimentary to sophisticated. This reality coincided with the fact that the use of Swahili was not uniformly distributed throughout the East African region. Perhaps the least competent in the language were the British commanding officers from Kenya, in particular. Kenya was a British settler colony and many of the settlers in the so-called White Highlands established commercial plantations of cash crops, especially tea and coffee. While their settlement was a colonial project of Britain in East Africa, many of the settlers themselves were motivated by the prospects of establishing cash crop plantations for commercial interests. Between the colonial administration, the missionaries, and the settlers, it was the latter who were the most ardent advocates of Swahili, as the language that would better link settler capital and African labor. Many of these Englishmen in the colonial days insisted on speaking Swahili to their employees partly as a way of maintaining social distance even if neither spoke Swahili well enough, while both spoke English to varying degrees of fluency.

This situation contributed to the formation of *Kisetla* (literally, "the settlers' way/variety"), a pidginized variety of British settler Swahili that reflected the power asymmetry between British master and African servants. A description of some of its linguistic features provided by Vitale (1980) includes drastic morphological attenuation of the verbal system, reduction of the morphological possibilities of Swahili's tense system, and, among others, a syntactic pattern that is more reminiscent of English in terms of the position of noun phrases and verb phrases. An important observation that Vitale makes is the correlation between the proportion of Swahili forms that appear in the speech of a settler and his/her familiarity with Standard Swahili (1980, 62), suggesting that the range of Kisetla varieties essentially reflected different approximations to the Swahili spoken by Africans themselves. Kisetla, then, is what many British commanding officers brought to the King's African Rifles between World War I and World War II.

Accompanying the linguistic preparation of settler-soldiers in East Africa was the production of language phrase books, Swahili phrase books in this case. "The selection process—which phrases to translate—was presumably derived partly from consultation with people with some military experience, partly drawn from existing travelers' phrasebooks, partly from editor's discretion, and partly from attitudes towards speakers of the language" (Languages and the First World War 2018). The prevailing British view of the African at that time was essentially that of a servant. The Army YMCA/British East Africa publication entitled *"First Aid" to the Swahili Language* is clearly demonstrative of this master-servant frame of Euro-African relationships. On page 12, for example, it has a list of Swahili words and phrases, shown in Fig. 3.1.

3 Swahili in Military Context: Between World War I and World...

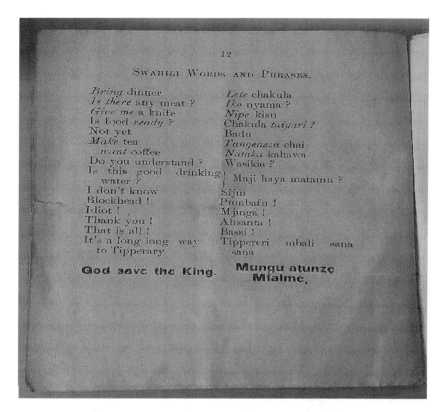

Fig. 3.1 Sample page from *"First Aid" to the Swahili Language*

The list clearly frames the racially defined relationship of a white master/mistress and African servant, all within a context that allows the British settler to affirm, in Swahili, the fact of coloniality in that popular phrase *Mungu atunze Mfalme* (God save the King). And it is from these kinds of phrase books and pamphlets that British officers who ended up in the army acquired their rudimentary knowledge of Swahili.

In this context, with British officers speaking Kisetla or no Swahili at all, and most African askaris (soldiers) having no more than a smattering of the language, a simplified variety of Swahili emerged that accorded the forces of KAR a distinct identity. This variety came to be known as *Kikeya* (literally, the KAR way, with the pronunciation of the acronym Swahilized). According to Mutonya and Parsons (2004, 111–112), it is "a variety of Swahili characterized by a relatively simplified structure and a distinct lexical borrowing of military terminology [...] laden with substrate influences of African languages." Kikeya seems to have persisted throughout the period before Swahili had a standard variety.

Kikeya or KiKAR became a consolidated variety partly because British officers of the King's African Rifles avoided recruiting men from the native Swahili-speaking communities of the Kenya coast, sometimes because they were considered "non-martial"—even though the KAR did enlist "several clerks/interpreters from the coast to improve the language skills of the battalion in Uganda" (Parsons 1999, 112). As a result, much of the recruitment focused on men from rural and agrarian communities from the upcountry with little or no proficiency at all in the Swahili language. Though by then Swahili had spread widely throughout East Africa, it was still primarily an urban phenomenon to which many rural communities of the interior had little exposure. These new recruits would then acquire Kikeya from other recruits who were already serving in the King's African Rifles and from African non-commissioned officers who served as language instructors and were often responsible for facilitating communication between the British officers and the African recruits (Mutonya and Parsons 2004, 116).

Osborne refers to a satirical piece in a colonial periodical intended to make a mockery of the Swahili of British officers who had served in the King's African Rifles (KAR). The piece opens with a chance meeting in London of two British veterans of KAR, Bill and Potter:

> Potter acts as though he has never left Africa, sprinkling his vocabulary with the broken Swahili of the KAR officers. When Bill attempts to leave–claiming he must get home to his wife–Potter responds: 'Oh, the little memsahib wouldn't mind *bado kidogo-ing* [waiting a little] while one effendi pots with another effendi.' (Osborne 2020, 303)

Osborne also provides an example of a fictional interview with a certain "Mr. Arbuthnot" in which "the subject is asked whether British men and women in East Africa should learn Swahili. 'No Sir!' he replies, 'Just give 'em [Africans] a good kick right up the backside! They do it twice as fast!'" (Osborne 2020, 303). While the limited Swahili command of

British soldiers depicted in the first anecdote may appear that it was a subject of some derision, that same linguistic limitation was an important marker of social distance between the British and their colonized subjects, a linguistic marker that the British would rather not have been bothered with if they could have achieved their objectives through other means.

The outcome of World War I was also an important factor behind the emergence of the very concept of Standard Swahili. Because the British now controlled Kenya, Uganda, Tanganyika, and Zanzibar, the idea of standardizing Swahili as an East African language became viable. Rivalries between the colonial powers themselves and Christian missionaries over which dialect among the East African varieties of the language to choose for such an enterprise ceased to be relevant after the ouster of the Germans from the East African space. Hitherto the native speakers of Swahili themselves used an Arabic-derived script in writing their language. European colonizers, both German and British, were hostile to the Arabic-derived script because of its association with Islam. As a result, German and British missionaries and colonial functionaries that were positively disposed to Swahili sought to replace the Arabic-derived script with Latin script. But there were many spelling inconsistencies resulting from the uncoordinated adoption of the Latin script.

In 1925, an education conference was convened by the British Governor of Tanganyika in the capital city of Dar es Salaam and it became an important landmark in the development of the idea of a standard Swahili orthography in the Latin script. In 1926, a number of proposals were made concerning spelling and word division in Swahili. Meanwhile, the 1925 conference had led to the establishment of a Central Publishing Committee. This body now demanded to be fully informed about projected textbooks for schools in an endeavor to avoid unnecessary duplication, but also to exercise colonial control over the Swahili they wished to emerge in their colonial space.

Kenya was also groping for some kind of standard orthography in the Latin script. It was in January 1928 that an interterritorial conference held in Mombasa, Kenya, confirmed the decision to adopt the dialect of Zanzibar as the basis of Standard Swahili. The Universities Mission to Central Africa had recommended the Zanzibar dialect in competition with the Church Missionary Society who were advocating the dialect of Mombasa, Kenya. Again, the whole enterprise of choosing a dialect from British-controlled East Africa as the basis of Standard Swahili became viable partly because, in the aftermath of World War I, Tanganyika was no longer controlled by a rival European power. The range of dialects to choose from would have been reduced to that of Mombasa and Zanzibar alone if a divided imperial presence had been an additional factor in the linguistic situation in East Africa. And it is conceivable that if German rule had continued in Tanganyika in the aftermath of World War I, there might have been a competing standard Swahili based on a dialect from German East Africa.

On January 1, 1930, the Inter-Territorial Language Committee came into being at last. This Committee became a paramount mechanism in the process of standardizing Swahili and ensuring its uniformity throughout the region. The initial composition of the Committee reflected the new post-World War I reality, with officers from British-controlled Kenya and Uganda, from Zanzibar, and from Tanganyika, once part of German East Africa. And during World War II, the Committee worked closely with the King's African Rifles and its military units in Kenya, Nyasaland (modern-day Malawi), Tanganyika, and Uganda especially, in an effort to increase Swahili language proficiency among the soldiers. In other words, the Committee's work became an important dimension of the British war effort.

In Uganda, the hold of Swahili was still relatively weak as compared with Kenya, Tanganyika, and Zanzibar. But even in Uganda, the fortunes of Swahili began, perhaps haltingly, to take a turn for the better following the defeat of Germany in Tanganyika. In the 1920s, Swahili in Uganda had at first seemed to be receding completely into the background. In 1925, A. W. Smith had observed that in Uganda "probably no person would favor the teaching of Swahili; Luganda is making headway in the provinces at the expense of the vernaculars" (1925, 12). In addition, the missionaries who dominated the educational system in Uganda at that time were hostile to Swahili because of its close cultural links with Islam.

In 1926, special committees on language policy recommended that three languages be promoted in schools in the country: In the north, Acholi should be used as the medium of instruction; in parts of the

3 Swahili in Military Context: Between World War I and World...

eastern province, Teso should be the medium of instruction; and in the rest of Uganda, Luganda should continue to dominate the education system. Swahili did not feature prominently in this planning. The full significance of Tanganyika's new status as a Mandated Territory under Britain had taken longer to reveal its implications for Uganda than it might have done. It was nearly seven years after World War I before Governor Williams Gowers of Uganda made the first major bid to pull Swahili into the mainstream of Ugandan society. According to Gadsden:

> Gowers argued that since Tanganyika had become a British mandated territory and communication in East Africa had improved, Uganda could not afford to isolate itself by ignoring Swahili which was understood in Kenya, Tanganyika, and as far as the Congo…. The possibility of federation [in East Africa] must have made the Swahili issue a matter of urgency for Gowers. But he confined his arguments to a more general discussion of the need for Uganda to integrate herself with general developments in East Africa, and the educational advantages of Swahili. (Gadsden 1971, 4)

The question of coordinating, if not integrating, the armed forces and the police of East Africa had also been examined. As indicated earlier, and in spite of the colonial belief that some ethnic groups were culturally better prepared for military combat than others, the King's African Rifles recruited from different groups throughout the region. On a global scale, the number of troops to be recruited from East Africa was indeed quite modest, but the recruitment covered a diversity of linguistic backgrounds. The KAR had already had to face the issue of the language of command even before the war. As suggested earlier, the issue was not absent even in the First World War when East Africa was the scene of battle between Britain and Germany over the possession of German East Africa. But with the imminence of World War II and the possibility of wider recruitment once again, the problem of a suitable language of command, effective enough for a multilinguistic unit of armed forces, assumed a new persistence.

In the ultimate analysis, there were three possibilities: first, a policy based on using a number of ethnic languages; second, a policy based on adopting English; and thirdly, a policy based on utilizing Swahili. The multiethnolinguistic solution had a number of disadvantages. Unlike those of the West African languages, such as Hausa and Yoruba, the native speakers of indigenous languages in East Africa were more modest in population. Even the larger ethnic groups, like the Gikuyu of Kenya and the Baganda of Uganda, were at the time little more than a million each, whereas Yoruba speakers in West Africa—let alone Hausa speakers—were to be counted in the several millions.

There was also the related argument that military command based on ethnic languages would bedevil the issue of command and promotions within each linguistic group. The officers commanding Baganda soldiers might need themselves to be Baganda; the officers commanding Acholi soldiers might need themselves to be Acholi. If they were not drawn from the same linguistic community, the officers would need to be versed in the appropriate language.

The adoption of English would help solve this problem of communication across ethnic lines but would inevitably drastically reduce the section of the population from which the soldiers could be recruited. In the 1930s and 1940s, only a small proportion of the population of the East African countries spoke even rudimentary English, and those who spoke it well would look toward recruitment as officer cadets from the beginning. The King's African Rifles knew they had to recruit from a wide section of the population of East Africa and could not at the time afford to have this area circumscribed by an insistence on some knowledge of the imperial language.

The third possibility centered on adopting Swahili as the language of the armed forces. This would eliminate the problem of each linguistic community producing its own officers and non-commissioned officers. An Acholi could command an army unit consisting of Akamba, Baganda, and Wadigo, for example. Neither boundaries between ethnic groups nor boundaries between colonies within the same region would need to be constraining factors in recruitment. It is true that knowledge of Swahili was not uniformly distributed throughout the region. Some communities spoke it more fluently than others. Some colonial territories preferred a more "sophisticated" version of Swahili than others. But a basic lingua franca, even if rudimentary, was already evolving. The armed forces could take advantage of the availability of such a lingua franca and could, in turn, strengthen its functions by providing, if need be, further courses in Swahili in the barracks.

In colonial Kenya, for example, a form of Swahili that came to be known as "Kibara," or upcountry Swahili, evolved out of the contact and trade relations between the coastal native speakers of Swahili and non-coastal Africans speaking a number of different languages, with Swahili serving as the trade language. This is the variety of Swahili that came to be dominant in the military. It is significant that F. H. Le Breton, the author of the booklet entitled *Upcountry Swahili*, had been a soldier himself during World War I and ended up becoming "a soldier-settler" in Kenya. As far back as World War I, the colonial War Council of Kenya not only concerned itself with the war and the problem of conscription (in which East Africa led the way in the Empire), but it sought to strengthen the European position in particular by devising a Soldier Settlement Scheme for the postwar period (Bennet 1963, 38–39).

At the end of World War II, the Kenya colonial government and the British government announced an agricultural settlement scheme for European soldiers released from the armed forces—"men and women of pure European descent, who were thus eligible to farm in the area reserved for Europeans, and whose war services a grateful country wished to recognize" (Blundell 1964, 63), all at the expense of the natives of that land, of course. It is from the ranks of these "soldier-settlers," then, that the author of *Upcountry Swahili* emerged.

In writing *Upcountry Swahili*, Le Breton was inspired by the need for an introductory book not on Standard Swahili that was based on the native-speaking coastal population, but on the kind of Swahili that was more common in the upcountry region. In Le Breton's words:

> Correct Swahili is a very complicated language native to Zanzibar and the coastal belt of East Africa. To the ordinary up-country native, Swahili is a foreign language of which he possesses only a very limited knowledge. This book aims at teaching, in a simple way, just that degree of Swahili that is understood and talked by the average intelligent up-country native. All previous Swahili books have dealt with correct coastal Swahili, but the average up-country native definitely does not understand the intricacies of correct Swahili, neither does any settler, miner, businessman or wife

attempt to speak it to him, and the official deals with him largely through interpreters into his own dialect. (1936, 3)

As the subtitle indicates, Le Breton's booklet was written "For the Soldier, Settler, Miner, Merchant, and their Wives And for all who deal with Up-country Natives without Interpreters" who were members of the British settler community in Kenya at that time. And to make sure that British officers in the King's African Rifles in Kenya benefited from the booklet, Le Breton provided a vocabulary of over 120 Swahili words that he describes as "Military Terms" (1936, 53).

The exercises that accompany the list of military terms shows clearly that, for Le Breton, this variety of Swahili, when used in the context of the military, was intended to serve primarily as a language of command. The English to Swahili translation exercises, for example, are replete with orders and commands, presumably given by British officers to African non-commissioned officers and other African subordinates. For example, learners are asked to translate the following English sentences into Swahili:

> Tomorrow you will send the recruits to the rifle range. They will fire at a hundred yards; see that they aim properly, and that they squeeze the trigger slowly...
>
> Stand properly! Shoulders back, stick out your chest, raise your chin, straighten your knees! What is the matter with you?
>
> Tell the sentry on the guns not to allow anyone to approach the ammunition with a cigarette because it is very dangerous.

And there are other sentences that give orders to discipline soldiers, to attend to the wounded, and more. In the process, military terms that are part of the British military experience, terms like ammunition, bullets, grenades, machine guns, and submarines, are all integrated into the exercises.

Of course, the history of Swahili military terminology goes all the way back to the precolonial period. The Swahili themselves had recurrent

3 Swahili in Military Context: Between World War I and World... 77

outbreaks of war between city-states framed in military language derived from the indigenous experience. But centuries of Swahili-Arab encounter, mainly a product of trade and later religious relations, resulted in the adoption of several military terms from Arabic. The context of the King's African Rifles between the two world wars opened up other sources of military terms in Swahili, including that of the English language (Adika Kevogo and Kevogo 2014).

In addition to serving organizational purposes as a language of command, Swahili also served to promote a sense of unity and even a new sense of identity tied to new loyalties. The role of Swahili for such inspirational purposes was particularly evident in the songs that the African soldiers sang in peace and war. Many of the songs reflected "new loyalties, first to a battalion and to an army, but later on to a colony or a new nation. Some were obviously officially inspired, but many others were a natural almost spontaneous expression of the wish of soldiers of different languages to identify themselves with the new loyalties and to communicate with each other" (Clayton 1978, 1). And if in West Africa the songs were of multilingual origin with "some songs being composed of words or lines of several languages," in East Africa they were based primarily on the region's lingua franca, Swahili (Clayton 1978, 3–4).

A good World War II song that served these multiple functions is "Haya Keya Askari" (Onward KAR Soldiers!), a marching song of the Kenya battalion of the King's African Rifles, intended to affirm a new interethnic loyalty anchored in the Third KAR battalion and its defining territorial base, the Kenya Colony. The song adopts the tune of "Men of Harlech" that was widely used as a regimental march song by the British Army and Commonwealth regiments. The lyrics, as reported by Clayton (1978, 48), are as follows:

Haya! Kenya Askari	Onward K.A.R. soldiers
Sisi kazi ya safari	Our role is to travel
Kazi yako kazi gani?	What is your job?
Vita kali leo!	Ferocious fighting today
Amri ya serekali!	Orders of the government
Keya tayari!	K.A.R. is ready!
Kali kama simba sisi,	We're as fierce as lions,

Askari wote ni hodari.	All the soldiers are skilled
Twende twende kupigana	Let's go and fight
Piga adui piga sana!	Strike the enemy, strike hard!
Haya! Keya askari,	Onward K.A.R. soldiers
Vita kati leo,	Heavy fighting today,
Toka! Toka! Manyumbani!	Get out, get out of your homes
Wacha bibi kitandani!	Leave your wife in bed!
Haya! Keya askari!	Onward K.A.R. soldiers!
Sisi third Keya.	We're the 3rd K.A.R.

The King's African Rifles was organized in battalions recruited from four British-controlled African countries: Kenya, Nyasaland (or modern-day Malawi), Tanganyika (today referred to as mainland Tanzania after Tanganyika's merger with Zanzibar), and Uganda. Two battalions, First and Second KAR, were grounded in Nyasaland. Another two, Third and Fifth KAR were Kenya-based. The latter were the battalions that made the most extensive use of KiKAR or Kikeya (Mutonya and Parsons 2004, 113). Fourth KAR and Sixth KAR were located in Uganda and Tanganyika, respectively. What we see in the song "Haya! Kena Askari" is not only the identification with the broader community of soldiers of the King's African Rifles, but also with the specific Kenyan battalion of the King's African Rifles, the Third KAR. In addition to this identitarian dimension, there is the inspirational side of the song, with the soldiers of Third KAR likening themselves to a band of fierce lions out to strike the enemy hard and move on to victory.

Of all the Swahili march songs of the King's African Rifles, however, none was more popular than Tufunge Safari (Let's prepare for the journey), which has again been recorded by Clayton (1978, 37):

> Tufunge safari, tufunge upesi
> Tufunge safari, tufunge upesi
> Kwa amri ya nani?
> Amri ya Bwana Kapteni, amri ya jeshi!
> > Tufunge safari, twende vitani,
> > Tufunge safari, twende vitani,
> > Tupigane tuwashinde maadui.
> > Maadui wanalala kwa mahandaki.

3 Swahili in Military Context: Between World War I and World... 79

Tukishinda maadui tutarudi kwetu
Na Watoto wanatungoja wakipiga makofi,
Tutaanza kulima mashamba yetu,
Na kuchunga ng'ombe yetu maisha,

> Let's prepare for the journey, let's prepare quickly
> Let's prepare for the journey, let's prepare quickly
> With whose order?
> Orders of Mister Captain, orders of the Army.
>
> Let's prepare for the journey, let's go to the war
> Let's prepare for the journey, let's go to the war
> Let's fight and defeat the enemy
> The enemy are sleeping in the trenches.
>
> When we have defeated the enemy, we shall return home
> And the children will be waiting for us, clapping
> We shall start tilling our plots of land
> And tending to our cattle forever.

Again, the song has an inspirational purpose, summoning the courage to fight the "cowardly" enemy pitched in their trenches, reinforcing the soldiers' sense of duty to finish the task at hand. But it also offers the soldiers hope for a postwar return to their homes, being greeted as heroes, to join their families once again, resuming their regular lives as farmers.

All these songs were relevant, of course, when the African regiments were fighting locally in East Africa. But during World War II, a significant proportion of East African soldiers was deployed outside East Africa, in parts of North Africa and the Middle East, South Asia, Madagascar, and Mauritius, among other places. In order to keep up morale in these contexts of war "and to legitimate the massive transfer of African military personnel to the aforementioned theaters of operation, the British colonial and military authorities built up a huge propaganda machinery. Directed at soldiers and civilians alike, Africans now became targeted audiences of the mass media in Britain's East African possessions" (Bromber 2010, 278). The colonial propaganda needs of the East African Command helped push Swahili to a new position as a language of written military media. In the process, African soldiers abroad were even able to debate various notions, for example honor (*heshima*) and shame (*aibu*), that would later come to frame postwar discussions for years (Osborne 2020, 306).

Bromber identifies three categories of Swahili military periodicals during World War II that were accessible to the East African contingents. The first was *Askari* (Soldier), which provided regular information about what was transpiring in the "various theaters of war and about the soldiers home territories." Then, following the example of *Askari*, were Swahili periodicals that focused primarily on the specific countries in which the soldiers were deployed. These included *Habari Zetu* (Our news) for soldiers located in the Horn of Africa, *Heshima* (Honor) for those deployed in South Asia, and *Pamoja* (Together) for Madagascar-based East African contingents. In the meantime, the Kenya Information Office "produced its own publication for troops from Kenya, *Kenya Kwetu*. *Kenya Kwetu* a monthly magazine in Swahili … concerned entirely with … such issues as the opening of schools and hospitals, agriculture, and the marriage of prominent individuals in the African community" (Gadsden 1986, 406). The third category included *Habari za Vita* (War News), *Askari Ugenini* (Soldiers abroad), and *Askari Wetu* (Our soldiers), which "targeted East African civilians and military personnel alike" (Bromber 2010, 279–280). *Habari za Vita* in particular was prompted by a government advisory committee report that there was a problem with a small number of Africans "who were mistranslating to others news from the English newspapers and so often causing disquiet among the African population" (Scotton 1978, 7). *Habari za Vita* began to be produced to combat these problems of "mistranslation." There was also *Baraza* (Forum), established in 1939 by the East African Standard Ltd. with the financial support and "at the instigation of the [Kenya] colonial government to bring news of the Second World War to non-English speakers" (Durrani 2006, 58). The East African soldiers deployed elsewhere also had regular access to civilian Swahili newspapers like *Mambo Leo* (Current events) and *Baraza* (Forum), which carried letters to the editors from the soldiers (Bromber 2010, 280) and which helped link the soldiers with their East African communities.

3 Swahili in Military Context: Between World War I and World... 81

In tandem with Swahili periodicals intended primarily for African soldiers were publications targeted at British soldiers. One of these was *Jambo* (Hello), published by the East Africa Command. The contributions to the periodical were all in English. But by using Swahili for the title, the periodical signaled the British presence in the African space. At the same time, however, the periodical allowed a few contributions by African soldiers with some command of English. Many of these African writers "used the venue to critique the conditions of their military service, argue about the sort of social ordering they desired in their home communities, and create an alternate narrative of the war" (Osborne 2020, 288).

In addition to news reports and letters, the periodicals, especially the civilian ones, regularly carried poems on the war experiences. The Swahili newspaper *Mambo Leo* was particularly noteworthy as an outlet for poetry from soldiers on the frontlines. In the words of Bromber: "The soldiers' access to civilian newspapers enabled them to actively or passively take part in a poetical discourse about the war which emerged in *Mambo Leo* immediately after the outbreak of hostilities" (2018, 124). In the Swahili verse tradition of "dialogic poetry," *Mambo Leo* also provided an opportunity for poetic exchanges on the war between the soldiers themselves and between the soldiers and their civilian communities at home. The poems revealed that the arena and implications of World War II were both global and local, and that the soldiers had to be prepared to traverse the space between the local and the global. With regard to the war effort against Japan, for example, a verse from a poem by Stephen M. R. Semsei declares:

Upesi pasipo shaka, amri tukapokea
Tukaondoka Afrika, upeso tukamwendea
Bandarini tukafika, bila ya yeye kujua
Japani ajililia, wengi wanaangamia (quoted by Bromber 2018, 128)

Quickly without doubt, we received the order
We left Africa, and rapidly advanced towards him
We arrived at the harbor, without him knowing
The Japanese are crying, many of them are perishing

Many of the poems gave a clear idea of where the soldiers were serving. We know, for example, that Semsei quoted above was deployed in Ceylon where he hoped the African troops would emerge as honorable. In his words:

> Heshima tutaipata hakika hapa Ceylon
> Tusifanye matata wakatuita wazimwe
> Hamu yangu ninataka uvumilivu yakini
> Tusiharibu heshima, wakatuita wajinga (quoted by Bromber 2018, 129)
>
>> Honor we shall receive, here in Ceylon,
>> Let's not cause trouble, lest they call us fools
>> What I wish for most is patience for certain
>> Let's not destroy our honor, with them calling us fools

In addition, between the local and the global, conceptions of participation in the war effort went beyond serving on the warfront. These included "increasing food production" and making "donations to the war fund," both considered to be "of equal importance" to serving in theaters of war abroad (Bromber 2018, 127).

Not all World War II poems came from soldiers, of course. Some were composed by civilians. Among the latter, none has received more attention than Shaaban Robert's *Utenzi wa Vita vya Uhuru* (Poem of the War of Liberation). Shaaban Robert was a leading and, in the area of Swahili prose fiction, even a pioneering literary figure in East Africa. Written between 1939 and 1945 with parts of it initially serialized in *Mambo Leo*, *Utenzi wa Vita vya Uhuru* (Narrative poem of the War of Independence) is a text of some 3000 stanzas, composed in the meter of the Swahili *utenzi* (narrative poetry). Robert makes manifest his objective of composing in Swahili in verse 13 of the poem:

> Nataka shairi hili
> Nilitunge Kiswahili
> Pasiwe na mushkeli
> Kutamka na kujua

3 Swahili in Military Context: Between World War I and World...

> I want this poem
> To be composed in Swahili
> To avoid any difficulty
> Of pronunciation and comprehension (Robert 1967, 2)

The poem then proceeds to narrate a history of World War II and the place of African troops in various theaters of war around the world. As the back cover of the book summarizes:

> Utenzi huu unasimulia habari za Vita Vikuu vya Pili–1939 mpaka 1945. Kwa utungo fasaha, Robert, yule mshairi mashuhuri wa Afrika Mashariki, anaeleza kwa nini vita hivi vilipiganwa na viliendeshwa namna gani na pande zote mbili. Karibu kila kitu muhimu cha vita hivi kinaelezwa katika utenzi huu. Hotuba muhimu zilizotolewa na viongozi mbalimbali, na hata simu walizopelekeana, zote zimo.

> This poem narrates the story of the Second Great War–1939 until 1945. Through this eloquent poem, Robert, that famous East African poet, explains why this war broke out and how it was fought by both sides. Critical speeches delivered by different leaders, and even the telegrams they exchanged, all of them are described here.

Unlike the metaphorical character of much of Swahili poetry at that time, we are told, again in the back cover description, that this poem "yametungwa kwa lugha nyepesi" (has been composed in simple language), all for ease of understanding.

According to Jan Knappert, this poem, "one of the longest ever written in Swahili, gives us a unique insight into how an African author who is widely regarded in his own country sees the history of the war and the attitudes of the belligerent nations" (Knappert 1969, 342). At the same time, however, the poem says little, beyond the conquest and counter-conquest of some African nations in the zones of war, about the African experience in the war. Apart from some passing mention of the presence of African troops abroad—as in stanza 215, for example—the nature of the African encounter with Europe in the theaters of war does not appear to have been on the poet's mind at all. What emerges prominently, rather, is the poet's support for the Allied powers against Germany.

Not only did members of the Swahili-speaking community, both soldiers and civilians, compose poetry to describe their experiences and perspectives of the war, sometimes they drew on existing poems to deal with the trauma of the war. A good example is the poem by Sayyid Abdalla bin Ali bin Nasir entitled *Al-Inkishafi* (The awakening of the soul), a text that the Swahili turned to reading frequently, in mosques and in homes, in the course of World War I. *Al-Inkishafi* is partly a meditation on the decline of the royal and the powerful in East African civilizations, constantly evoking images of collapse and decay. Might this degree of ruin also be the destiny of the world, of human civilization in the aftermath of the "vita vikuu," great war (world war)? Witnessing the destruction all around, the poet confronts his own heart/soul, urging it to turn away from vanity—the kind of vanity that fuels the ideological engines of war—and seek the spiritual path instead. In the context of World War I, then, this celebrated Swahili poem became an important source of refuge at a time of great fear and precarity.

In the meantime, East Africans in the colonial military were also acquiring new skills, including literacy, some in Swahili, some in English, and some in both these languages. The Swahili periodicals of the World War II period were quick to capitalize on the potential of the military experience for the upward mobility of ex-soldiers. Sometimes the periodicals provided specific examples of ex-soldiers who became successful, not by returning to rural farming as intimated by the conclusion of the song of Tufunge Safari (Let's prepare for the journey), but by assuming positions in urban spaces, even though the topic of the ex-soldier as an agent of modernization continued to be a contested one within colonial circles (Bromber 2010, 290–292).

Conclusion

It could be stated that military service contributed to the rise of a political awareness in Africa as a whole partly because of the expanding horizons of experience in areas far from home. The expanding horizons obtained as a result of seeing other parts of the world and of knowing the white man as a fellow soldier in combat, and of seeing his weaknesses as well as

3 Swahili in Military Context: Between World War I and World... 85

strengths at close quarters, began the process of humanizing the white man and of discovering that he was indeed fallible. A large number of African soldiers

> expanded their horizons as they sojourned in India where the nationalists were demanding that the British should quit their country, on in Italy where they saw the immense destruction one group of white men could visit on another. When they returned to their countries they did so with ambitions for themselves and their children that were utterly different from those they had when they first stood before the recruiting officer. (Crowder 1993, 99)

It is partly because of this factor that in the history of nationalism in the Africa of those days as a whole, ex-servicemen after world wars contributed to the general feeling of unrest that remained unassuaged by mild constitutional reforms. Soldiers, laborers, and carriers who had been uprooted from their village life during the war now had a major impact on their societies upon their return. Most significantly, the aftermath of the wars saw a rise in demands for participation in the process of governance and in the new politics imposed on them by Europeans. As a result, in both Kenya and Tanganyika, Swahili began to gain ground as a language of political mobilization in individual nations.

In addition to the acquisition of new skills, the military experience fostered a sense of national consciousness but might also have stimulated the emergence of regional consciousness, complete with the promotion of Swahili among the members of the security forces of Kenya, Tanganyika, and Uganda. This sense of panregional consciousness was facilitated partly by the transterritorial method of recruitment into the King's African Rifles. In the police and army, perhaps even more than any other services, two factors were combined: an attempt to maintain a balance in the number of people recruited from each territory and an attempt to minimize the significance of the territorial origins of a new recruit in determining where he was to serve. As late as 1971 when General Idi Amin Dada toppled the Ugandan government in a military coup, in the security forces of Uganda there were still personnel from the other two East African countries (Mazrui 1975, 141). What was critical in the military experience as a space that fostered both national and regional East African consciousness was the crucial role that Swahili played in making "joint command" feasible, and in facilitating interterritorial recruitment into the armed forces.

References

Adika Kevogo, Stanley, and Alex Umbima Kevogo. 2014. Swahili Military Terminology: A Case of an Evolving Non-Institutionalized Language Standard. *Research on Humanities and Social Sciences* 14 (21): 609–630.
Bennet, George. 1963. *Kenya: A Political History: The Colonial Period.* New York: Oxford University Press.
Blundell, Michael. 1964. *So Rough a Wind.* London: Weidenfeld and Nicholson.
Bolton, Caitlyn. 2016. Making Africa Legible: Kiswahili Arabic and Orthographic Romanization in Colonial Zanzibar. *The American Journal of Islamic Social Sciences* 33 (3): 61–78.
Bromber, Katrin. 2004. German Colonial Administrators, Swahili Lecturers and the Promotion of Swahili at the Seminar Für Orientalische Sprachen in Berlin. *Sudanic Africa* 15: 39–54.
———. 2010. Correcting Their Perspective: Out-of-Area Deployment and the Swahili Military Press in World War II. In *The World in World Wars: Experiences, Perceptions, and Perspectives from Africa and Asia*, ed. Heike Liebau, Katrin Bromber, Dyala Hamzah, and Ravi Ahuja, 277–297. Leiden: Brill.
———. 2018. Sasa, pote, Masheji yetu diniani: Swahili Poetry and the Translocal Moment of World War II. In *Translocal Connections Across the Indian Ocean: Swahili Speaking Networks on the Move*, ed. Francesca Declich, 121–131. Leiden: Koninklijke Brill.
Brumfit, Ann. 1980. *The Rise and Development of a Language Policy in German East Africa.* Hamburg: Helmet Buske.
Clayton, Anthony. 1978. *Communication for New Loyalties: African Soldiers' Songs*, Papers in International Studies, African Series 34. Athens, OH: Ohio University Press.
Crowder, Michael. 1985. The First World War and Its Consequences. In *General History of Africa. VII. Africa Under Colonial Domination 1880–1935*, 283–311. London: Heinemann.

———. 1993. Africa Under British and Belgian Domination, 1935–1945. In *General History of Africa. VIII. Africa Since 1935*, ed. Ali A. Mazrui, 76–101. London: Heinemann.
Durrani, Shiraz. 2006. *Never Be Silent: Publishers and Imperialism in Kenya 1884–1963*. London: Vita Books.
Fabian, Johannes. 1986. *Language and Colonial Power: The Appropriation of Swahili in the Former Belgian Congo 1880–1938*. London: Cambridge University Press.
Gadsden, Fay. 1971. Language Politics in Uganda: The Search for a Lingua Franca 1912–1944. USSC Conference, Makerere University, December 15–17, 1971.
———. 1986. Wartime Propaganda in Kenya: The Kenya Information Office, 1939–1945. *The International Journal of African Historical Studies* 19 (3): 401–420.
Gooden, Phillip, and Peter Lewis. 2014. *The War of Words: World War II in a 100 Phrases*. New York: Bloomsbury Publishing.
Kapanga, Andre M. 2001. Recreating a Language. A Socio-historical Approach to the Study of Shaba Swahili. *Cultural Survival* 25 (2). https://www.culturalsurvival.org/print/3160.
Kapanga, Mwamba Tshishiku. 1991. Language Variation and Change: A Case Study of Shaba Swahili. Ph.D. diss., University of Illinois, Urbana-Champaign.
Knappert, Jan. 1969. A Swahili Epic. *The Journal of African History* 10 (2): 341–342.
Le Breton, F.H. 1936. *Up-Country Swahili Exercises; For the Soldier, Settler, Miner, Marchant and Their Wives*. Richmond: R. W. Simpson and Company.
Mazrui, Ali A. 1970. Africa's Experience in Nation Building: Is It Relevant to Papua New Guinea? *East Africa Journal* 7 (11): 15–23.
———. 1975. *The Political Sociology of the English Language: An African Perspective*. The Hague: Mouton.
Mutonya, Mungai, and Timothy H. Parsons. 2004. KIKAR: A Swahili Variety in Kenya's Colonial Army. *Journal of African Languages and Linguistics* 25: 111–125.
Osborne, Myles. 2020. British Visions, African Voices: The "Imperial" and the "Colonial" in World War II. *Itinerario* 44 (2): 287–315.
Parsons, Timothy H. 1997. "Kibra Is Our Blood": The Sudanese Military Legacy in Nairobi's Kibera Location, 1902–1908. *The International Journal of African Historical Studies* 30 (1): 87–122.

———. 1999. *The African Rank-and-File: Social Implications of Colonial Military Service in the King's African Rifles, 1902–1964*. Portsmouth, New Hampshire: Heinemann.

Polome, Edgar C. 1967. *Swahili Language Handbook*. Washington, DC: Center for Applied Linguistics.

Pugach, Sara. 2012. *Africa in Translation: A History of Colonial Linguistics in Germany and Beyond, 1814–1945*. Ann Arbor: The University of Michigan Press.

Robert, Shaaban. 1967. *Utenzi wa Vita vya Uhuru: 1939 hata 1945*. Nairobi: Oxford University Press.

Samson, Anne. 2021. Language in East Africa During the First World War. In *Multilingual Environments in the Great War*, ed. Julian Walker and Christopher Declercq, 32–43. New York: Bloomsbury Publishing.

Scotton, James F. 1978. Tanganyika's African Press, 1937–1960: A Nearly Forgotten Pre-Independence Forum. *African Studies Review* 21 (1): 1–18.

Smith, A.W. 1925. Memo on the Proposed International Bureau of African Languages and Literature. Edinburgh House, May 1925.

Vitale, Anthony J. 1980. KiSetla: Linguistic and Sociolinguistic Aspects of a Pidgin Swahili. *Weekly Review*, September 21, 1984.

Whiteley, Wilfred H. 1969. *Swahili: The Rise of a National Language*. London: Methuen.

Wright, Marcia. 1971. *German Missions in Tanganyika: 1891–1941*. Oxford: Clarendon Press.

4

Swahili and Imperial Britain: Colonial Creation/African Appropriation

Alamin Mazrui

In Chap. 3, we saw how British colonial interest in Swahili in the interwar period was partly inspired by the development of the King's African Rifles (KAR) as an interterritorial force and the need for a language that could help serve organizational military purposes. Indeed, the work of the Swahili Inter-Territorial Language Committee, which had begun in the early 1930s, became integral to British war efforts during World War II. At the same time, however, the overall British "policy" on Swahili and other African languages was part of a broader imperial project of conquest and control. Colonial agents turned "alien ways of speaking into objects of knowledge, so that their speakers could be made subjects of colonial power" (Errington 2008, vii). What emerged from this colonial context was a linguistic war of a sort as part of a wider civilizational clash, one that eventually influenced both the substance and function of Swahili to one degree or another. And as Caroline Elkins (2022) documents, such civilizational wars in the annals of British imperial history were regularly bolstered by violence and brutality, often systematic, even as colonial Britain continued to tout the gospel of liberalism.

The (Re)Construction of African Languages and Identities

At the forefront of this linguistic war of conquest and control in its initial phases, often framed as a war of civilizations, was a wide array of Christian missionary operatives from different churches and nations. In the process, this "contact between Christian missionaries and the so-called indigenous and African peoples" led to the emergence in African languages "of Christian-lects, a set of linguistic discourses and instruments that were used as a mechanism of domination by framing people and languages in specific ways, inventing and naming local languages, inventing ethnolinguistic categories that overlapped ethnicity and language using literacy as a framework to define what counts as language, and translating several Christian discourses to 'local' languages that, in turn, helped frame the 'local' in specific ways" (Makoni et al. 2020, 221). Missionaries, administrators, and other colonial functionaries wrote grammars and textbooks that were based on very particular constructions of languages rather than the local languages used by the natives themselves, contributing to the Christianization of "indigenous" languages (Isichei 1995; Renck 1990).

It is important to bear in mind that European colonialism in Africa not only introduced European languages to the continent and imposed them on its peoples. In many cases, it proceeded to (re)construct and even "invent" languages and organized them in hierarchies. These hierarchies were of a pyramidal structure, with the European languages themselves at the very top, followed by a select few African languages that were "developed" and instrumentalized for colonial administrative purposes, and then the thousands of other local languages at the very bottom that were increasingly marginalized. Such colonial linguistic interventions were often an integral part of the process of the formation and configuration of the colonial state itself. Many of the widely spoken African languages that we know of today have been a product of such reconstruction – in the name of codification and standardization – carried out by colonial anthropologists, missionary workers, and administrators.

Following the development of linguistics in their own nations, Europeans introduced into their colonies an artefactual image of language as something "bounded, nameable and countable unit, often reduced to grammatical structures and vocabulary and called by names such as 'English,' 'French' and so on" (Blommaert 2010, 4). The process of demarcation of languages into discrete units that are then named and enumerated created a particular colonial cartography of the colonial space and its colonized subjects. In the process, as Makoni, Griffler, and Mashiri show in relation to the colonial situation in Southern Africa, "native speakers of southern African languages were displaced and rendered irrelevant to the process of codifying their 'own' languages, the alleged repositories of their cultural authenticity …. The direct source of the constructed languages were, therefore, at best, second-language speakers of the languages they were recording" (2007, 30). Colonial records then proceeded to assign these constructed languages to communities of speakers to whom the very logic of the linguistic assignments was vague at best. Named and bounded, these languages could now be more efficiently controlled and managed.

In the process of these efforts of linguistic construction and invention, European colonial agents also introduced into the African space the notion of indivisibility of language, race/ethnicity, and geographical location. The invention of languages, then, resulted in the crystallization of new categories of identity and with them language attitudes and language ideologies that fed directly into African nationalist discourses. Core to these discourses of African nationalists has been the idea that just as European languages are bearers of a peculiarly European civilization, "indigenous" African languages are the guardians of and the only ones capable of giving "authentic" expression to African cultures and the true spirit and worldview of African people. The battle of ideas between relativism and universalism in the field of linguistics came to play out in the African linguistic landscape within a political framing that pitted imperialism against its nationalist other.

Assigning to themselves the role of brokers of cultural capital, the British also created ethnic identities that served military interests. In their recruitment of African soldiers, the British invented "martial traditions" that they imposed selectively on African ethnic groups, as discussed in Chap. 3. In time, elites among some African communities found it expedient to "manipulate martial identity for their own purposes." In Kenya, for example,

[t]he label 'Kalenjin,' a term for the linguistically related Elgeyo, Kipsigis, Marakwet, Nandi, Pokot, Tugen, and Terik peoples of the central Rift Valley, was invented, in part, by African soldiers during the Second World War who disliked being referred to as 'Nandi-speaking tribes' by the army. 'Kalenjin' (meaning 'I tell you') came into widespread use as an opening salutation during wartime radio broadcasts to African servicemen. Kalenjin cultural brokers adopted the term to counter the influence of the more populous Luo and Kikuyu peoples in post-war Kenya. Military officials sympathized with the goal. The new label encouraged martial pride and sharpened divisions between askaris and more politically active ethnic groups. (Parsons 1999, 55)

Once a reference to people speaking different languages that are related to each other as members of the Southern Nilotic branch of languages, Kalenjin had now become a supraethnic identity with all the deadly implications that such a construction would end up having for postcolonial Kenya.

Dis-Islamization/Europeanization of African Languages

When it came to the promotion of Christianity, generally seen as a core element of Western civilization in spite of the fact that Christianity had arrived in Africa (Ethiopia) long before it set foot in Europe, the impulse was not always to introduce European languages for the missionary purpose. There was certainly the school of thought that widely shared the view that the most effective and direct way of reaching the African natives spiritually was through their own native languages. For these missionaries, neither English nor any other European language was adequately equipped to guide Africans from their indigenous spiritual beliefs to the "universal" tenets of the Christian faith.

On the other hand, there were many missionaries who believed that native African languages were too saturated with associations and connotations drawn from an indigenous religious experience very much removed from Christianity. After all, as early as 1545, the Council of

Trent was cautioning missionaries about the dangers of translating the Word of God into the languages of "pagans" and the need to "safeguard the key words of the doctrine from confusion with native beliefs and terminologies." A. R. Barlow of the Church of Scotland Mission, for example, was often frustrated in his attempts to find Gikuyu equivalents for fundamental religious concepts. In translating the word "sin," for example, Barlow considered the Gikuyu word *thahu*,

> ... the dangerous 'ritual cleanliness' which Gikuyus thought troubled them when they transgressed rules that kept life and sex separate from death and blood, bush out of the homestead, and wild game away from domestic stock... For Barlow [however] *thahu* failed as 'sin' because it did not prescribe a sense of individual grievance toward God: uncleanliness brought suffering on the transgressor, but not divine condemnation. (Paterson 1997, 266)

Missionaries had learned, therefore, that "pagan" words might not be easily disentangled from pagan worlds (Errington 2008, 42). The utilization of these ethnic languages for biblical studies, therefore, supposedly carried the risk of serious conceptual distortion.

But then there was another class of African languages at the disposal of the European missionaries – languages of wider transethnic communication, some of which had been extensively enriched by Arabic. By the beginning of European colonialism in Africa, Islam had already established itself solidly in some regions of the continent for centuries. In the process, Arabic as the language of Islam – of the Qur'an and Islamic ritual especially – had come to influence several of the languages of Muslim-majority African communities, including Hausa in West Africa and Swahili in East Africa. In addition, some of these languages had adopted the Arabic script, often modified to meet the phonetic needs of local languages, and produced a significant range of written materials in it, some of great historical and epistemological significance. In parts of West Africa, this African version of the Arabic script came to be known as Ajami.

Was the Islamic association of these languages an asset or a liability for Christianity in Africa? This was certainly a question that challenged the minds of colonial missionaries and even divided them in policy. A number of missionaries felt that since both Islam and Christianity were monotheistic religions drawn from the same Middle Eastern ancestry, and share a considerable number of spiritual concepts and values, these languages would serve well as transmitters of biblical lessons and Christian values precisely because they could already cope with the religious universe of Islam. Because of their presumed Islamicity and their role as transethnic media of wider communication, they were seen by some as the best available options for reorienting the African "natives" from their presumed fear of spirits and the unknown toward Christian notions of paradise and hell.

On the other hand, the African languages so influenced by Arabic were not seen as representing the true spirit of the African peoples whose souls the missionaries had come to capture, but of an "Eastern other" that had long been regarded as antithetical to Western Christianity and civilization. Ironically, in the Arabic-speaking world, Arabic had been used as a language of Christianity and the Christian Bible from the pre-Islamic period to the present. But when it came to its influence in Africa, "the colonial regime of language systematically correlated Arabic with Islam and, in effect, Arabic became indexically 'the' carrier of a dangerous discourse" (Makoni et al. 2020, 217). Its influence was often seen as a dangerous liability to the European missionary agenda of communicating the Christian message. Bishop Alfred R. Tucker, for example, was very critical of his missionary colleague, Bishop Alexander Mackay, for his advocacy of Swahili as a potential language of Christianity. In Tucker's words:

> Mackay ... was very desirous of hastening the time when one language should dominate Central Africa, and that language, he hoped and believed, would be Swahili .... That there should be one language for Central Africa is a consummation devoutly to be wished, but God forbid that it should be Swahili. English? Yes! But Swahili, never. The one means the Bible and Protestant Christianity and the other Mohammedanism ... sensuality, moral and physical degradation and ruin. Swahili is too closely related to Mohammedanism to be welcome in any mission field in Central Africa. (Tucker 1911, 262)

For missionaries like Tucker, then, and in spite of the areas of convergence between the two religions, Christianity and Islam belonged to totally different universes of experience, one Western and one Eastern, that could not be linguistically reconciled through the use of languages like Hausa and Swahili.

As we saw in Chap. 2, these views in British colonies were also found in German colonies of Africa. Prior to the war of resistance against colonialism on the German side of East Africa, for example, an important section of the colonial establishment regarded Swahili as a reservoir of an Islamic spirit and was openly opposed to its use in the translation of the Bible. According to one colonial ideologue of the time, H. Hansen, Islam and Swahili together constituted not only the mortal adversaries in the transmission of the Christian message, "but also, in Africa, the unrepentant enemies of colonial politics" (quoted by Pike 1986, 231). The existence of *An-Najah* (The Redeemer), a Swahili journalistic venture using the Ajami script openly agitating against German colonial rule, was seen as a vindication of Hansen's position.

In fact, in the British colonial imagination, nothing was more demonstrative of the material influence of Arabic and Islam on the Swahili language than the Ajami script. As indicated in Chap. 3, the British colonial administration made use of Ajami in mobilizing support for the Swahili-speaking community in its World War I efforts. After the war, however, and in a deliberate attempt to erase Swahili's Islamicity, a new scriptural ideology was advanced. The Latin script was now projected as superior, more practical and better equipped to represent the sounds of the Swahili language than Ajami. The process of scriptural dis-Islamization of Swahili now began in earnest, with leading members of the Swahili society condemning this colonial move altogether. For the Swahili, the Latinization of their language was a direct affront to their identity, religion, and cultural values related to linguistic expression. To the colonizer, it was one more symbolic victory of the West over the native, over Islam, in their attempted transformation of Africa (Bolton 2016).

In German East Africa, a missionary who was particularly attracted to this idea of dis-Arabizing the Swahili of Christianity was Dr Karl Roehl. Roehl argued that "the Arab expressions are linked up with Moslem ideas, which are very often strongly divergent from the corresponding Christian ones" of the West (Roehl 1930, 197). As a result of Roehl's campaign, representatives of four different German missions resolved in 1914 that a new translation of the Bible be produced that would be suitable for the whole of German East Africa. A main objective of this exercise was "to purify Swahili…by eliminating the majority of the Zanzibar Arabic words, which are either not used, or imperfectly understood, by the natives of the coast, and are quite unintelligible to those in the interior" (Mojola 2001, 516).

This anti-Arabic sentiment was to continue well into the postcolonial period. In the guise of using an informal style of Tanzanian Swahili, for example, the Biblica online Swahili translation of the Bible seems to make a deliberate effort to minimize "Arabisms," preferring the Latin-derived *Lusifa* (from Lucifer), for example, to the more commonly used Arabic-derived *Shetani* for the Devil. According to the late Kennedy Walibora Waliaula of Riara University, Nairobi, for example, one of the translators of Biblica displayed outright hostility toward Arabic influences in Swahili during his interview with Waliaula on QTV's *Sema Nami Program* on February 22, 2014. In fact, in an email communication on Wednesday, September 9, 2015, Waliaula stated that he suspected that the recent translations of the Bible that claim to use "Tanzanian Swahili" or "Kenyan Swahili" were, in effect, attempts to dis-Arabize "biblical" Swahili.

In short, then, sections of colonial Europeans made deliberate attempts to erase the Arabo-Islamic component in African languages, and inscribe in its place a European presence. African languages that had been heavily influenced by Arabic were now systematically dis-Arabized in their lexical composition, and Ajami, the Arabic-based African script, was often replaced with the Roman alphabet. In these efforts to construct Swahili as a colonial lingua franca, the language "had to be decontextualized from its origin as a language of the Swahili societies of the East African coast, in which the language was inscribed with Islamic cultural meanings, literary tradition, linguistic sophistication and intellectualism, making it a 'nobody's language'" (Beck 2018, 13). The emergence of what came to be known as Standard Swahili was, to some extent, a product of these twin politico-linguistic processes of dis-Arabization, on the one hand, and Europeanization and Christianization, on the other. This is why some

Muslim leaders, like Sheikh Al-Amin bin Ali, became vocal critics of the Standard Swahili that was now being taught in schools, urging his own Muslim community to boycott this new variety of the language "kilicho-haribiwa na Wazungu" (that had been disfigured by Europeans) (*Al-Islah*, June 20, 1932).

Of course, the Swahili that was promoted by colonialism through schools, published materials, and the media interacted with Swahili's own momentum of spread among the common folk to assume a great variety of forms/lects in actual linguistic practices of East Africans. Ethnicity, class, race, gender, and even generation have continued to interact in various dynamic ways to produce a multilayered continuum of Swahili varieties that are evident throughout the Swahili-speaking region, but especially in Kenya. What is important for our purposes, however, is that many of these non-native dialects of Swahili are often seen as informal variations of the Swahili that began to be promoted during the colonial period.

Swahili and the Foundations of Anti-Colonial Nationalism

Far from boycotting the new Swahili that had been constructed by colonial Europeans and the varieties that emerged from the language's colonial contexts, many East Africans essentially appropriated it, a process by which a language "is seized and re-placed in a specific cultural location" (Pennycook 2017, 267), moving it from the confinement of colonial control to the arena of struggle and liberation from European colonial rule. In the process, the appropriation of language, of Swahili in our case, came to "include a struggle beyond the language itself to engage with broader battles around culture, knowledge and inequality" (Pennycook 2017, 269).

These battles, however, presupposed particular conditions that favored the emergence of anti-colonial nationalism in East Africa: de-ethnicization and class formation. The record has shown that Swahili played an important role in these two processes. In both cases, Swahili helped expand the capacities of East Africans as social and political creatures in ways that contributed to their struggles to end colonial domination.

By de-ethnicization we mean not the disappearance of ethnic loyalties, but their absorption into a wider network of allegiances. It is not a process by which people stop thinking of themselves as Luo, or Baganda, or Chagga, or Bakongo. There is little evidence yet in Eastern Africa that those who are associated in "ancestry" with those particular groups have stopped thinking of themselves in terms of those groups. De-ethnicization rather has to be seen in a somewhat different context. First, it could take the form of changes in custom, ritual, and rules, and a shift toward a more cosmopolitan style of life. In behavior, a particular Muganda or Luo or Chagga may no longer be guided by the heritage of values and rules of his or her rural, ethnic community, but in loyalty and identification, the person may be even more ferociously a Muganda or Luo or Chagga than ever. It is therefore possible to have declining "ethnic" behavior as one becomes increasingly cosmopolitan, but stable or even increasing ethnic loyalty in terms of emotional attachment. The other sense of de-ethnicization concerns the emergence of new loyalties, not necessarily to supplant older ones, but more often to supplement them in complex ways. These new loyalties could be in terms of social class, or religious affiliation, or racial identity, or national consciousness. Our position is that Swahili has indeed facilitated both these senses of de-ethnicization.

Swahili's role in supplementing East African allegiances was initially linked to its place in Islamization and Christianization. The coastal regions of Kenya and Tanzania, in particular, were substantially Islamized several centuries before European colonial rule. Swahili facilitated social intercourse among Muslims from different ethnic groups and regions, and gradually built up a comprehensive culture of its own over and above language as a mere medium of communication. Swahili culture was born with its own form of Islam, its own worldview, its own dress culture, its own cuisine, its own ethics and aesthetics. At the same time, the language itself was providing further communication between the Swahili people and other groups, and was contributing to the expanding network of affiliations of the peoples of the coast of Eastern Africa.

With the coming of Christian missionaries in the later century and their activities from then on, Swahili gradually acquired the additional role of becoming a language of Christian mission, as suggested earlier. There was reluctance on the part of some missionaries to use Swahili, since it had been so substantially associated with Islam. But once strategies for its dis-Islamization were in place, the language quickly became ecumenical, serving the religious needs of Muslims as much as of Christians. This role of Swahili in the Church, once again, helped broaden the social and human horizons of East Africans beyond the confines of their ancestral ways. In the meantime, as we saw in Chap. 3, recruitment into the King's African Rifles in colonial East Africa was both transethnic and transterritorial. As a result, Swahili played a key role in the emergence of transethnic national armies and security forces.

In the process of de-ethnicization, the role of Swahili is also linked to the process of urbanization. Certain forms of urbanization have the effect of expanding the scale of social interaction. Urbanization in Eastern Africa has also been a major factor behind the erosion of rural ethnic custom and ritual, though it has not necessarily eroded ethnic loyalty and identity. Groups of different ethnic origins have intermingled in places like Dar es Salaam, Lubumbashi, Mombasa, and Jinja. Many of the customs of the rural areas have declined in these urban or semi-urban conditions, even though ethnic loyalty has persisted. Swahili has been a facilitating factor behind such urbanization and has served as a lingua franca among the different ethnic communities. It has also been, quite often, the most important language of the workplace and the marketplace among average citizens in the towns. Once again, this is a role that has both expanded the network of allegiances and eroded some ancestral traditions of rural life.

After World War II, the towns and cities also became major centers for the new politics of African nationalism in direct opposition to European colonialism. A growing race consciousness was spreading among East Africans. They were not only sensing their own original ethnic identity as Kamba or Acholi and Haya, they were also recognizing, in a new way, that they were a people sharing a history of exploitation and domination by people belonging to other "races." It is important here to distinguish between race consciousness and racism. Race consciousness is, at a minimum, an awareness, in a politicized fashion, of one's membership of a particular "race." Racism, on the other hand, is usually a hostile or contemptuous attitude toward people of other races. The rise of anti-colonial nationalism in Eastern Africa was more a case of race consciousness than a case of racism against Europeans. Africans in Dar es Salaam, Zanzibar, and Nairobi heard speeches from the new breed of African politicians, agitating for African rights, including, by the 1950s, the right to self-determination and independence. Politics in Tanzania, Kenya, and parts of Zaire became more and more national, partly with the communicative facility of Swahili as a lingua franca.

In addition to the racial boundaries of the new nationalism in East Africa, there were also the emerging territorial boundaries. East Africans were thinking of themselves not merely as people belonging to the African continent, but also as Tanganyikans, Ugandans, Kenyans, and Congolese. A new complex relationship based on territorial nationality was in the process of being born, and Swahili played its part in the process. The struggles to end colonialism often manifested this interplay between race consciousness and territorial consciousness.

As discussed in Chap. 3, the British colonial government sought to standardize and promote Swahili in the interwar period, in part to facilitate its military needs. This pro-Swahili policy was now seen to have precipitated unforeseen circumstances, with the growth of national consciousness and anti-colonialism in East Africa benefiting directly from the availability of a grassroots transethnic language like Swahili. Political consciousness was now regarded as a dangerous "postwar epidemic" and as a result, in East Africa, colonial administrators moved more decisively against "over-promoting Swahili." As Tarsis Kabwegyere noted:

> In the light of … the African awakening in the post-war period, it is not unreasonable to assert that the stopping of Kiswahili was a strategy to minimize intra-African contact. In addition, intensive anglicizing followed, and East African peoples remained separated from each other by a language barrier …. What this shows is that whatever interaction was officially encouraged remained at the top level and not at the level of African population. That the existence of one common language at the level of the masses would have hastened the overthrowal of colonial domination is obvious. The withdrawal of official support for a common African language was meant to keep the post-war 'epidemic' from spreading. (Kabwegyere 1974, 218–19)

De-ethnicization, the weakening of ancestral practices, can occur not only under the influence of new cultural horizons precipitated by forces like religion and urbanization, but also as a product of new ties of economic production. This factor relates to new social class formations. The expansion of social horizons need not entail the disappearance of family allegiance, or the ties of the clan, the bonds of ethnicity, or the consciousness of racial affinity. But the process does include an important moderation of those allegiances by the class factor in society. Africa is continuing to move from a culture of the primacy of kinship to a culture of the primacy of class.

Swahili played a role in that transition in Eastern Africa toward further de-ethnicization. It was a significant player in the history of proletarianization, in the emergence of modern industrial or urban working classes. Swahili facilitated labor migration in Eastern Africa and, as indicated, very often became the primary language of the workplace and marketplace. From its past association with the Swahili aristocracy and the East African slave trade, to serving as a language of command and organization in colonial armies, Swahili now became a crucial agent toward the emergence of a working-class consciousness.

In Kenya, the most important Swahili-speaking city was for a long time Mombasa. The city was also essentially the birthplace of militant collective bargaining in Kenya and the utilization of strike action. A number of factors went toward making Mombasa a breeding ground for organized labor agitation and relatively effective collective bargaining. One factor concerned the role of Mombasa as East Africa's most important port, which was then under British control. Like their counterparts in a number of countries elsewhere, including many other parts of Africa, dockworkers in Mombasa became leaders in labor organization and protest.

The ethnic mixture of the labor force in Mombasa during this colonial period was quite diverse. While very few coastal people trekked into the interior of Kenya to look for jobs during those years, many people from "upcountry" descended on the coast for employment. This trend affected Swahili in two ways. First, the ethnic mosaic in Mombasa against the background of Swahili culture made the language more necessary than ever in this hive of labor agitation and class consciousness. Second, as

Sharon Stichter put it: "Over half of Mombasa's work force were Kikuyu, Luo, Baluhya, Kamba, and other long-range migrants from upcountry. The time, effort, and money that had to be invested in transportation made long-distance migrants more dependent than short-distance ones on the wages they could make, and typically, they stayed in employment for longer lengths of time" (1975, 31). As a result, precisely because many of the workers from "upcountry" had to invest considerable time in their jobs in Mombasa, there was ample time and opportunity for them to improve or even enrich their Swahili. Under these circumstances, then, Swahili was increasingly becoming the language of the emergent Kenyan proletariat.

Across the border in Dar es Salaam in what was then Tanganyika, a similar interaction between proletarianization and Swahilization was taking place. Dar es Salaam, like Mombasa, was of course a port, and also like Mombasa, it was part of the heartland of Swahili culture. And, also like Mombasa, Dar es Salaam was a magnet attracting workers from long distances, holding them for long periods, and Swahilizing them in the process. Once again, the interplay between working conditions in a port and diversified ethnicity both sharpened class consciousness and necessitated an effective lingua franca like Swahili. Labor unrest following World War II culminated in the Tanganyika strike of 1947, reenacted artistically in the novel *Kuli* by Shafi Adam. In the words of John Iliffe:

> The strike was the high point in the dockers' history. They initiated it. They won impressive gains both in their working conditions and in their organization and confidence. Briefly, they led the most wide-spread protest in Tanzanian history between the end of the Maji Maji uprising and the formation of Tanu… The astonishing success of the seething discontent it demonstrated, undoubtedly influenced…wage increases variously estimated at 40–50 percent of existing pay …. The 1947 award made the dockers a privileged group among Tanzanian workers, the best paid, most formidable labor force in the country. It was won by the first real exercise of African power in Tanzania since the end of Maji Maji–an exhilarating and enlightening experience for those who participated. (Iliffe 1975, 62–65)

Once again, urbanization, proletarianization, and Swahilization converged, giving the Swahili language one more role in the emerging process of class formation in East Africa. In Uganda also, Swahili had its proletarianizing role. This took two major forms. One concerned the immigration of workers from neighboring countries, especially from Kenya. Trade unionism in Uganda was partly the product of labor migration from Kenya. Luo workers, especially, organized themselves and sought to involve Ugandan workers in the new techniques of collective bargaining and economic leverage. The lingua franca between the immigrants and the Ugandan workers was more often Swahili. The other role that Swahili played concerned migrant labor from northern Uganda into the city of Kampala and the industrial center in Jinja. Again, on balance, northern Ugandans and Kenyan workers operating in Ugandan cities utilized Swahili as the major medium of the workplace and the marketplace. Indeed, the spread of Swahili in Uganda was due much more to migrant workers than to priests and school teachers (Mazrui and Mazrui 1995, 14).

It is important to bear in mind that throughout the colonial period, leading trade unionists like Fred Kubai regarded the trade union movement as an instrument of political struggle against colonialism. Swahili was its medium of action. One of the most active and visible trade unionists in East Africa at that time – when there was already a sizable population of East Africans of South Asian origin – was Makhan Singh, himself of Indian, Punjabi background. Singh was constantly trying to transcend the color line that had been established by the racial laws, policies, and practices of the British colonial government in order to make common cause between his Indian compatriots and the African population. Partly in an effort to achieve this objective, he urged the South Asian communities in Kenya to do their best to learn Swahili, "the language of the people" (Dasgupta 2021).

In sum, then, Swahili played a critical role in the de-ethnicization of East Africans at a crucial moment in politico-economic history. It accomplished this transition especially through the processes of urbanization and class formation. In doing so, it managed to facilitate the emergence of both national consciousness and class consciousness among East Africans, which became crucial in their mobilization in the political war against British colonialism.

Parties, Periodicals, and Protest

The most liberal phase of British rule in East Africa might well have been the last ten to fifteen years or so of colonialism. During this phase of colonial power, situated in the postwar period, African nationalists could agitate for self-government and independence, sometimes with the support of important members of parliament in London. No doubt Britain continued its efforts to repress dissent, often under the cover of laws that justified use of force, arrests, and imprisonment: "If Britain's civilizing mission was reformist in its claims, it was brutal, nonetheless. Violence was not only the British Empire's midwife; it was endemic to the structures and systems of British rule. It was not just an occasional means to liberal imperialism's end; it was a means of and an end for as long as the British Empire remained alive" (Elkins 2022, 13). On the whole, however, there was a level of openness and frank agitation in the last decade or so of British colonial rule that stood out in some contrast to previous decades. And Swahili, as it evolved into the primary language of politics in Tanzania and Kenya especially, was part of the process through which the masses in these countries became increasingly involved in national agitation for African rights. A national political constituency emerged partly because Swahili as a national lingua franca was operating in these societies.

In Kenya, of course, there was the Mau Mau Emergency (1952–1959), an example par excellence of the violence and terror at the heart of Britain's so-called civilizing mission in Kenya (Elkins 2005). From the point of view of the Swahili language, the Emergency created additional complications. The core of the Mau Mau war of liberation against the British was the Gikuyu, though there was participation by members of other ethnic groups. By the 1930s and 1940s, many in the Gikuyu society were already suspicious of Swahili as "part of a much wider rejection of all things introduced by or associated with Europeans" (Whiteley 1969, 348). The British colonial rulers now decided to isolate the Gikuyu from the mainstream of the political process in the course of the Emergency as a way of depoliticizing them. Their confinement in appalling spaces inspired some of the verses in Salim Kibao's *Utenzi wa Uhuru wa Kenya* (Narrative poem of Kenya's independence). As Kibao writes:

Matata yaliposhuka
Kenya ikasukasuka
Ikawa ni pata shika
Na watu wakapotea
    When trouble began
    And Kenya was shaken
    All became uncertain
    With people disappearing
Watu wengi wakashikwa
Nyayani wakenda wekwa
Mwahali msimofikwa
Hata kwa kuangalia
    Many were arrested
    And confined in enclosures
    In unreachable places
    Beyond eye's vision
    (Kibao 1972, 15)

This relative isolation of the Gikuyu in the 1950s also partially arrested their Swahilization. Of course, there were several (suspected) members of the Mau Mau who either were already proficient in Swahili or acquired the language in their interaction with prison wardens during their confinement in Swahili-speaking areas like Lamu. Overall, however, the colonial targeting of Kenyans of Gikuyu origin encouraged a temporary retreat to bonds of ethnic solidarity under the pressure of counter-insurgency techniques inaugurated by the British. Gikuyu isolation lessened their involvement in national affairs and slowed down the process of Gikuyu Swahilization.

If the colonial state sought to alienate the Gikuyu from the Swahili language, however, it did not prevent it from galvanizing the language in its propaganda war to win public support against the Mau Mau. One colonial strategy was to produce published materials intended to provoke outrage against the Mau Mau. For example, one such publication, entitled *Mau Mau*, had a cover that featured a bright red background, with a hand holding a machete next to a baby's corpse, severed in two. Written in Swahili, it provided black-and-white photographs of white women and children '*Kazi ya Mau Mau*,' ran one caption: 'The Work of Mau Mau.' Other photographs showed amputated feet, bodies with heads partially severed, and disemboweled cattle. '*Hebu, angalia watoto hawa wawili! Pengine wakikuwa wako!*' ran another caption: 'Here, look at these two children! They could be yours!' (Osborne 2015, 83)

The strategy here and in other early propaganda materials of the colonial state, then, was to depict Mau Mau as a terrorist organization with its combatants as "subhuman savages capable of almost any act of depravity" (Osborne 2015, 84).

A later strategy of the colonial propaganda machinery against the Mau Mau was to attempt its erasure from the public mind, to have the public shift to a media source in which the topic of Mau Mau would not feature at all. It is partly in this context that the British colonial Department of Information came to support the establishment and operation of the new radio station, Sauti ya Mvita (Voice of Mombasa) with the Kenyan coastal Muslim population as its target audience. Because of its neo-Islamic cultural universe, this audience often tended to listen to Cairo Radio, which broadcast in both Arabic and Swahili. In its Kenyan broadcasts, however, Cairo Radio demonstrated its support for the Mau Mau liberation cause. With Sauti ya Mvita, this Swahili-speaking constituency could now have its own programming that is at once attuned to its cultural tastes and preferences and, with the intervention of the colonial government, free of Mau Mau news, allowing the Swahili public to hear no Mau Mau (Osborne 2015, 95–97).

In the meantime, the fact that Gikuyu seclusion might have curtailed their access to and enhancement of their proficiency in Swahili did not, of course, prevent Swahili writers from being inspired by the Mau Mau war. An example is *Mkuki wa Moto* (Spear of fire), a Swahili play by Farouk Muslim and Said Mzee (1980). The authors give an explanation of their choice of Swahili in writing this play:

> *Vita vya kupigania Uhuru ni moja kati ya matukio makubwa katika tarekhe ya Kenya. Watu wa kila aina walijitolea kwenye juhudi ya vita hivi kwa njia*

4 Swahili and Imperial Britain: Colonial Creation/African... 107

ambazo mpaka leo hazijakamilika kusimuliwa hasa kwa sababu masimulizi mengi yamekuwa kwa lugha zisizo lugha ya taifa jipya la Kenya. Mchezo huu ni mojawapo ya juhudi za kusimulia vita hivi kwa lugha inayotumiwa na watu wa nchi ya Kenya. (i)

The war of Independence was one among great episodes in the history of Kenya. People from all walks of life volunteered in this war effort in ways that until today have not been fully narrated especially because most of the narratives have been in languages other than the language of the new Kenyan nation. This play in one attempt to provide a narration of this war in a language that is employed by the people of Kenya.

The play seeks not only to be "true" to the Mau Mau historical record but also to memorialize the movement in a language that "the people" understand.

The earliest and best known among Swahili literary works on the Mau Mau, however, is *Kaburi Bila Msalaba: Hadithi ya Vita vya Mau Mau* (Grave without a cross: a story of the Mau Mau war) by Peter M. Kareithi (1969). Kareithi was himself a witness to the Mau Mau war and tries to give a semi-fictionalized account of the experience especially during the moment of the Emergency. As Kareithi states:

Hadithi hii ni ya kweli. Ni vitendo ambavyo wengi wetu tunavijua, kwani vilitendeka hapa kwetu. Watu wengi watakaoisoma hadithi yeyewe pengine watapajua mahali ambapo pametajwa. Ingawa hivyo, hii si hadithi ya mahali pamoja, ni hadithi ya yale yaliyotendeka kote nchini Kenya, na hasa katika Jimbo la Kati la nchi ya Kenya. (vi)

This story is true. The events are ones known to many of us because they occurred right here. Many people who might read the story will perhaps recognize the place named. Nonetheless, this is not a story of a single place; it is a story of what happened throughout the country, especially in the Central Province of Kenya.

Among the colonial actions narrated by Kareithi is the mass arrest and confinement of people of Gikuyu ethnicity. Indeed, "the British colonial government had managed, by the end of 1955, to detain nearly the entire Kikuyu population—a feat that was unprecedented in the empire save for the Chinese population in Malaya" (Elkins 2022, 563). This state of confinement under unbearable conditions, as explained earlier, was one of the factors that restricted Gikuyu exposure to and acquisition of Swahili for a period of time.

If the Mau Mau Emergency limited direct and open Gikuyu participation in the national politics of the time, it increased the visibility of other ethnic groups. And since trade unionism in Kenya was substantially led by members of these other ethnic communities, especially the Luo, the Mau Mau Emergency created a fusion between proletarian economic movements, on the one hand, and the nationalistic political movements and parties, on the other. Class consciousness and the new race consciousness were in alliance, partly because leadership in both movements was essentially in the hands of the same people.

Perhaps the most illustrious figure to emerge in this dialectic between proletarian and African nationalism was the late Tom Mboya. He grew up on a sisal estate in Kilima Mbogo, near Thika, in what was referred to as "White Highlands," reserved for European settlers. Mboya was a trade union leader who rose to become one of Kenya's most eloquent political spokespersons in the last decade of British rule. He was an orator both in English and in Swahili. Internationally, his impressive command of the English language was a major factor behind his impact on liberal opinion in the UK and the USA. But domestically in Kenya, it was his command of Swahili that gave him access to transethnic mass opinion and created for him an impressive national constituency ripe to be galvanized against British colonialism in Kenya.

Throughout East Africa, publications of one kind or another became one of the most important instruments used by both trade unions and political organizations to mobilize their constituencies against colonial rule. In Uganda, the most prominent anti-colonial publications were not in Swahili, but in Luganda, a language seen by the Baganda to have been in competition with Swahili for potential national status. Far from embracing Swahili as a language that could potentially unite East African nations in their common struggle against British rule, Baganda nationalists would sometimes publish attacks against the colonial administration for appearing to be promoting Swahili, "a rootless and fatherless language seen as a threat to Buganda kingdom and its Luganda language" (Scotton 1978, 223).

Ironically, if the Baganda in Uganda were reluctant to adopt Swahili in their publications, it was a diaspora Muganda, Erica Fiah, who launched the first Swahili periodical, *Kwetu* (Our home), in the neighboring country of Tanganyika under British rule. Believing in the power of an African periodical, in the mantra that "Without our own paper we are really nonentities," Fiah's message was that of "urban radicalism," seeking to promote an anti-colonial agenda among Africans throughout the region. *Kwetu* regularly targeted not only the British colonial administration for its racist and discriminatory policies, but also the emergent African elite that he described as alienated, opportunistic, and unconcerned about the welfare of the African people. As a result, Fiah constantly attracted the ire of both the British colonial government – as high up as Sir Harold MacMichael, the then governor of Tanganyika – and members of the African elite affiliated with what was then called the African Association (Scotton 1978, 2–6). On the other hand, as critical as Fiah was of the colonial government, he remained "loyal to the British Empire" (Robinson 2022, 117).

Though *Kwetu* ceased circulation by 1942 or so, the journalistic seeds it had planted in Tanganyika began to sprout after World War II. Now "a new group of African newspapers in some larger communities in Tanganyika continued Fiah's arguments" not on a wider regional basis as Fiah had done, "but on a territorial basis" (Scotton 1978, 2). Many of these newspapers were sponsored directly by pre-independence African political parties. Though many of these papers were bilingual, combining material in Swahili and English, Swahili was increasingly taking center stage, gaining ground as the lingua franca, and enhancing its credentials as the potential national language of what would become the independent state of Tanganyika.

The leading postwar political party in Tanganyika became the Tanganyika African National Union (TANU), headed by Julius Nyerere who was destined to become the president of the country at independence. TANU began by issuing periodic leaflets and pamphlets in Swahili, including *Sauti ya TANU* (Voice of TANU). Later it established the widely circulated paper *Mwafrika* (The African), which had a definite anti-colonial agenda. There was also *Zuhra* (The star/Venus), which, though independent, was strongly pro-TANU. Writing in conversational

Swahili, the editor of *Zuhra* always "got straight to the point...and pushed it without qualification in simple terms which even the semi-literate reader could understand easily. By the mid-1950's *Zuhra* was strongly pushing TANU's political arguments and often quoted Radio Moscow in attacking colonialism" (Scotton 1978, 11).

The political context of the struggle for independence expectedly gave rise to a full-scale propaganda war, all carried out in the Swahili language. The position of *Mwafrika* and *Zuhra* was met with a counter-offensive that was carried in publications of the colonial government, especially the magazine *Mambo Leo* (Daily news) and daily news sheets under the name *Mwangaza* (Light). The issue of immediate African self-rule that was demanded by *Mwafrika* and *Zuhra* was particularly contentious in this propaganda war. And when these periodicals seemed unrelenting in their campaign, "British authorities used the sedition laws in an attempt to silence them" (Scotton 1978, 16), clearly demonstrating that *Mwafrika* and *Zuhra* had the upper hand in the propaganda war in colonial Tanganyika.

In considering the trend in Swahili publications in Kenya, one must begin by highlighting the fact that, unlike both Uganda and Tanzania, the country experienced a settler form of colonialism. It had a sufficiently large population of European settlers who wielded power and proceeded to use it to promote and protect their own interests, sometimes with the support of the metropolitan government in London and at times at odds with it. British settler rule established an apartheid-style racial structure that privileged members of the White community above all others. This racial structure tended to foster an alliance between trade unionists and political activists of Indian background and those of African background. In the area of publishing, this partnership was especially crucial because printing presses were predominantly in the hands of entrepreneurs of South Asian – or, as they are often called in Kenya, Indian – origin. In fact, many newspapers in colonial Kenya were "started by South Asians in this period, and a tradition grew among them to publish not only in English, the colonial language, but in South Asian languages such as Gujarati, Hindi, and Punjabi as well. Many papers were also published in Kiswahili, reflecting the growing link between progressive South Asian

4 Swahili and Imperial Britain: Colonial Creation/African... 111

and African peoples" (Durrani 2006: 36). Frederiksen mentions the Swahili newspapers *Habari za Dunia*, edited by F. M. Ruhunda, and *Mwalimu*, edited by Francis Khamisi, as examples of this South Asian–African collaboration (Frederiksen 2011, 164).

Perhaps more than in Uganda and Tanzania, anti-colonial periodicals in Kenya demonstrated a close link between trade unions and political organizations. For example, the influential Swahili paper *Sauti ya Mwafrika* (Voice of the African) that began to be produced in the 1940s was an organ of the Kenya African Union (KAU), the leading nationalist organization of the time. At different times in its development, the paper was under the editorship of prominent trade unionists. These included Fred Kubai, leader of the Kenya Transport Workers Union and East African Trade Union Congress, who was also among the Kapenguria Six – members of KAU who were arrested in 1952 and tried and imprisoned on charges of organizing the Mau Mau – and Chege Kibachia, an influential leader in the African Workers Union, which later changed its name to African Workers Federation (Durrani 2006, 70).

As in other East African countries, the reality of anti-colonial struggle made propaganda war inevitable in Kenya. For the British, the radio was perhaps the most important propaganda tool because it was exclusively under the control of the colonial government. But the colonial administration also made use of print media. *Baraza*, first established in 1939 to support the war effort, later became an important propaganda tool for the colonial establishment targeted especially at winning the hearts and minds of Africans. After World War II, when the British supposedly began to take an interest in the welfare of Africans, the colonial government "launched several educational and edifying publications for Africans in Swahili and vernaculars that were handed out free of charge .... Propaganda grew and diversified in the late 1940s as the anti-colonial struggle intensified and took the shape of the Mau Mau organization. With African and Indian nationalism, the Mau Mau revolt and the prospect of independence, Kenya became the site of a virtual information and propaganda war" (Frederiksen 2011, 163). And when the colonial government appeared to be losing that propaganda war, it once again resorted to coercive means of silencing African voices, like banning the *Nyota ya*

Kirinyaga (the Kirinyaga Star) and other periodicals (Durrani 2006, 191). Despotism had now given way to a kind of rule of law that employed "legal codes and procedures" as the crucial "legitimating instrument" for sanctioning repression (Elkins 2022, 13).

Conclusion

We started this chapter by looking at how Swahili became part of the colonial culture war on East African natives. European missionaries and colonial administrators took charge of the language, in time reconfiguring it – especially through the twin processes of dis-Arabization and dis-Islamization – and promoting it in their colonial territories in order to serve colonial ends. In this reconfigured form, Swahili became an important tool of British colonial command and control of African military personnel, as discussed in Chap. 3. As the language gained momentum, however, it began to acquire new and unforeseen roles that helped precipitate the anti-colonial winds of change. It played a role in broadening the horizons of East Africans and enriching the complexities of their loyalties and allegiances, and became a significant factor in the emergence of class consciousness. These formations that Swahili helped unleash were crucial to the emergence of the kind of racial nationalism that declared a war against British colonialism in East Africa.

Audre Lorde is known to have said that "the master's tools will never dismantle the master's house." Yet, Africa and several other parts of the world offer many examples of how the languages of the colonizer were appropriated and galvanized by the colonized as tools of struggle against colonialism. Frantz Fanon described how French in Algeria, for example, once seen as an enemy language of oppression, became liberated from its historical meanings in the service of the Algerian combatants fighting to gain independence by assuming a more universal dimension of truth and justice. In the words of Fanon:

> The French language lost its accursed character, revealing itself to be capable of transmitting, for the benefit of the nation, the messages of truth that the latter awaited. Paradoxically as it may appear, it is the Algerian

Revolution, it is the struggle of the Algerian people, that is facilitating the spreading of the French language in the nation…Used by the voice of the combatants, conveying in a positive way the message of the Revolution, the French language also becomes an instrument of liberation. (1967, 89–90)

The French language thus became purged of its oppressive meanings by the forces of liberation and was put into the service of a nationalist struggle.

A phenomenon similar to that described by Fanon in relation to French in Algeria was at play in East Africa in the concluding decades of British colonialism. As indicated above, though an African language, Swahili was seized and transformed by the colonizer to serve colonial ends – from Christian attempts to capture the souls of Africans, to its role in providing labor for colonial settlers and the colonial economy and askaris for the King's African Rifles. Once the anti-colonial struggle exploded, however, Swahili was reappropriated and put into the service of African liberation. Between nationalist publications of one kind or another and speeches at political rallies, the language lost all semblance of colonial influence. If *uhuru* once referred primarily to the state of freedom from enslavement or human bondage, it now became an East African war cry for national sovereignty and self-determination. The struggle against colonialism in East Africa had heralded a new phase in the development of the language.

References

Beck, Rose Marie. 2018. Language as Apparatus: Entanglements of Language, Culture and Territory and the Invention of Nation and Ethnicity. *Postcolonial Studies* online, April, 1–222.

Blommaert, Jan. 2010. *The Sociolinguistics of Globalization*. Cambridge: Cambridge University Press.

Bolton, Caitlyn. 2016. Making Africa Legible: Kiswahili Arabic and Orthographic Romanization in Colonial Zanzibar. *The American Journal of Islamic Social Science* 33 (5): 61–78.

Dasgupta, Arko. 2021. Makhan Singh: The Punjabi Radical Who Fought for Freedom in Not One but Two Countries. *Scroll.* https://scroll.in/article/984131/makhan-singh-the-punjabi-radical-who-fought-forfreedom-in-not-one-but-two-countries. Accessed 3 July 2022.

Durrani, Shiraz. 2006. *Never Be Silent: Publishers and Imperialism in Kenya 1884–1963*. London: Vita Books.
Elkins. 2005. *Imperial Reckoning: The Untold Story of Britain's Gulag in Kenya*. New York: Henry Holt and Company.
Elkins, Caroline. 2022. *Legacy of Violence: A History of the British Empire*. New York: Alfred A. Knoff.
Errington, Joseph. 2008. *Linguistics in a Colonial World: A Story of Language, Meaning and Power*. Oxford: Blackwell.
Fanon, Frantz. 1967. *A Dying Colonialism*. Trans. Haakon Chevalier. New York: Grove Press.
Frederiksen, Bodil Folke. 2011. Print, Newspapers and Audiences in Colonial Kenya: African and Indian Improvement, Protest and Connections. *Africa: Journal of the International African Institute* 81 (1): 155–172.
Iliffe, John. 1975. The Creation of Group Consciousness Among Dock Workers of Dar es Salaam 1929–1956. In *The Development of an African Working Class: Studies in Class Formation and Action*, ed. Richard Sandbrook and Robin Cohen, 49–72. Toronto: University of Toronto Press.
Isichei, E. 1995. *A History of Christianity in Africa*. Lawrence, NJ: Africa World Press.
Kabwegyere, Tarsis. 1974. *The Politics of State Formation: The Nature and Effects of Colonialism in Uganda*. Nairobi: East African Literature Bureau.
Kareithi, P.M. 1969. *Kaburi Bila Msalaba: Haditi ya Vita vya Mau Mau*. Nairobi: Phoenix Publishers.
Kibao, Salim A. 1972. *Utenzi wa Uhuru was Kenya*. Nairobi: Oxford University Press.
Makoni, Sinfree, Janina Brutt-Griffler, and Pedzai Mashiri. 2007. The Use of 'Indigenous' and Urban Vernaculars in Zimbabwe. *Language and Society* 36 (1): 25–49.
Makoni, Sinfree B., Christine G. Severo, and Ashraf Abdelhay. 2020. Colonial Linguistics and the Invention of Language. In *Language Planning and Policy: Ideologies, Ethnicities, and Semiotic Spaces of Power*, ed. Ashraf Abdelhay, Sinfree B. Makoni, and Christine G. Severo, 211–228. Newcastle upon Tyne: Cambridge Scholars Publishing.
Mazrui, Ali A., and Alamin Mazrui. 1995. *Swahili, State and Society: The Political Economy of an African Language*. Nairobi: East African Educational Publishers.
Mojola, Aloo Osotsi. 2001. The Swahili Bible in East Africa from 1844–1996: A Brief Survey with Special Reference to Tanzania. In *The Bible in Africa: Transactions, Trajectories and Trends*, ed. Gerald O. West and Musa W. Debe, 51–523. Leiden: Brill.

Muslim, Farouk, and Said Mzee. 1980. *Mkuki wa Moto*. Nairobi: East African Publishing House.
Osborne, Myles. 2015. "The Rooting Out of Mau Mau from the Minds of the Kikuyu Is a Formidable Task": Propaganda and the Mau Mau War. *Journal of African History* 56: 77–97.
Parsons, Timothy H. 1999. *The African Rank-and-File: Social Implications of Colonial Military Service in the King's African Rifles, 1902-1964*. Portsmouth, New Hampshire: Heinemann.
Paterson, Derek. 1997. Colonizing Language? Missionaries and Gikuyu Dictionaries, 1904 and 1914. *History of Africa* 24: 257–272.
Pennycook, Alastair. 2017. *The Cultural Politics of English as an International Language*. London: Routledge.
Pike, Charles. 1986. History and Imagination: Swahili Literature and Resistance to German Language Imperialism in Tanzania 1885–1910. *International Journal of African Historical Studies* 19 (2): 201–234.
Renck, G. 1990. *Contextualization of Christianity and Christianization of Language: A Case Study from the Highlands of Papua New Guinea*. Erlangen: Verlag der Luth-Mission.
Robinson, Morgan J. 2022. *A Language for the World: The Standardization of Swahili*. Athens: Ohio University Press.
Roehl, K. 1930. The Linguistic Situation in East Africa. *Africa: Journal of the International Africa Institute* 3 (2): 191–202.
Scotton, James F. 1978. Tanganyika's African Press, 1937–1960: A Nearly Forgotten Pre-Independence Forum. *African Studies Review* 21 (1): 1–18.
Stichter, Sharon. 1975. The Formation of a Working Class in Kenya. In *The Development of an African Working Class: Studies in Class Formation and Action*, ed. Richard Sandbrook and Robin Cohen, 21–48. Toronto: University of Toronto Press.
Tucker, Alfred R. 1911. *Eighteen Years in Uganda and East Africa*. London: Edward Arnold.
Whiteley, Wilfred H. 1969. *Swahili: The Rise of a National Language*. London: Methuen.

5

Swahili and the Wars of the Great Lakes Region

Alamin Mazrui and Kimani Njogu

In the Eastern African context, the term "great lakes" usually refers to six water reservoirs: Lake Victoria, Lake Tanganyika, Lake Kivu, Lake Edward, Lake Albert, and Lake Kyoga. The area lying around these lakes is what is generally called the Great Lakes region, though the narrow sense of the term and the one employed in this chapter restricts the region to four countries: Uganda, Rwanda, Burundi, and the Democratic Republic of the Congo. This is an area known for its favorable natural and ecological conditions that have led to dense populations and vibrant economic activities and exchanges. Equally distinctive perhaps, as Archie Mafeje (1998) shows, is the fact that the region has a long history of pre-colonial kingdoms: Buganda, Bunyoro, Burundi, and Rwanda, among other monarchic states that competed with and occasionally fought each other. With the advent of colonialism and its governance practices, including enclosing these kingdoms in confined spaces, the climate for more intense competition and potential conflict increased tremendously, sometimes exploding into civil wars and/or interstate wars. And in each of these nations, armies and military encounters became crucial in the (re)shaping of the state.

The Great Lakes region, in the narrow sense employed here, borders both Kenya and Tanzania, the two countries most intimately associated with the origins and expansion of Swahili. As the more stable neighbors, Kenya and Tanzania came to play important roles in some of these regional conflicts – supporting one warring party against another, initiating and coordinating peace negotiations, and always playing host to hundreds of thousands of refugees from one or more of the countries of the region. The geographical location of Kenya and Tanzania in the constellation of countries of the Great Lakes region and the various parts played by the two countries in the conflict situations of those countries were to have a direct or indirect impact on the regional fortunes of the Swahili language.

In the postcolonial dispensation, the politico-military developments in Uganda had a direct impact on the postcolonial history of Rwanda and its military formations. In turn, the complex situations that unfolded in both Burundi and the Democratic Republic of the Congo were related to the dynamics in Rwanda in multiple ways. For these reasons, Uganda becomes a good entry point into the discussion of the conflicts of the Great Lakes countries and the spread of Swahili in the region.

Uganda and the NRA Effect

With Uganda's independence, Swahili continued to serve as the language of the armed forces and the police with a purely instrumental function as the language of command. The armed forces of Uganda from 1961 to 1986 were simultaneously multiethnic and largely uniregional. The soldiers were overwhelmingly from the north of the country, but the north was multiethnic, though predominantly of the Nilotic branch. This composition of the army was a legacy of British colonialism that constructed identities and assigned attributes to communities. In this case, they regarded the northerners as being among the "martial races" of Uganda. The multiethnic nature of the armed forces created the instrumental need for a lingua franca like Swahili. But the uniregional (northern and mostly Nilotic) nature of the army eventually created a sentimental attachment to Swahili, seen by other Ugandans as a northern lingua franca. In the cultural divide between the mainly Nilotic northern Uganda and the mainly Bantu southern Uganda, it was paradoxically the northerners who embraced and espoused Swahili, a Bantu language, as their own.

Almost from the outset, the leadership of Prime Minister Milton Obote, himself a northerner, was in a state of tension with the then President of the country, Mutesa II, who was also the Kabaka/King of the Buganda Kingdom. Since Milton Obote "came from the Lango northern ethnic group that had been marginalized by the British, while the President was Mutesa II, ruler of the Buganda kingdom whose Baganda people had been favoured under colonial rule, the army was soon at the center of the sharp power struggle" (Prunier 2017, 100–101). Soon the army had intervened on behalf of Milton Obote, eliminating the position of prime minister, and installing Obote as the president. With the army assuming the role of a political power broker in this ethnically framed context, its ethnicization intensified, with northern, mainly Nilotic soldiers and officers growing in rank and authority. Expectedly, then, as a language associated with the military throughout this period, Swahili acquired a particularly negative image and was broadly viewed as a tool of oppression among many Bantu peoples of Uganda.

Until the soldiers first captured political power on January 25, 1971, and in spite of Baganda antipathy toward the language, Swahili retained its other role, serving more as a language of economic interaction than of political participation. Swahili was widely used in trade, commerce, and industrial activities. It helped expand the wage sector of the economy and facilitated the emergence of a modern working class. But in practice the language was hardly utilized in national politics between Independence in 1962 and the military takeover in 1971 (Mazrui and Mazrui 1998, 130). Of course, President Milton Obote himself was convinced that the promotion and use of Swahili in Uganda would be a great asset to the country in its political development as well as in terms of its relationship with its regional neighbors. He intended to introduce it as one of the compulsory languages to be learnt in his proposed National Service, and "announced at Makerere University in October 1970 his intention to promote its teaching in the schools of Uganda. But he never got around to fulfilling these promises of a new language policy in the educational system of Uganda. He never even fulfilled the promise to introduce Swahili on Radio Uganda, which he had considered doing for many years" (Mazrui 1975, 142).

The military takeover of 1971 under the leadership of General Idi Amin Dada was, almost by definition, a reduction of political participation by the masses. Parliament and political parties were abolished, and student politics gradually ground to a standstill. Yet, in a paradoxical twist, this shrinking of the political space was accompanied by a quick expansion of the use of Swahili, with the military now increasing Swahili's chances of participation in Uganda's national life. Radio and television employees were ordered to use Swahili for the first time as one of their languages. As Mazrui commented at that time:

> Within less than three weeks of the coup Swahili was on Radio Uganda and on Uganda Television. Indeed, on Radio Uganda Swahili has acquired almost the status of a national language. It is the only news bulletin in an African language to be read simultaneously on both channels of Radio Uganda. The old attachment to Swahili which the armed forces had shown, and which was a residual symbol of the connection between military service and East African integration, had found yet another manifestation. On taking over power in Uganda, the soldiers decided that one of their first policies was indeed to introduce Swahili in the mass media of the country. (Mazrui 1975, 143)

The military regime proceeded to formally confer upon the language the status of a national language. The soldiers, meanwhile, precisely because they were in power, increased the use of Swahili in their own contacts with the general public, fostering a certain consolidation of the language in social interaction throughout the Idi Amin years.

During the years of his rule (1971–1979), Idi Amin became notorious for his brutality, among other excesses. Nepotism, ethnic persecution, political repression, gross human rights abuses, and regular extrajudicial killings were some of the main features of his years in office. In 1972, he expelled Ugandans of Indian origin from Uganda and embarked upon a redistribution of commercial enterprises. This expulsion and redistribution, referred to as "Operation Mafuta Mingi," led to widespread migrations. Within the army, he purged some of the northern ethnic groups, like the Lango and the Acholi, and increased the numbers of other northern ethnic groups, like those from the West Nile region. In spite of these changes in the army, however, Swahili continued to be associated with northerners and, under Idi Amin, with a brutal military dictatorship.

It was during this period of Idi Amin's misrule that Tanzania and Kenya, two of the major Swahili-speaking countries in the region, experienced an ever-increasing flow of Ugandan refugees and political exiles. Milton Obote, Uganda's president who had been overthrown by Idi Amin, had himself found refuge in neighboring Tanzania. Because of Obote's longstanding friendship with the then president of Tanzania, Julius Nyerere, and the growing tensions between Idi Amin's Uganda and Tanzania, many political opponents of Idi Amin – real, potential, or imagined – also ended up seeking asylum in Tanzania. But some of the exiles also fled to Kenya and Sudan, and later to other African countries, Europe, and North America. In the meantime, Uganda's economy was in shambles because of mismanagement, resulting in a massive wave of Ugandan refugees in Kenya and other neighboring countries. As the bedrock of anti-Amin opposition, many of these exiles later constituted themselves into a united, armed front, the Uganda National Liberation Front (UNLF). With its base in Tanzania, and reliant on Tanzanian support at the state and community level, members of the UNLF began to embrace Swahili as a language of their own UNLF identity.

With Uganda's deteriorating relationship with Tanzania, mounting economic and political problems, and dissension within the ranks of his army, Idi Amin ordered the invasion of Tanzania in October 1978. Ugandan soldiers moved into the Kagera Salient, looting and killing civilians in the process. Tanzania declared a state of war, with its Tanzania People's Defence Force (TPDF) responding with a counterattack in what came to be known in Tanzania as the beginning of the Kagera War. By December 1978, the TPDF had managed to repulse the invading forces and pushed them all the way back to the Uganda side of the border. The reprisal had received the support of Ugandan groups, including the Front for National Salvation (FRONASA) under Yoweri Museveni and his colleagues, and Kikosi Maalum, which was dominated by Obote supporters.

It was at this point that Tanzania decided to assist the anti-Amin exile groups in Uganda and elsewhere to unite under the banner of the Uganda National Liberation Front (UNLF). Tanzania now provided members of the UNLF financial support and military training and helped arm them for an attack on Uganda. Together with the armed wing of the UNLF, the Uganda National Liberation Army (UNLA), the Tanzanian forces now proceeded to launch a full-scale offensive into Uganda. With rapidly declining morale, the Ugandan army began to disintegrate, allowing the combined forces of the TPDF and UNLF to advance all the way to the main city, Kampala. By May 1979, the Ugandan army had been completely vanquished and General Idi Amin fled, first to Libya and later to Saudi Arabia.

The Kagera War soon inspired Henry Muhanika to compose his poem of some 1271 verses on the subject. Entitled *Utenzi wa vita vya Kagera na anguko la Idi Amin Dada* (The narrative poem of the Kagera War and the fall of Idi Amin Dada), the poem traces the entire course of the war, beginning with the rise of Idi Amin, to his tensions with Julius Nyerere, to the invasion of Tanzania and the eruption of the war, to the final fall of Kampala and the end of Idi Amin's regime. It is significant that the poet makes specific mention of the coalition of Ugandan rebel groups attacking from Tanzania, united under the name of Uganda National Liberation Army (UNLA), with names of some of its leaders and massive support from the Tanzanian army. As the poet puts it (1981, 138–139):

Tanzania ikaona	(And) Tanzania sensed
Hali ya hatari yaja	(That) the danger was imminent
Uamuzi ikafanya	(So) It made a decision
Vita ikamalizike	To take the war to completion
Na janga liepukike	And get rid of the nightmare

Na U.N.L.F. pia	And U.N.L.F. also
Jeshi lake ikaunda	Created its own army
U.N.L.A. liliitwa	U.N.L.A. it was named
Uganda kuikomboa	To liberate Uganda
Kwa bunduki kutumia	By means of guns

Kamanda wa U.N.L.A.	(For the) U.N.L.A. commander
Okelo alichaguliwa	Okelo was selected
Kwa cheo huyu Titus	In rank, this Titus
Alikuwa ni Kanali	He was a colonel

Msaidizi Kamanda	A deputy commander
Naye alichaguliwa	Was also elected
Nafasi aliyeshika	And the one installed
Ni William Oraria	Is William Oraria
Wengine wanakamati	Other council members
Viongozi wa vitani	In the war leadership
Oyite Ojok nataja	I mention Oyite Ojok
Maruru naye nataja	as well as Maruru
Na Yoweri Museveni	and Yoweri Museveni
Wapinzani zake Idi	The anti-Idi forces
Hasa wale Askari	especially the soldiers
Wakaungana pamoja	now became united
Chini ya hii UNLA	Under this UNLA
Na vijana kwa mamia	And hundreds of young people
Waganda namaanisha	Ugandans, I mean
Wakawa wamiminika	Arrived in droves
Kujiunga na UNLA.	To join UNLA.

The idea then was that once the liberation front and its armed wing were announced, the ranks of Ugandans who volunteered to join the effort would multiply rapidly. The economic and social consequences of the war for Tanzania also became the subject of the play *Lina Ubani* (It has incense), in which the playwright, Penina Muhando (1984), depicts the scarcity of basic and essential commodities such as flour, sugar, and soap and the rise of the black market resulting from the war.

For a while, the ouster of Idi Amin seemed to hold even better prospects for the future of Swahili in Uganda. The thousands of Tanzanian soldiers walking the streets of Uganda, interacting with the people in Swahili, were seen as heroes and liberators of the Ugandan people from Idi Amin's tyranny. The national language of Tanzania, the Swahili language, suddenly acquired a new positive image in the minds of many Ugandans precisely because of the positive role that the national army of Tanzania was seen to have played in ending Idi Amin's bloody era. The fortunes of Swahili now seemed boundless indeed. The political climate indicated new possibilities of Tanzanian personnel, both military and otherwise, coming into Uganda on a large scale to help in the reconstruction of the country. This move would certainly have helped in the greater Swahilization of Uganda.

This positive image of Tanzania due to its perceived role in Uganda's liberation, however, declined as rapidly as it had arisen. This is when it appeared that Nyerere's involvement in Uganda's political affairs was based less on the noble principle of freedom and liberty for the people than on a hidden agenda to reinstate his friend Milton Obote as Uganda's president, essentially to replace Idi Amin's dictatorship with Obote's dictatorship. Tanzania's image as a liberator of the people of Uganda now gave way to the image of a betrayer of the democratic aspirations of the Ugandan people. The Ugandan population began to turn hostile toward Tanzania, and with this change in political opinion the Swahili language lost a golden moment in its political history in Uganda.

The fall of Idi Amin in 1979, the return of civilian rule under Milton Obote, and the changed attitudes toward Tanzania now combined to threaten the gains that Swahili had made under the rule of the military. But the 1980 edition of the manifesto of Milton Obote's political party, the Uganda People's Congress (UPC), gave advocates of Swahili a new glimmer of hope. According to the manifesto:

> UPC will seek to promote an African language such as Kiswahili to the status of a national, unifying language. At the same time, UPC will encourage and foster the development and teaching of various indigenous languages as proof of our heritage. English shall remain the official language. (UPC 1980, 4)

While the statement by no means demonstrated a commitment on the part of UPC to promote Swahili in particular, it at least left the impression that the party, with its political history now more intimately linked to Tanzania, was seriously willing to consider that option.

By the time Milton Obote was ousted from power in 1985, however, it was only the English part of UPC's pledge that was in effect. The English language did indeed continue to serve as the official language of Uganda. Neither Swahili nor any of the local languages of Uganda gained

5 Swahili and the Wars of the Great Lakes Region

from UPC's return to power. Admittedly, the new UPC government did not repeal Idi Amin's decree making Swahili the national language, nor did it terminate Swahili programs on Uganda's radio and television. But neither did it initiate any moves to promote the language in the country.

Soon after assuming the office of President of Uganda for the second time – a period that is popularly referred to as Obote II in Uganda – major political rifts arose within what was once a united front against Idi Amin. In particular, there were charges that Milton Obote and his Ugandan and Tanzanian supporters rigged the 1980 presidential elections in favor of Obote. The political fallout triggered a long guerilla war between Obote's Uganda National Liberation Army (UNLA) and a variety of groups, the most prominent being the National Resistance Army (NRA), led by Yoweri Museveni. The initial core of the NRA was composed of fighters from Museveni's own Front for National Salvation (FRONASA), a group that was formed in Tanzania in the early 1970s and continued to organize and train in that East African country for years before joining the Tanzanian army in the war against Idi Amin's forces in Uganda. As a result of this background, the NRA core was also the most Swahilized linguistically and continued to make Swahili the main medium for its organizational needs. As an editorial in Uganda's *Weekly Topic* (October 1, 1986) put it: "Faced with a practical problem of communication and unity while in the bush, the NRA was bailed out by Swahili."

As a guerilla army, the NRA depended heavily on the surrounding civilian population for support. Therefore, it initiated a system of democratic governance of villages in the Loweero Triangle, with full participation of the villagers themselves in decision making on matters related to their relationship with and support of the NRA. The NRA was thus "a guerilla group whose commitment to popular support deepened into democratic village management during the course of its civil war. The significant causal factors in deepening this commitment were its ideological conviction, relative military strength, dependence on civilian material assistance, and need for accommodation with civilian preferences in its operational area" (Kasfir 2005, 271). In this political exercise, Swahili became a useful medium to the NRA, though it was often used side by side with other languages of the area. And these practices of democracy at the village level helped in the consolidation of Swahili in Uganda beyond the urban areas.

The NRA's use of Swahili, however, was not restricted to organizational and operational needs. Sometimes Swahili was galvanized for inspirational purposes. This was clearly evident in the kind of Swahili "bush songs" that the NRA combatants sang during the course of the war. For example, the song "Endesheni Mapambano" (Onward with the struggle) urged the fighters to advance and accomplish the objectives that the NRA had set for them. The chorus of the song is as follows:

Endesheni mapambano	Onward with the struggle
Tutengeneze Jeshi la Obote	Let's teach Obote's army a lesson
Tujenge Uganda mpya.	And build a new Uganda

Stanzas of the rest of the song open with a new line each followed by the chorus. These lines include the following:

Wananchi wa Uganda—Songeni	Citizens of Uganda—Move on
Fukuzeni Obote huyo—Songeni	Chase away that [Milton] Obote—Move on
Fukuzeni Smith huyo—Songeni	Chase away that [Brig] Smith [Opon of UNLA]— Move on
Fukuzeni Ojok huyo	Chase away that [Maj. Gen Oyite] Ojok [of UNLA]
Fukuzeni Rwakasisi huyo	Chase away that [Hon. Chris] Rwakasisi. Minister, UPC government
Fukuzeni ukabila	Chase away tribalism
Fukuzeni huku na huko	Chase away, here and there

("NRA Bush War Song: Endesheni")

From the song, then, combatants were inspired to understand their mission to move on to complete victory, not only to rid the country of the leaders of UPC and UNLA, but also to transform the society into a more inclusive order that accepts unity in diversity.

An equally popular Swahili "bush song" of the NRA was "Wazalendo wa NRA" (Patriots of NRA.) Unlike "Endesheni Mapambano," which focuses on what is to be accomplished, "Wazalendo wa NRA" predicates the necessity of victory on recollecting the ultimate sacrifice that so many combatants had made. Here are some of the lyrics of the song:

Wazalendo wa NRA—Pamoja	Patriots of the NRA — Together
Ushindi wetu ni wa lazima	Our victory is a must!
Wazalendo—Pamoja	Patriots — Together
Wazalendo—Pamoja	Patriots — Together
Wazalendo	Patriots
Ushindi wetu ni wa lazima	Our victory is a must!
Seguya alikufa kwa mapambano	[Major Ahmad] Seguya died fighting
Ushindi wetu ni wa lazima	Our victory is a must!
Rubereza alikufa kwa mapambano	[Major Fred] Rubereza died fighting
Ushindi wetu ni wa lazima	Our victory is a must!
Mugabi alikufa kwa mapambano	[Major Hannington] Mugabi died fighting
Ushindi wetu ni wa lazima	Our victory is a must!
Tumuhairwe alikufa kwa mapambano	[Enock] Tumuhairwe died fighting
Ushindi wetu ni wa lazima	Our victory is a must!
Kakwezi alikufa kwa mapambano	[Sam] Kakwezi died fighting
Ushindi wetu ni wa lazima	Our victory is a must!
Wazalendo—Pamoja	Patriots — Together
Wazalendo—Pamoja	Patriots — Together
Wazalendo	Patriots
Ushindi wetu ni wa lazima	Our victory is a must!
	("NRA Bush War Song: Wazalendo")

These "bush songs," then, demonstrate how Swahili had become not only an essential tool for inspiring and mobilizing the combatants in their guerilla war with the Obote regime, but also a medium for memorializing the heroes who sacrificed their lives for the liberation of Uganda. Spirits of fallen heroes were invoked by name, one at a time, to emphasize the principle that without our victory their sacrifices would have been in vain. Swahili therefore continued to be an important medium of transethnic communication in the National Resistance Army throughout the period of struggle against government forces.

As indicated earlier, the Ugandan military was hitherto dominated by northerners of Nilotic and, especially during Idi Amin's rule, Central Sudanic background. The ascendency to power of the NRA in 1986 changed this ethnic–military equation in Uganda. Because the NRA, in the popular consciousness of Ugandans, was a movement intended to end the continued tyranny of Nilotic and Central Sudanic people, it mostly attracted Bantu speakers to its ranks, especially those from the western region. For a while, the confrontation between the NRA and the Ugandan government's army was seen as an ethnic confrontation between speakers of Bantu languages and speakers of Nilotic and Central Sudanic languages. And when the NRA became victorious, a new ethnic–military equation had emerged in the politics of Uganda. Precisely because speakers of Bantu languages are not themselves a homogenous group, Swahili continued to feature as an important language of the new military setup. And in spite of continued Baganda opposition to Swahili, the language acquired a new image and gained a new momentum in Uganda precisely because the NRA, as a liberation force, had been victorious.

Rwanda, Burundi, and the RPF Effect

There is a sense in which Rwanda and Burundi can be considered members of a cluster in a way that other countries of the Great Lakes region cannot. Both countries were once colonies of Germany as part of German East Africa and later of Belgium. In spite of the presence of the Twa minority in Rwanda and Burundi, the national identities of both nations have continued to be framed in terms of a duality, of the Hutu–Tutsi ethnic divide, with the Hutu constituting the majority in both. In addition, while the local national languages of the two countries bear different names, Kinyarwanda and Kirundi, they are essentially varieties of the same language.

In exploring the theme of Swahili and war in these two nations, one must begin with the racial construction of Hutu–Tutsi identity during the Belgian colonial period. Prior to and during the Belgian Trusteeship, the Tutsi–a minority community in the centralized state–wielded much political power over the majority Hutu. Under the late 1800s rule of

Mwami Kigeli Rwabugiri (c.1840–1895), a Tutsi, the fundamental characteristics of modern Rwanda were fixed. While social identities in precolonial Rwanda were fluid and malleable, the social hierarchy and power asymmetry between communities were encouraged and solidified over time by the Belgians, who treated the Hutu and Tutsi as two racially distinct groups, notwithstanding the fact that they spoke one language (Kinyarwanda). The Belgians succeeded in entrenching in the collective consciousness of community members the belief that the Hutu were Bantu on account of their physical features, and the Tutsi were Afro-Asiatic (the "other"/the "foreigners"/the "newcomers"). In the words of Gerald Caplan (2007, 20):

> In the colonial era, under the German and then the Belgian rule, Roman Catholic missionaries, inspired by the overly racist theories of nineteenth-century Europe, concocted a bizarre ideology of ethnic cleavage and racial rankings that attributed superior qualities to the country's Tutsi minority. This 15 percent of the population, it was announced, were approaching, however gradually, the exalted level of white people, in contrast with the declared brutishness and innate inferiority of the 'Bantu' majority. Because the missionaries ran the colonial-era schools, these pernicious values were systematically transmitted to several generations of Rwandans along the more conventional Catholic teachings.
>
> The alleged differences between the ethnic groups were arbitrary and baseless, yet they soon took on a life of their own. The Belgians made the *Mwami's* complex structures more rigid and ethnically inflexible. They institutionalized the split between the two groups, culminating in the issuance to every Rwandan of an ethnic identity card. This card system … became the instrument that enabled Hutu killers in urban areas to identify the Tutsi who were its original beneficiaries.

This systematic colonial construction of the Hutu–Tutsi dichotomy, with accompanying symbols and ramifications for access to political power, was to have devastating consequences.

As the push for decolonization gained momentum in the 1950s, democracy came to be associated with majority rule. In the case of Rwanda, the notion of majority was defined ethnically. The colonially constructed ethnic divisions were invoked in earnest, and toward the end of the 1950s, the Belgian government and the Catholic Church encouraged a revolt of the Hutu against the Tutsi-led monarchy. In November 1959, the Tutsi monarchy was overthrown and Grégoire Kayibanda became Rwanda's first president, under the Party for Hutu Emancipation. The Tutsi aristocracy now lost their position of political power as well as much of their wealth to members of the Hutu nationalist movement. "In the process, tens of thousands of Tutsi were killed and many more inhabitants were displaced. By the time the UN recognised Rwanda's independence in 1962, somewhere between 40 and 70 per cent of the entire Tutsi population was thought to have fled" (Reed 1996, 481). The majority of these Tutsi refugees ended up in Uganda.

After years of residence in various countries, the Tutsi refugees made attempts to blend into their respective host communities. Except in rare circumstances, however, none of these efforts to belong in their new homes away from home (Rwanda) succeeded. In what was then Zaire and in Tanzania, Rwandan refugees continued to be regarded as foreigners, a status that especially limited their employment opportunities in state and parastatal agencies. In Uganda, in the meantime, following "the overthrow of Amin and the beginning of what has become known as the Obote II regime, Rwandans living in Uganda were blamed for supporting Amin, and Obote sought to fan anti-Rwandese sentiments as a way of building support for himself. In the process, their lands and cattle were often confiscated, and many were summarily dismissed from public employment" (Reed 1996, 483–484).

These circumstances that contributed to a life of increasing precarity among Rwandan refugees in Uganda made them potential and willing recruits for an armed struggle against the Obote II regime. Thus, when Yoweri Museveni retreated into the Luweero Triangle with his National Resistance Army (NRA), the initial and rapidly growing population of its combatants was in fact drawn from the Rwandans: "As attacks against the Rwandan community in Uganda escalated, more and more members of the diaspora joined the NRM and its military wing, the National Resistance Army (NRA), which recruited anyone who was willing to fight, regardless of nationality" (Reed 1996, 484–485). The NRA leadership itself came to include prominent Rwandan refugees of Tutsi origin, like Paul Kagame who later became its Chief of Military Intelligence and

Fred Rwigyema who served as the Deputy Army Commander-in-Chief. Indeed, in spite of their minority status in Uganda, it is estimated that by the end of the Ugandan Civil War in 1985, perhaps as much as "30 percent of the NRA was made up of Rwandese refugees, most of whom were born in Uganda after the 1959 Hutu revolution in Rwanda and the ensuing waves of exiles" (Prunier 2017, 104). Because Swahili had risen to become the NRA's official medium of communication, these Rwandan members of the NRA were bound to develop some proficiency in the language in the course of the eight-year "bush war" of resistance in Uganda.

With the NRA's victory and the rise of Yoweri Museveni and his National Resistance Movement to power in Uganda, and against the backdrop of the crucial role of Rwandan refugees in securing this victory, the expectations were high that Uganda would now be home for its Rwandans, and that the Rwandans would now be accepted as fellow Ugandans. These expectations, however, were never to materialize in practice, in spite of Museveni's declaration that refugees of Rwandan origin who had resided in the country for at least ten years could become citizens. On the contrary, the Rwandan presence in the NRA itself now became a liability as it "progressively developed into a major political problem in the country" (Prunier 2017, 104).

Under these circumstances, the ranks of Rwandan refugees seeking to reclaim a home in Rwanda through acts of armed insurrection continued to increase. These militant efforts eventually crystallized into a more or less united front under the banner of the Rwandan Patriotic Front (RPF). This RPF was dominated by Rwandan veterans of Uganda's bush war. As Prunier points out, "One hundred percent of the Ugandan men (and some women) who invaded Rwanda in October 1990 were former NRA soldiers" (2017, 103). The resolve of the RPF to take over power in Rwanda increased tremendously following the Tutsi genocide that was triggered by the death of President Juvenal Habyarimana, himself of Hutu background, when his plane was shot down on April 6, 1994. It now proceeded to launch a full-scale invasion and, by the end of July 1994, had achieved complete victory. A transitional Government of National Unity was formed with Pasteur Bizimungu, a Hutu, as President, and Paul Kagame, a Tutsi, as Vice President. Because many of the new leaders and fighters had been in exile in Uganda and Tanzania, and many were born in those host countries, they had acquired both Swahili and English. The victory of the RPF, then, opened up the space in Rwanda for further Swahilization and Anglicization of the society.

A particularly important factor in the genocide of 1994 is that of religion. During the violence in this predominantly Catholic nation, the church failed to serve as a sanctuary as priests and nuns were themselves complicit in the violence, opening the gates of the churches to the Hutu militia. But the Swahili-speaking Muslim minority gave the victims protection in mosques and in their homes. Writing about the role of the Muslims ten years after the genocide, Marc Lacey says:

> When 800,000 of their countrymen were killed in massacres that began 10 years ago this week, many Rwandans lost faith not only in their government but in their religion as well. Today, in what is still a predominantly Catholic country, Islam is the fastest growing religion. Roman Catholicism has been the dominant faith in Rwanda for more than a century. But many people, disgusted by the role that some priests and nuns played in the killing frenzy have shunned organized religion altogether, and many more have turned to Islam. (*New York Times*, April 7, 2004)

Elsewhere in his article, Lacey explains that the Muslim community now had so many converts that it had to embark on a crash campaign to build new mosques to accommodate all of the faithful. Mosques were rapidly built across Rwanda and although no accurate census has been done, Muslim leaders in Rwanda estimated that they may have had about a million followers, or about 15 percent of the population. This percentage would represent a doubling of their numbers in a decade. Because Swahili was the primary language of these Rwandan Muslims, the positive image of their community went hand-in-hand with a positive image of the Swahili language. Rwanda's Swahilization was now accompanied by some degree of Islamization, and this religious conversion in turn consolidated the position of Swahili.

Since the 1994 genocide, Rwanda has been deliberate in promoting reconciliation and redefining its collective identity through language, shared culture, territory, history, discouraging ethnic identification, and

5 Swahili and the Wars of the Great Lakes Region 133

vocalization of a self-identifying national belonging devoid of ethnic "divisionism" (Englebert and Dunn 2013, 84). By developing a post-genocide alternative language policy, the government sought to minimize the salience of ethnicity as a site of identity and in political engagement. Toward this new direction, the Constitution of Rwanda stipulates that Kinyarwanda is the national language and a co-official language alongside French, English, and Swahili. While French and English had attained official status in 2003, it was on February 8, 2017, that Parliament passed a law making Swahili one of the official languages of Rwanda. This decision was aligned to the sociolinguistic direction that the post-genocide government took to accelerate economic and political integration within regional and international community. There was political will, and in the words of Wallace Mlaga (2017, 9):

> *Utashi huu wa kisiasa katika kipindi hiki unaweza kuelezwa kuwa ulisababishwa na mambo muhimu matatu: nguvu ya kundi la watu waliorejea Rwanda baada ya mwaka 1994, ushirikiano wa nchi za Ukanda wa Maziwa Makuu, na Jumuiya ya Afrika Mashariki. Sababu hizi tatu zinafungamana pia na ustawi wa kijamii, kisiasa, na kiuchumi wa nchi ya Rwanda. Hivyo basi, serikali ilichukua uamuzi wa kuunga mkono jitihada za kustawisha Kiswahili kutokana na misukumo hiyo.*

This political will in this period [1996–] was a result of three factors: the power of the returnees to Rwanda after 1994, the cooperation between the countries in the Great Lakes region and the East African Community. These three factors are tied to Rwanda's social, political and economic progress. Therefore, the government decided to support the development of Swahili on the basis of these factors.

Developments in Rwanda came to have a direct impact on Burundi. Even Burundi's own independence and extraction from the Rwanda-Urundi nomenclature that was part of the German and Belgian colonial legacy followed on the heels of the Rwanda Hutu uprising of 1959. Like Rwanda, Burundi experienced cycles of violence with ethnic cleavages that have resulted in forced migration to neighboring countries, notably Rwanda, Tanzania, Uganda, and the Democratic Republic of the Congo. In some ways, Burundi became "the inverted twin of Rwanda" (Prunier

2017, 105). If the victims of genocide in Rwanda were predominantly Tutsi, the initial victims of genocide in Burundi were predominantly of Hutu descent. As a result, the majority of refugees from Rwanda have been Tutsi, while the majority of Burundi refugees have tended to be Hutu. In the 1972 war that was triggered by a rebellion led by Hutu members of the gendarmerie and resulted in the first Burundi genocide, over 200,000 refugees from Burundi migrated to Tanzania and settled in camps for at least a decade. While some of them returned, others stayed on. As migrants, they were exposed to the Ujamaa philosophy and Tanzania's rich culture whose linguistic core is the Swahili language.

Another migration to Tanzania and other host countries began in 1993 after the assassination of President Melchior Ndadaye and during the 1996–1997 civil war. The refugees settled in camps and learned Swahili as they interacted with their hosts. Meanwhile, the rebel group Front National de Libération continued to wage war on the government in Burundi even after the main insurgent group, the Conseil National Pour la Défense de la Démocratie, took power in 2005. When the refugee camps were closed, refugees returned to Burundi. According to the United Nations, by 2003 – a decade after the 1993 civil war had begun – over 500,000 refugees (drawn from the 1972 and 1993 out-migrations) were living in official camps in Tanzania. Again, in 2015 during yet another political crisis, over 400,000 Burundians fled to neighboring countries, especially Tanzania (which accommodated at least 50 percent of them), Uganda, and the Democratic Republic of the Congo. In all cases, the refugees went back with new linguistic competencies, in English and Swahili especially, which they acquired in Tanzania, and with new networks of relationships that continued to link them to Tanzanian society.

After the victory of the RPF in Rwanda, many Burundi refugees and exiles moved to Rwanda. In fact, it is in Rwanda that the main Burundi rebel groups – like the Front National de Libération and the Républicaines du Burundi (FOREBU) – were constituted. These groups received direct support from the Rwandan government and military. In time these rebel groups became positively predisposed to the Swahili language partly because their host country, Rwanda, had itself Swahilized significantly after the RPF came to power.

One of the sociolinguistic features resulting from this forced migration to Tanzania and other countries was group labeling. According to Schwartz:

> In 2014, several years after the return had completed, villagers in Makamba [Burundi's southernmost district, on border with Tanzania], still identified groups in their community by their previous migration history ... [First] there were the *Abaguhunguste* (Kirundi for 'those who came back') ... Second were the *Abasangwa* (Kirundi for 'those who were here and welcomed others.' (2019, 126)

Some of the returnees only spoke Swahili, while others switched between Swahili and Kirundi. Burundians also used the Swahili term *Sabini na mbili* ('seventy-two') in reference to the migrants as Tanzanians on account of having lived across the border since 1972. This assignment of a new identity on account of a lived forced migration experience underscores a consciousness of "otherness" and legitimacy on account of the war. The stereotypes played into lack of trust in ethnic relations. In the words of Schwartz (2019, 127):

> The differentiation, between these groups, fueled narratives about which group had better claims to national legitimacy. People would use labels such as 'the Tanzanians' to differentiate returnees from Tanzania (as opposed to those from the Democratic Republic of Congo), but also to deride returnees' claims of belonging in the homeland. For example, as one returnee said. 'I thought when I came to Burundi, I would face many problems due to loss of culture. We don't speak Kirundi. They say people who do not speak Kirundi are not Burundian.'

The returnees did not speak Kirundi but rather Swahili, which gave them another identity at variance with that at "home."

Perhaps partly because of the influence of the returnees, Swahili began to make some gains in Burundi. According to the Burundi National Gazette of 2014, Kirundi is the national language of Burundi and serves, with French and English, as a co-official language of the country. But Swahili is recognized as the language of regional communication. In this Francophone country, English and Swahili have become common subjects in the school curriculum. This educational development is meant to accelerate the integration of Burundi with the rest of East Africa.

Compared to Kirundi, Swahili is asserting itself and attaining some valorization as the language of urban life and the creative industries among the youth. It is used in television dramas, music, video, and other forms of entertainment. It is also the language of cross-border commercial activities especially with Tanzania. What is certain is that the changing status of Swahili in Burundi is intimately linked to wars and enforced migrations arising from wars to and from neighboring countries.

From Zaïre Back to the DRC

Zaïre is the name that Mobutu Sese Seko gave to what was then the Democratic Republic of the Congo (DRC) after he, as Chief of Staff of the Army, overthrew the first elected postcolonial government of Patrice Lumumba in 1965 with the aid of the CIA and Belgium. He is well known for his ideology of "Authenticity" and initiating a process of "Zaïrianization" through nationalization and privatization. When his mineral resources program Société Zaïroise pour la Commercialisation de Minérais faced difficulties, he took advantage of the Cold War tensions of the time and presented himself as an ally of Western powers. But his reign was riddled with violations of human rights and suppression of freedom of expression. When, in May 1990, university students organized demonstrations and demanded democratic reforms, the government responded violently and over 300 students were killed. This action led to tensions between the Mobutu government and its key allies, notably the USA and France. Amid calls for democratic reforms, Mobutu became more vicious and dictatorial as he tightened his grip on political and military power.

As suggested in Chaps. 1 and 3, Swahili in the Congo/Zaïre prospered best in such mining areas of the country as Shaba, Upper Zaïre, and Kivu. In many cases the multiethnic composition of the labor force in the mines favored the use of Swahili as a lingua franca. In many homes in these mining areas, Swahili became more important than the original ethnic language. Swahili was thus domesticated, moving from the workplace to the home.

At one level, this was a case of regional integration, linguistically linking the Congo and other parts of Eastern Africa. But for a while, Swahili also seemed to reinforce the separate identity of provinces like Shaba (previously Katanga). Indeed, the very name Shaba (meaning copper) was a Swahili word for the province. Was this provisional separatism detrimental to national integration? Was Swahili in the Congo performing the paradoxical task of helping East African regional integration, on the one hand, and harming the internal national integration of the country, on the other?

As Mazrui and Mazrui (1998, 183) argue, it is significant that some of the earliest armed challenges to Mobutu's rule came from a region like Shaba/Katanga where Swahili had taken root. In the 1960s Moïse Tshombe attempted to pull the province out of the Congo altogether. Indeed, Tshombe is best remembered in the history of the Congo as a secessionist who was also complicit in the murder of Patrice Lumumba that took place precisely in that province of Katanga. In the 1970s, Shaba rebelled twice against the central government of Mobutu Sese Seko. On one of these occasions the Shaba rebellion had to be put down by imported Moroccan troops, aided by the French and American logistical support. Were the Shaba rebellions, an important base of the Swahili language in the Congo, detrimental to national integration, or were they pro-democracy revolts?

In the midst of internal resistance in the early 1990s, Mobutu was faced with additional challenges emanating from the Rwandan genocide of 1994, sketched above. After the Rwandan Patriotic Front under Paul Kagame took over political power, more than one million Hutus–including militiamen – the Interahamwe – are believed to have fled to the DRC. According to the International Crisis Group:

> This exodus was peculiar in that entire army units crossed the border, as did government and political leaders. The Hutu refugees, having crossed an international boundary, came under the protection of the international community especially UNHCR (United Nations High Commissioner for Refugees), which set up huge camps to house them near the Rwandan

border. These camps were controlled by the same political structures and leaders which had previously been in command in Rwanda and had organized the genocide. Furthermore, the camps became bases from which guerilla attacks were launched against the new regime in Rwanda. (ICG Congo Report No.3, May 21, 1999: 4)

The presence of the refugees heightened tensions in the eastern region around Kivu. Furthermore, the Mobutu government, which had been allied to that of Habyarimana when he was president of Rwanda, provided tacit support to the Hutu as they attacked Rwanda. The Banyamulenge – a subgroup of Tutsi in South Kivu – and the Banyarwanda – who populated the Kivu region – were under immense pressure from the Mobutu government, which on April 28, 1995, stripped them of their Congolese nationality.

Rwanda was concerned about the activities in Eastern Congo and warned that it would not allow another case of ethnic cleansing. Rwanda and Uganda felt increasingly threatened by groups operating from the Congo: the Interahamwe, the ex-Armed Forces of Rwanda, the Lord's Resistance Army, the West Nile Bank Front, and the Allied Democratic Forces, among others. Paul Kagame and Yoweri Museveni focused their strategy on ousting Mobutu and decided to reach out to small, exiled groups, some of which were based in Tanzania. It is in this context that the Alliance des Forces Démocratiques pour la Libération du Congo (AFDL), under Laurent Désiré Kabila, was born. Kabila had a long history of anti-Mobutu protests and had been a zone commander in the revolutionary redoubt Hewa-Bora (Swahili for "better air") in South Kivu during the 1964–1965 Congo Rebellion that was supported by Che Guevara and other Cuban revolutionaries. He had also gained the support of Julius Nyerere and Yoweri Museveni. Kabila spoke Swahili well and was part of the Tanzanian troops that joined the Ugandan exiles in ousting Idi Amin from power in 1979.

Under these circumstances, in 1996 and 1997, Kabila mobilized the Swahili language as the medium of command in a multiethnic army of rebellion, aided and abetted by Rwanda and Uganda (Shiner 1997). The anti-Mobutu armed rebellion of 1996 actually started with the local Tutsi of Zaïre, the Banyamulenge, but escalated not only into multiethnic revolt but also into a multinational movement, with Kabila as its leader. Already the Banyamulenge had increasingly emphasized the regular use of Swahili rather than Kinyarwanda in their own postcolonial homes precisely in order to prevent being mistaken for Rwandan immigrants. Swahili had become a kind of linguistic asylum for many Tutsi to reduce their own ethnic vulnerability as speakers of the "language of Rwanda," Kinyarwanda. While they could not entirely conceal their being Tutsi, they could at least de-emphasize it in the face of ethnic prejudice (Duke and Rupert 1997), which Swahili allowed them to do. In this context, Swahili became increasingly important, not only because many of the fighters who were recruited already had a command of Swahili, but also because of the secret participation of training officers and possibly troops linked to Rwanda's RPF and Uganda's NRA. As indicated earlier, the RPF as the basis of the Rwandan army was mainly Anglophone and Swahili-speaking.

As the AFDL marched to Kinshasa, joined by the Banyamulenge soldiers, they were received enthusiastically by the public, who saw them as a liberation force that had ended Mobutuism and ushered in the beginning of new freedoms. The defeated Mobutu fled into exile in May 1997 and Laurent Kabila was declared President on May 29, 1997. Having lived in eastern DRC and Tanzania, and because of his fluency in Swahili, Kabila's ascendancy to the presidency was a clear boost to the language. Though his presidency was short-lived, his political tenure in the highest office helped strengthen the position of the language in the country.

Kabila did not do enough to open up the democratic space, protect fundamental liberties, and encourage political dialogue, or contain militia such as the Maimai and Bembe. The militia groups continued to attack the governments of Rwanda and Uganda from eastern DRC. The tensions between these countries were heightened by accusations and counter-accusations that peaked when Rwanda and Uganda began a revolt against Laurent Kabila on August 2, 1998. At the same time, the Armée Nationale Congolaise stated that they no longer recognized Kabila as their leader. Under intense local resistance with the support of Rwanda, Kabila sought and received aid from Angola, Namibia, Zimbabwe, Sudan, Libya, and Chad. War was halted but only for a while because of the restlessness of the Swahili-speaking eastern DRC.

Fortunately for Swahili, it was Joseph Kabila who assumed the presidency of the DRC soon after his father, Laurent Kabila, was assassinated. Joseph Kabila was even more a child of Tanzania than his father was. He was largely raised and educated in Tanzania, speaking Swahili as his only African language. He had no knowledge at all of Lingala, one of Congo's lingua francas, or any other Congolese language for that matter except Swahili. There is no doubt that his eighteen years in office (2001–2019) helped consolidate the status of Swahili in the country. Like Moïse Tshombe, Joseph and Laurent Kabila were originally from the Shaba region. But unlike Tshombe, the father and son tried to mobilize their Swahili not only to bring the Congo closer to the other countries of East Africa, but also to pursue an integrationist agenda internally, unsuccessful as their efforts were.

Under Joseph Kabila, the DRC adopted a revised constitution. According to Article 1 of the 2006 Constitution of the Democratic Republic of the Congo, Swahili is identified as one of the country's four national languages. The other three are Kikongo, Tshiluba, and Lingala, while French continues to serve as the official language. The national currency, the franc congolais, carries three languages – French, English, and Swahili. Although French is used widely in administration, the national languages are also commonly used on radio and television. The linguistic trends underscore the triglossic nature among national, official, and community languages. Today, over 50 percent of the population of the Democratic Republic of the Congo speaks a variety of Swahili. These varieties include Lumbubashi Swahili/ Katanga Swahili (also referred to as Copperbelt/Shaba Swahili); Kisangani Swahili (subsumed under Kingwana); Kivu Swahili; and Bunia Swahili. They are associated with the major cities of Lumbubashi, Bukavu, Goma, and Bunia.

When Félix Tshisekedi of the Union for Democracy and Social Progress was elected President in January 2019, he found a nation that had political, linguistic, and social linkages with East African countries. He moved quickly to consolidate the linkages and piloted his country to formally join the East African Community (EAC) on April 8, 2022. Having become a member of the East African Community, the Democratic Republic of the Congo is now poised to work closely with Kenya and Tanzania in consolidating the use of Swahili. In doing so, it will draw on the varieties currently in use.

Swahili, Refugees of Wars, and Regional Integration

As shown in the discussion so far, political instability, insecurity, and loss of livelihood due to violent conflicts in the countries of the Great Lakes region over the years have led to the production and hosting of millions of refugees in the East and Central African region. To refugees from the Democratic Republic of the Congo, Burundi, and Rwanda must be added those from Somalia and South Sudan, two other nations of the greater Eastern African region. The main refugee-hosting countries have been Kenya, Tanzania, and Uganda, in camps such as Nyarugusu Camp in the Kigoma region of Western Tanzania – set up in 1996 and accommodating refugees from the DRC and later in 2015 from Burundi – and Daadab Camp and Kakuma Refugee Camps in Kenya. After the refugees are settled in the host countries, they are incorporated into the educational system.

In East Africa, the integration process includes the learning of English and Swahili in the refugee camps (Nchimbi et al. 2020; Khasandi-Telewa 2007). The provision of language education for the refugees follows the mainstream national policy. In the case of Kenya, for example, the language of the local catchment area is used in the first three years of education and then English takes over from Grade Four onwards. Tanzania's commitment to the liberation struggles was anchored in the Arusha Declaration, the national political, economic, and social blueprint. Indeed, for Nyerere "the refugee question was a simultaneous moral and ethical, as well as humanitarian, responsibility for Tanzania" (Mazrui and Mhando 2013: 167). Refugees were provided with an education just like Tanzanians. They learned Swahili and integrated into the community. In Tanzania, early childhood education is offered in Swahili, which is the language widely spoken in all communities. In situations where older refugee children originate from Burundi and the Democratic Republic of the Congo, they have some prior knowledge of Swahili, but not English. As a result, they end up being placed in classes with younger children and fall behind in age-appropriate academic levels (Le 2021, 19–20). Whatever the case, they learn Swahili and use it to interact with others in the community.

Swahili is widely used in the Tanzanian refugee camps and taught as a language in classrooms, alongside English or French depending on the origin of the refugees. For example, refugees from Burundi, Rwanda, and the DRC would communicate in Swahili and French. The location of the refugee camp has an impact on the Swahili dialect that is acquired. In Nyarugusu Refugee Camp, for example, the dialect used is different from the standard variety derived from the Zanzibar dialect. At the Camp, the dialect used integrates lexical items from French because many refugees are from Burundi and the DRC.

Notwithstanding the linguistic accommodation, most of the refugees in the Great Lakes region make headway with learning Swahili. Other than those from South Sudan or Somalia, most refugees in East Africa are speakers of Bantu languages, including Lingala, Kinyarwanda, Kirundi, and Luganda, which are structurally close to Swahili. The languages share important features such as noun classification with grammatical implications in morphological formation, syntax, and semantics, making the learning of Swahili by refugees to neighboring countries easy. Commenting on the Swahili in refugee camps, Nchimbi et al. (2020, 95) observe:

> The teaching, learning and use of Swahili in East African refugee camps should be made ongoing and sustainable. Swahili is used as a lingua franca and acts as an instrument that unifies various refugee groups from different nations who speak different languages. Swahili also facilitates mutual understanding between refugees and local residents. For example, Nyarugusu Refugee Camp hosts refugees from various countries such as Burundi and DRC. Although refugees from both countries speak French, Swahili language is another possible instrument to unite them on the basis of commonalities in their Bantu mother tongue languages, and on the basis of shared cultural traits.

Most children born in Kenyan or Tanzanian refugee camps acquire Swahili as a first language alongside their mother tongue and use them in social, religious, economic, educational, artistic, and cultural activities. They continue using the acquired languages even after being relocated.

As indicated earlier, the countries that served as the primary hosts of most of these refugees of war from the Great Lakes region were Kenya,

Uganda, and Tanzania. These three countries, in turn, were the original members and have continued to be the central core of the East African Community, a body intended to promote some degree of political, economic, and educational integration among member states. The Swahili language has been integral to the identity of the East African Community. Article 137 (2) of the East African Community Treaty states that Swahili will be developed as the lingua franca of the Community and Member States are expected to put in place mechanisms for the promotion of the language.

From their host countries, many of the refugees became leaders or members of militant groups aimed at changing the political orders of their respective countries of origin. Carrying with them the new dimensions of identity from their host countries, including knowledge of Swahili, these refugees became crucial in stimulating a postwar consciousness in the countries of their origin/return toward regional integration. Added to the fact that Kenya, Uganda, and Tanzania have all been critical players behind these changes in the Great Lakes region, almost all of the new postwar regimes, including those of South Sudan and Somalia, have felt a strong affinity with and sought to associate with the three nations by becoming members of the East African Community. As a result, the East African Community that started with the three East African nations of Uganda, Kenya, and Tanzania has now grown into a seven-member organization since Rwanda, Burundi, South Sudan, and the Democratic Republic of the Congo were admitted into the body.

Conclusion

Membership to the East African Community (EAC) is seen as a possible path toward strengthening new cross-border identities in the Great Lakes region. In Rwanda, for example, the colonially constructed ethnic identities of Hutu, Tutsi, and Twa were interrogated and rejected. In their place, a national identity of "being Rwandan" was affirmed legally and within the educational system. Post-1994 Rwanda has been deliberate in systematically crafting a new collective identity of "being Rwandan," and discussion of ethnic affiliations is strongly discouraged. The concept of "genocidal ideology or divisionism" that is articulated and banned by law is meant to minimize the ethnic identity tendencies of "being Hutu or Tutsi" that were a precursor to the 1994 genocide (Englebert and Dunn 2013, 84). The concept was a response to the legacy of a divisive history based on ethnicity and its consequences. The institutionalized tinkering to reduce the potency of ethnicity in political participation, the rejection of ethnic identity as a site of belonging, and the celebration of national identity are being propelled through political, social, and linguistic decisions.

Therefore, when in 2007 Rwanda joined the East African Community, it was reconfiguring its regional identity. This was an expression of the desire to solidify the political, economic, social, cultural, and linguistic links with Kenya, Uganda, and Tanzania nurtured in the period preceding the genocide and soon after. In 2009, Rwanda joined the Commonwealth despite not having been a British colony and built new global alliances. The edging out of French in Rwanda was clearly on course and its space was being taken over by English and Swahili.

The motivation to join the East African Community has necessarily encouraged countries like Rwanda, Burundi, Congo, and South Sudan to take a special interest in providing Swahili language instruction to their citizens. This is in full swing in Rwanda. Similar educational efforts are on the rise in the other newer member states: Burundi, South Sudan, and the Democratic Republic of the Congo.

In sum, then, although the Swahili language had diffused into Uganda, Rwanda, Burundi, and the Democratic Republic of the Congo since the mid-1800s, it was only after the 1980s that it started consolidating itself. Major contributors to this linguistic trend have been the cycles of war, forced migrations to Swahili-speaking countries, and the political goodwill emanating from a leadership that lived in exile. Even countries in Southern Africa – especially Mozambique, Zimbabwe, Namibia, and South Africa – have expressed interest in and solidarity with Swahili because of the support they received from Tanzania, primarily, and Kenya, to a lesser extent, during their wars of liberation. They are also slowly integrating the language within their educational systems.

References

Caplan, Gerald. 2007. Rwanda: Walking the Road to Genocide. In *The Media and the Rwanda Genocide*, ed. Allan Thompson, 20–37. London: Pluto Press.
Duke, Lynne, and James Rupert. 1997. Power Behind Kabila Reflects Congo War's Tutsi Roots. *International Herald Tribune*, May 29, 7.
Englebert, Pierre, and Kevin C. Dunn. 2013. *Inside African Politics*. Boulder, CO: Lynne Rienner Publishers.
Kasfir, Nelson. 2005. Guerillas and Civilian Participation: The National Resistance Army in Uganda, 1981–1986. *Journal of Modern African Studies* 43 (2): 47–65.
Khasandi-Telewa, Vicky. 2007. *English Is a Must to Us: Languages and Education in Kakuma Refugee Camp, Kenya*. PhD thesis, University of Warwick.
Lacey, Marc. 2004. Since '94 Horror Rwandans Turn Toward Islam. *The New York Times*, April 7. https://www.nytimes.com/2004/04/07/world/since-94-horror-rwandans-turn-toward-islam.html.
Le, Hang M. 2021. Language, Education, and Power in Refugee Camps: A Comparison of Kakuma Refugee Camp (Kenya) and Thai Myanmar Refugee Camps. *Current Issues in Comparative Education* 23 (1): 15–30.
Mafeje, Archie. 1998. *Kingdoms of the Great Lakes Region*. Kampala: Fountain Publishers.
Mazrui, Ali A. 1975. *The Political Sociology of the English Language: An African Perspective*. The Hague: Mouton.
Mazrui, Ali A., and Alamin Mazrui. 1998. *The Power of Babel: Language and Governance in the African Context*. Oxford: James Currey.
Mazrui, Ali, and Linda L. Mhando. 2013. *Julius Nyerere: Africa's Titan on a Global Stage: Perspectives from Arusha to Obama*. Durham, NC: Carolina Academic Press.
Mlaga, Wallace. 2017. Historia ya Kiswahili Nchini Rwanda: Kielelezo cha Nafasi ya Utashi wa Kisiasa Katika Ustawi wa lugha ya Kiswahili. *Kioo cha Lugha* 15 (1): 1–19.
Muhando, Penina. 1984. *Lina Ubani*. Dar es Salaam: Dar es Salaam University Press.
Muhankia, Henry R. 1981. *Utenzi wa Vta vya Kagera na Anguko la Idi Amin Dada*. Dar es Salaam: Dar es Salaam University Press.
Nchimbi, Fokas, Sterling Roop, Jay Boss Rubin, and Sarah Delaney. 2020. The Use of Swahili in Refugee Camps in East Africa. In *Migrations in Contemporary World: A Case of Africa Cultural and Social Issues*, ed. Helena E. Myeya and Maciej Ząbek, 71–102. Bernardinum: Pelplin.

"NRA Bush War Song: Endesheni Mapambano." n.d.. https://www.youtube.com/watch?v=tjGtzIlQeZE.
"NRA Bush War Song: Wazalendo wa NRA." n.d.. https://www.youtube.com/watch?v=eGc1xPu1Ie0&t=6s. Accessed 20 Aug 2022.
Prunier, Gerard. 2017. The Armies of the Great Lakes Countries. *Prism* 6 (4): 98–111.
Reed, William Cyrus. 1996. Exile, Reform, and the Rise of the Rwanda Patriotic Front. *The Journal of Modern African Studies* 34 (3): 479–501.
Schwartz, Stephanie. 2019. Home, Again: Refugees Return and Post-Conflict Violence in Burundi. *International Security* 44 (2): 110–145.
Shiner, Cindy. 1997. Kabila: A Study in Paradox. *The Washington Post*, May 19.
Uganda People's Congress. 1980. *Manifesto of the Uganda People's Congress.* Kampala, Uganda.

6

Swahili in the Context of Cold Wars

Alamin Mazrui

We can define a "cold war" as a state of mutual hostility between nations or communities short of military action and one that is often punctuated by propaganda and threats. In this chapter, we look at the place of Swahili in three cold wars. The first, often considered "the Cold War," is the ideological conflict between the USA and its allies, on the one hand, and the Soviet Union and its allies, on the other, pitting a capitalist ideology against a communist one. The second is a racial cold war that took place especially in the USA with the emergence of the Black Power movement of self-affirmation and against institutionalized racism. And the third is the more recent economic cold war that has continued to unfold between the USA and China. In each of these cold wars, culture – languages, books, art, and so forth – has been part of the arsenals.

The Ideological Cold War

The Cold War between East and West has generally been regarded as an ideological battle that was essentially global in geopolitical scale. To that extent, this cold war played out in many different ways in several spaces throughout the world. One of these spaces was East Africa, encompassing mainly the countries of Kenya, Tanzania, and Uganda as they gained their independence from British colonial rule in the 1960s. The Cold War often framed the political dynamics both within and among the East African states, and each struggled to avoid being a (mere) pawn in superpower rivalries of the time. What was the place of Swahili in this war of global proportions? And how did the Cold War and its various local articulations affect the destiny of Swahili, both within East Africa itself and beyond?

The nation of Tanzania looms large in almost any mention of the modern development of the Swahili language. Among the East African countries, it was initially Tanzania that seriously attempted to change the colonial linguistic legacy that had privileged English in education and the state. In 1967, Tanzania launched the Arusha Declaration that essentially announced its politico-economic shift toward Ujamaa socialism, and adopted the proposed developmental policy of its president, Julius Nyerere, on "Education for Self-Reliance" designed to provide an education for life that would be relevant to the needs of the Tanzanian nation, and not alienate the educated from the common citizen. With this development, Swahili quickly expanded its demographic scope and gained functional momentum in Tanzania, becoming an official language of the state and government and the medium of instruction initially at the primary school level. Swahili now became central not only in the articulation of Tanzania's socialist aims, but also in the implementation of its socialist policies and programs at the mass level.

It is true, of course, that Ujamaa was framed as an economic experiment that was different from that of the so-called Communist Bloc, one anchored in an African universe of experience. In addition, Nyerere was a leading figure in what came to be known as the nonaligned movement of developing nations that sought to refrain from adopting foreign positions out of superpower sympathies. Yet it is difficult to see the evolution of both Ujamaa and nonalignment outside the context of the Cold War. Politics of the Cold War were the stimulus for both. After all, it is unlikely that there would have been a nonaligned coalition without the Cold War. And by the time the country had become the United Republic of Tanzania after its 1964 merger with the nation of Zanzibar following the island's

6 Swahili in the Context of Cold Wars 149

communist-inspired revolution, the capital city of Dar es Salaam had turned "not just into a Mecca for liberation movements, but also a critical site of Cold War competition" (Roberts 2021, 27). It is against this backdrop that we connect the ascendancy of Swahili in Tanzania of the 1960s and 1970s to the dynamics of the Cold War moment.

The role of Swahili as the lingua franca of East Africa and the policy consolidation of the language in left-leaning Tanzania quickly brought the language to the attention of the Cold War competitors. In the USA, in particular, the attention to Swahili, among many other languages of Africa, the Middle East, and Asia, was directly related to the discipline of Area Studies in the US academy. This is not to suggest that the Cold War is what gave birth to Area Studies, since we know that Area Studies had been in existence in some form or other even before World War I and World War II. But it was during the Cold War that the aims and objectives of Area Studies became directly linked to the political interests of the American state. For many American politicians, the Cold War made Area Studies more palpable as a state project worthy of state funding. This financial support for Area Studies came under Title VI of the Higher Education Act of 1965. Title VI encompassed the International and Foreign Language Education program of the Federal Department of Education intended to support the teaching of foreign languages and their respective area and international studies. And this is how African Studies, as a component of Area Studies, came to gain ground in the USA while expanding the space for the study of Swahili in the American academy.

But why should East Africa have been of concern to the USA at all in its Cold War with the Communist Bloc? What were the political dynamics in East African states in the immediate aftermath of their independence from colonial rule that became central in drawing Cold War competition to the region and resulted in Swahili acquiring additional instrumental value internationally because of its potential utility as a medium of contending ideological messaging? In actual fact, each of the countries of Swahiliphone East Africa had its own peculiar dynamics at play that ended up making it subject to Cold War politics.

With regard to Kenya, in particular, there was the familiar tension between leaders – including Jomo Kenyatta and Tom Mboya – of the then ruling party, the Kenya African National Union (KANU), on the one hand, and those like Jaramogi Oginga Odinga and Bildad Kaggia, of the new opposition party, the Kenya People's Union (KPU), on the other. The fault line between the two parties was essentially ideological, with KANU seeking to pursue a capitalist path of development and KPU a populist, quasi-socialist one. In fact, the leader of KPU, Jaramogi Oginga Odinga, proceeded to cultivate a special relationship with both the Soviet Union and the People's Republic of China. Expectedly, the USA came out openly in support of KANU. There is no better testimony of the American position on the unfolding of Cold War politics in Kenya than *The Reds and the Blacks*, the autobiography of William Attwood (1967), the first American ambassador to Kenya. Attwood reveals in no uncertain terms the machinations and intrigues of his office in Nairobi, designed to prevent Kenya from falling into the communist sphere of influence.

It was against this backdrop that, in 1967, the Kenyan Government moved to ban, in addition to other quasi-socialist materials, Chinese publications translated into English and Swahili – the two transethnic national languages of the country – and released by the Peking Foreign Languages Press. These included *Cheche Moja Yaweza Kuanzisha Moto Mbugani*, a Swahili translation of Mao's *A Single Spark Can Start a Prairie Fire*, and the so-called *Little Red Book* of Mao's quotations that was available in both English and Swahili translations (Lal 2014, 97). Suspicious of the entire Foreign Languages Press's project, the Kenyan Government proceeded to place a ban on "the importation of all past and future publications purporting to be published by the Foreign Languages Press, Peking" (Colony 1962, 855–56). This ban remained in place until the beginning of the political reform movement in Kenya that led to the new 2010 Constitution of Kenya.

Then there were America's Cold War concerns with Tanzania that started even before the nation had adopted a socialist path of development. It all started with the Zanzibar revolution of 1964. Under the leadership of Abdulrahman Babu and his fellow "comrades" who had connections with Cuba, it was clear that the bloody revolution was intended to usher in a communist dispensation in the island nation. As a result, it has been suggested, and with good reason, that the very union of Tanganyika and Zanzibar to form the United Republic of Tanzania was in part endorsed by the American Central Intelligence Agency (CIA) precisely to neutralize the communist hold on Zanzibar (Wilson 1989). In spite of the wishes and intrigues of the US government, however, the Zanzibar revolution became an added pressure for the union of Tanzania to move to the left toward socialism, increasingly consolidating its links with the People's Republic of China.

The Zanzibar revolution had a great impact on the spread of the Swahili language to the Arabian Gulf. The violence and bloodshed that accompanied this civil war in Zanzibar forced many native speakers of the Swahili language to flee and seek asylum in Oman and other countries of the Emirates. Within a short time, this first major wave of Swahili-speaking immigrants had become quite visible in capital cities like Muscat, though the Swahili language proficiency of subsequent generations of the Swahili Diaspora seems to have waned. Later the waves of Swahili-speaking migrants continued not only in the Arabian Peninsula, but also in countries of the West – in Europe, the USA, and Canada – where, as immigrants, they became an important resource for the teaching of Swahili in schools and colleges and in media promotion of the language.

In its first few years after Independence in 1962, Uganda did not appear to have concerned the USA much in terms of its Cold War interests, as it showed no signs of leaning toward socialism or seeking alliances with the Communist Bloc. Then in 1969, its first president, Milton Obote, succeeded in adopting policies arising from the document of his political party, the Uganda People's Congress (UPC), entitled *Common Man's Charter: First Steps for Uganda to Move to the Left*. This development was an immediate red flag to the CIA. However, two years later the Obote government was toppled by the Uganda military under the leadership of General Idi Amin Dada. It has been suggested that this military coup had the tacit support of the USA, Israel, and Great Britain (Mamdani 1983), precisely because of Uganda's intended "move to the left."

In general, then, from the time they achieved their independence from colonial rule to the 1970s, the political orientation of all three East African countries tended to show that the capitalist system that was part of the legacy of European colonialism was being contested. This evolving situation became one of the reasons for American attempts to influence the politico-economic direction of the East African nations. It also became a factor in motivating the US government to support the teaching of Swahili, among other languages, and the continuing growth of the proportion of Americans interested in Swahili Studies in the American academy.

Outside the academy, there was also a significant group of Americans that came to study Swahili during the period of the Cold War. This was the group of Peace Corps volunteers that was assigned to service in Kenya and Tanzania. The American Peace Corps was itself a product of the Cold War, launched in part in response to Soviet presence in and aid to a number of countries in the world through which it was seen to be spreading its ideology. Thus, the Peace Corps was established partly to serve as a transmission belt of American political and economic values. In other words, the Peace Corps

> was an outgrowth of the Cold War. President Kennedy pointed out that the Soviet Union 'had hundreds of men and women, scientists, physicists, teachers, engineers, doctors, and nurses … prepared to spend their lives abroad in the service of the world of communism.' The United States had no such program, and Kennedy wanted to involve Americans more actively in the cause of global democracy, peace, development, and freedom. ("Peace Corps")

From this global project of the American state, and because so many Americans opted to join the Peace Corps rather than be subject to the military draft to go and fight in the Vietnam War, thousands of young Americans ended up learning Swahili. A glimpse of this history of the Peace Corps is captured in the 2020 documentary film *Swahili on the Prairie*, by David Asher Goldenberg.

The Cold War also affected, though to a much lesser extent, the destiny of Swahili in the Soviet Union. It is true that African Studies in general had been a discipline of study in Soviet universities since the 1930s. However, together with the study of Swahili, it picked up greater momentum in the 1960s, especially as one African nation after another attained its independence from European colonial rule. This is the time when the Soviet Union began trying to establish a presence in Africa in competition with the USA. In the process, several Swahili books were translated into Russian as a way of exposing Russians to the cultures of Africa (Gromov 2018, 165).

The ideological Cold War was also evident in shortwave radio broadcasting. Spurred by Lenin's message of world revolution, the Soviet Union established Radio Moscow as early as 1929. But to "meet the escalation of tensions between the Soviet Union and the west, Radio Moscow continued to increase its broadcast capabilities and target populations" (Winek 2009, 102). In the meantime, the US government established Voice of America, initially as a propaganda organ aimed at an international audience during World War II. Later, however, it gave way "to the Cold War and to the specter of a new and powerful enemy. It was felt that the forces of democracy needed a shortwave arsenal to combat the thundering propaganda brigades of Russian communism, so the Voice of America was continued during peacetime…" (Uttaro 1982, 103). As African countries began to get embroiled in the Cold War, Swahili, among other African languages, came to have an important place on the airwaves of both Radio Moscow and Voice of America.

Naturally, the ideological Cold War came with its own language and vocabulary that had to find expression in the Swahili language. Societies now had to be conceptualized in terms of their politico-economic systems, with the conflict between communism and capitalism (sometimes arising from a feudal base) as a central construct. Adopted directly from English, *ukomyunisti* became the Swahili equivalent of "communism." The term *bepari* was in wide use in Swahili to mean "businessperson." Tanzania's president, Julius Nyerere, quickly and successfully reconfigured it to mean "capitalist" and its corollary, *ubepari*, to stand for capitalism. *Ukabaila*, a preexisting term that denoted a system of social prestige based in lineage, now came to be used for feudalism.

In spite of his leftist inclinations, Nyerere was among the new African leaders who were at the forefront of nonalignment, now rendered in Swahili as *usoufungamano*. Against this backdrop in the context of the Cold War, he imagined for his country a move toward a socialism rooted in African cultural traditions. For such a system, Nyerere employed the word *ujamaa*, which originally meant the fellowship of kinship ties with all the mutual obligations, responsibilities, and protections that such a fellowship implied. Now a "whole universe of ethical principles was compressed within that single Swahili word *ujamaa*. Nyerere's skills in transvaluation [translation of values from one culture to another] and transverbalization [translation of words from one language to another] had merged to produce the beginnings of a language of socialism in East Africa" (Mazrui 1975, 120).

Swahili had to engage in a new articulation of not only politico-economic systems but also of new notions of class that had arisen from the colonial encounter with the West and the global discourses of the Cold War. The very idea of social class came to acquire a new meaning and a new Swahili designation, semantically extended from the word *tabaka*, which hitherto simply meant a "level." With class also came the Marxist idea of class consciousness, or *urazini wa kitabaka*, and class struggle, *mapambano ya kitabaka*. Social classes of the bourgeoisie, workers, and peasants all came to develop their own Swahili terms – *mabwanyenye*, *wafanyi-kazi*, and *mafalahi*, respectively. And *unyonyaji* (exploitation), derived from the Swahili *nyonya* to mean "suck," is, of course, the term that came to define the relationship between the *mabwenyenye* and some of the other classes.

Cold War itself, *Vita Baridi*, was translated quite directly from English to capture the tensions between the two *mataifa makubwa* (superpowers). We know that later Mikhail Gorbachev introduced reforms to the politico-economic system as well as in the nature of Cold War relations with the West that entered the Cold War vocabulary. These too came to gain currency in Swahili, and existing terms like *marekebisho* or *matengenezo* (perestroika), *uwazi/ushauriano* (glasnost), and *mtulizano* (détente) acquired new meaning and currency in Swahili media.

The Ideological Cold War in Swahili Translation

The propaganda efforts of the USA and the Soviet Union also extended to the translation of works written originally in English and Russian to the Swahili language. In his brilliant book *Archives of Authority: Empire, Culture and the Cold War* (2012), Andrew N. Rubin demonstrates how the USA, during the Cold War period, patronized the arts in a way that aimed to reinforce its ideological onslaught against the Soviet Union. An important American initiative of this time was the state sponsorship of the translation of George Orwell's *Animal Farm* into various languages of especially the South, as a propaganda tool against perceived communist incursions (Rubin 2012, 24–46). One of these US-sponsored translations became *Shamba la Wanyama*, the Swahili rendering of *Animal Farm* by a Tanzanian national, Fortunatus Kawegere. According to the University of Kansas Libraries Exhibit, the Swahili translation too was "underwritten by United States Information Service" (KU Libraries Exhibits 2015), even though there seems to have been a general agreement that these US-sponsored translations should "contain no references to the Information Department of the Embassy or the United States Information Exchange" (Rubin 2012, 38).

Animal Farm (1945) is a satirical animal fable ostensibly about a group of animals who, through conspiracy, launch an armed revolution to oust their human owners from the farm on which they live. They then run the farm themselves on the agreed revolutionary principles of "Animalism" that distinguish them from humans and human rule. Within a short period, however, animal rule degenerates into a brutal tyranny, erected on the deliberate erasure of the history of the revolution, muzzling of political dissent, a growing personality cult, corruption, and ruthless exploitation. The revolution has been betrayed. Orwell intended *Animal Farm* to be an exposure and critique of the dangers of the Soviet totalitarian government under Joseph Stalin.

Events in postcolonial Tanganyika – as mainland Tanzania was then known before its merger with Zanzibar – provided the immediate political context for the translation of *Animal Farm*. As Venuti points out, the inscription of local target-community interests in the process of translation "begins with the very choice of a text for translation, always a very selective, densely motivated choice" (Venuti 2004, 486). In this case, however, it was not the betrayal of a revolution that had already taken place but the fear of an impending (socialist) revolution that became the inspirational force for *Shamba la Wanyama* as part of an anti-communist offensive during the Cold War.

It is true that the socialism of Ujamaa was not formally launched, and the ruling Tanganyika African National Union (TANU) did not become the Chama cha Mapinduzi (Revolutionary Party) until 1967, precisely the year that the Swahili translation of *Animal Farm* appeared. But the idea of a quasi-socialist state had certainly been in gestation as early as 1962, if not earlier, when the then president of the country, Mwalimu Julius Nyerere, released his pamphlet entitled *Ujamaa: The Basis of African Socialism*. America's fears of a socialist turn of events in Tanganyika were further reinforced when on April 26, 1964, the country merged with the independent island state of Zanzibar to form the United Republic of Tanzania. This merger came barely three months after the violent Zanzibar Revolution whose aims – given the central role of the Marxist-led Umma Party as its architect – were seen by many, especially by the US government, as essentially communistic. It was even feared that Zanzibar would be an African Cuba of a sort, poised to influence the rest of the region (Wilson 1989). A Swahili translation of *Animal Farm* acquired additional urgency due to the unfolding tensions between pro-socialist and pro-capitalist political camps throughout the East African region.

Critics generally agree that Kawegere's translation is poised toward domestication (Traore 2013, 21; Herrington 2015). It is not clear whether the decision to domesticate the text was made independently by Kawegere himself or, as happened in other parts of the world, was a product of some American influence. In their attempts to construct their authority of the "Third World," Rubin notes, both the American and British governments favored the adaptation of *Animal Farm* to local contexts and conditions:

> In Malaya, where the British fought its longest postwar conflict, there was an effort to produce a less 'English' version of *Animal Farm*. In Egypt, too, where British authority faced mounting anticolonial challenges to King Farouk, the IRD [Information Research Department, a secret unit of the British Foreign Office] viewed *Animal Farm* as particularly 'relevant' to conditions there. Reducing the Arabic language to Islam, Ernest Main wrote Ralph Murray that translating *Animal Farm* is 'particularly good for Arabic in view of the fact that both pigs and dogs are unclean animals to Muslims.' (Rubin 2012, 38)

Domestication, in other words, was seen as adding to the anti-communist propaganda value of translations and adaptations of *Animal Farm*. And whether or not Kawegere came under the influence of the US sponsors on his mode of translation, there is no doubt that the domestication of the text was in conformity with the wider imperial agenda.

However, while Kawegere produced *Shamba la Wanyama* for his own compatriots in socialist-leaning Tanzania, ironically enough it was in capitalist Kenya that the translation came to score its greatest success. The Kenyan revolutionary movement that can be compared most closely with that of *Animal Farm* is perhaps the Mau Mau movement against British settler colonial rule. Known as the Kenya Land and Freedom Army by its combatants, the Mau Mau war broke out in 1952 under the leadership of Dedan Kimathi. The expropriation of much of the best land in the country for European settlement, accompanied by a series of labor laws and regulations forcing Africans to provide ill-compensated labor for the settlers, made land and labor the most burning issues in the struggle for independence. And under oppressive colonial conditions, Mau Mau became precisely the kind of revolutionary movement that partly inspired Orwell to write *Animal Farm* (Ingle 1993, 75–76). It was a violent, conspiratorial revolution with a popular following. And while Mau Mau's military leaders may not have been known to be power-hungry, those who claimed its political mantle and leadership and eventually assumed the reins of power when the country became independent in 1963 obviously were. In other words, like Orwell's characterization of the Russian Revolution, the Mau Mau too was a revolution that quickly opened the gates to its own betrayal, as Oginga Odinga, Kenya's first vice-president, came to argue in his controversial book *Not Yet Uhuru* (1967).

The central themes of *Animal Farm* are the rewriting of history to distort the objectives of the revolution in general and the role of Snowball, its selfless intellectual spirit in the struggle for animal liberation, in particular. This political exercise as it relates specifically to the history of the Mau Mau came to be the hallmark of successive Kenyan regimes in the postcolonial era. Until recently, the silent policy was "Speak No Mau Mau; Hear No Mau Mau," in which Kenyans were led to develop a culture of amnesia about the movement and its leaders. On October 20, 2001, for example, over seventy Kenyans were arrested and charged with unlawful assembly. The party had apparently angered the government of the day by celebrating October 20 not as Kenyatta Day – as officially named to mark the arrest of Jomo Kenyatta by colonial authorities – but as Mau Mau Day in honor of Kenya's freedom fighters. Similarly, the Kimathi Cultural Centre was denied permission to hold celebrations in honor of Dedan Kimathi, the military leader of the Mau Mau, on February 18, the day of his execution by the British colonial government (*Sunday Nation*, February 19, 2006, p. 4). This was early in 2006 when Kenya was regarded to be at its most open in political space.

In the same period of Cold War rivalry, the Soviet Union launched the Swahili translation of Gorky's *Mother*, the Russian novel described by Katerina Clark as

> that post, or station, where Bolsheviks coming out of the old intelligentsia tradition were able to stop and take on fresh horses to bear them on into Socialist Realism itself. *Mother* provided a system for translating the clichés of tsarist radicals into the determining formulas of Bolshevism. (Clark 1981, 52)

The Swahili translation – *Mama* – was sponsored by the Department of Progress (Idara ya "Maendeleo") of the USSR. Besides the information that the book was published in the Soviet Union (kimechapwa katika Soviet Union), there are no details of the publisher or year of publication. According to Gromova, *Mama* was among the earliest Soviet texts rendered into Swahili by Swahili-speaking East Africans who were then living in the Soviet Union, either studying or working with Radio Moscow or the Foreign Languages Press. These included Hussein Abdul-Razak, Herman Matemu, and Ben Ombuoro (Gromova 2004).

The Swahili translator of *Mother*, specifically, was Badru Said, a Tanzanian of Zanzibari origin who was then residing in the Soviet Union. Described by Kasim Suleiman[1] in an interview in 2015 as an extremely brilliant student from his earliest years of education, Badru Said left Zanzibar soon after his graduation from high school to go to China to

---

[1] Personal interview in 2015 with Kasim Suleiman who was a friend of Badru Said and was in the Soviet Union before, during, and after Said left for Zanzibar. Suleiman now lives in Zanzibar.

study political economy in 1960. In fact, he was among the first batch of African students to visit Communist China for academic reasons. By 1962, however, he and many other African students had left China allegedly because of "undesirable political indoctrination, language difficulty, poor educational standards, inadequate social life, outright hostility, and racial discrimination" (Larkin 1971, 142). He later went to Moscow to continue his studies. It was during this period that he was approached by an agent of the Foreign Languages Press to produce a Swahili version of Gorky's *Mother*. Because he was not yet sufficiently proficient in Russian, Badru based his translation on the already existing English translation of Gorky's text.

Mother is the story of the daily struggles of the average proletariat in the Soviet Union who were protesting against the czar and the capitalists of the time, stimulating conditions toward the October Revolution of 1905. Pelageya, the protagonist, is the wife of a factory worker who ignores the political upheaval in her country, focusing her energies on her family instead. In this regard, she represents thousands of workers who, partly out of fear, are simply concerned with living their lives. Pelageya's son Pavel, on the other hand, joins the revolutionary movement that inspired so many. But when Pavel is arrested, Pelageya is herself transformed into a revolutionary activist, standing by her son against the oppressive state. The plot itself "fuses historical reality and revolutionary myth in a coherent political allegory. The novel describes an actual incident, a May Day demonstration that took place in the Volga town of Somov" and its immediate aftermath (Clark 1981, 52).

The cover of the Swahili translation of the book deserves special note. The front cover with an all-white background presents a sketch of a young plant – perhaps alluding to the status of Tanzania as a new nation. The plant is red and its branches and leaves are all blowing "backwards." The impression created by the sketch, then, is one of a (red) flag in a "forward" march against an unseen force of wind. Though the image takes one back to the May Day march of workers in the Volga Region in which Pavel was holding a red banner, the representation could conceivably also refer to Tanzania's move to the socialist left in spite of the challenges on its path.

The back cover is not the usual description of the book and the author along with quotes by reviewers. This information is found on the inner cover of the book, with a photograph of Maxim Gorky himself (alias Aleksei Maksimovich Peshkov). Rather, the back cover bears two photographs of people who existed in real life during Gorky's lifetime, each accompanied by a caption. The first is that of Anna Kirillovna Zalomova, and the other of Pyotr Zalomov and his wife Josefina Zalomova. The captions explain that it is the activist life of Anna Zalomova and Pyotr Zalomov that inspired two of Gorky's main characters in the novel, Pelageya Nilovna Vlassova, the mother, and Pavel Vlassov, the son. The back cover ends by quoting Gorky's own words:

Je, Bi Nilovna alikuwako kikweli? ... Yapasa kujua kwamba akina mama pia walishiriki katika maandalio ya mapinduzi na katika harakati za kisiasa za kichinichini. Bi Nilovna ndiyo taswira ya kifasihi iliyobuniwa na mwandishi yenye kummathilisha mama Pyotr Zalomov. Mama huyo alikuwa akishughulika katika jumuiya ya kisasa na kusambaza maandishi huku na huko, akijifanya kama mhajiri ... Wala hakuwa ni mhusika wa kipekee.

So then, did Lady Nilovna truly exist? ... It is important to understand that women too participated in preparing for the revolution and in underground political activities. Lady Nilovna is the literary image created by the author as the example of mother Pyotr Zalomov. That mother was active in modern society and in distributing pamphlets here and there, [on the move] like a migrant. And she was not alone in this. (own translation – AM)

These words are intended to underscore not only the working-class dimension of that revolutionary moment, but also the important role that women played in its planning and execution.

The Swahili translation also has a foreword by Boris Bursov, the distinguished Soviet literary scholar who was a member of the Communist Party of the Soviet Union and served as professor first at Leningrad University and later at the Herzen Leningrad Pedagogical Institute. Bursov opens his foreword with the following words: "Katika fasihi ya kila taifa kuna vitabu venye kuambatana na nyakati za mabadiliko katika maendeleo yake" (In the literature of every nation there are books that accompany the moments of change in its development) (my translation) (Bursov n.d., 3). Gorky's *Mother* was certainly one such book in Soviet history. And the Swahili *Mama* was perhaps intended to encourage a socialist revolutionary choice in Tanzania.

As political life began to change in post-Cold War Tanzania, however, *Mama* and other texts from the Soviet Union began to disappear. But if the book went out of circulation in Tanzania, its African relevance was most clearly demonstrated in post-Cold War Kenya, especially with regard to the events that followed the disputed Kenyan presidential election results of December 27, 2007. This is when Kenya erupted into weeks of bloody violence, pitting poor Kenyans against poor Kenyans, seemingly along ethnic lines. When calm finally returned with the intervention of the peace-mediating team led by the former Secretary General of the United Nations, Kofi Annan, over 1000 people had been killed – some in a brutal manner – and hundreds of thousands displaced from their homes. These developments in a country once considered an island of peace in a sea of turmoil sent shock waves throughout Kenya and the international community, resulting in intensive multilateral efforts for national reconciliation and healing. In addition to numerous diplomatic shuttles from all over the world, there were local initiatives from the business community, trade unions, faith-based organizations, civil society groups, hip-hop artists, and so forth, all directed toward the need to create an enabling political, socioeconomic, and cultural environment that would make a united and peaceful Kenya more sustainable.

In Kenya's largest slum, Kibera, where the poor turned on each other only to add misery to their suffering, a different kind of post-violence response was taking place. A multiethnic group of young artists was meeting every afternoon in a corner of a partially destroyed community hall partly to reflect on and make sense of what had transpired in the immediate aftermath of the elections. They expressed their horror and anger at how successful the "Mafuta Mingi" – those with a lot of fat, the rich – of Kenya had been in ethnicizing the face of poverty to a point where the poor were rendered blind and could no longer see who their real enemy was. They seemed clear about the economic roots of what was projected on the surface as ethnic conflict, springing from the long-burning question in Kenya about who owns and controls land in the different parts of the country. They reminisced over a Swahili saying that "ndovu wawili wakipigana, ziumiazo ni nyasi" – when two elephants fight, it is the grass that suffers. And when a deal was finally brokered for the contending factions of the political class to share power, the Kibera youth added that even when "ndovu wawili wakitombana, ziumiazo ni nyasi" (when two elephants are copulating, it is (still) the grass that suffers).

As a result, this group of young artists from the Kibera slum decided to inject a different kind of message into the political discourse of peace and reconciliation that had come to dominate the nation in the aftermath of the violence: That no member of the "Mafuta Mingi" could be expected to address the concerns and needs of the poor; that there can be no genuine peace and reconciliation without socioeconomic justice; and that what Kenya needs is a complete political and economic overhaul. Toward this end, members of the group, calling itself Matigari,[2] spent hours reading tattered photocopied pages of the Swahili *Mama*. Each chapter of the novel became a point of animated discussion and reflection on their perceived state in Kenya. In the process they were busy crafting a dramatized version of the Swahili translation of the novel, which they intended to perform on stage in various parts of the country to propagate their message of revolution. In a sense, the group vindicated the words of Satish Kalseker when he wrote that "the day *Mother* waited for has not come yet. The struggle for its survival, too, has not ended. It is possible that we need to fight for it incessantly; and will have to prepare ourselves for a long-drawn struggle. We all, and the next generations to come will have to read *Mother* again and again" (Kalseker, quoted in Pansare 2012, 228).

The Swahili translations of Orwell's *Animal Farm* and Gorky's *Mother*, then, share interesting facts of history. They were both products of imperial agendas, one American, the other Soviet. They were both initially intended for a Tanzanian audience, one as a counterhegemonic text

---

[2] Matigari, of course, is the revolutionary hero of Ngũgĩ wa Thiong'o's Gikuyu novel, *Matigari ma Njurungi*. The leader of the group of seven people, Chris Opiyo, is someone who had served as my research assistant in previous field work in Kibera, and it is he who invited Alamin Mazrui to the meetings of the group. They solicited Mazrui's assistance in procuring funds to enable them to put up the play in Nairobi and other towns. Three of the seven were university graduates.

against the country's turn to the left, and the other in support of it. Once they migrated to the neighboring country of Kenya, however, the two translations immediately freed themselves from the imperial project implicit in the Cold War. Now they became the voices of the local population against local exploiters even if, as suggested in one reading of the Swahili translation of *Animal Farm*, the local exploiters were somehow linked to more global forces of capitalist exploitation. If in Tanzania the two texts, as Cold War imperial projects, confronted each other in relation to *Ujamaa*, in Kenya they both became independent articulations in opposition to capitalism *à la* Kenya.

The Racial Cold War

Related to ideological Cold War dynamics in the USA was the racial cold war that became prominent especially with the rise of the Black Power movement, an outgrowth of the civil rights movement that became particularly prominent in the 1960s with emphasis on Black self-determination in matters of identity, cultural practice, education, and the economy. The Black Power movement and the civil rights movement of which it was a part were often regarded as elements of American domestic politics. In reality, however, the movement also had an internationalist dimension in at least two different if interconnected ways. First, as Rasberry (2016) amply demonstrates, it provided an opportunity to challenge the US government and expose its hypocrisy in its Cold War efforts against communist totalitarianism, selling the message of liberty abroad while continuing to uphold Jim Crow laws at home. Under the leadership of Elijah Mohamed, for example, the Nation of Islam was increasingly seen as a threat to the very ideological foundations of American liberalism with its anti-communist interventions against political dissent at home and abroad (Curtis 2019). Second, the global impact of Cold War politics gave rise to forms of anti-colonial Black internationalism that sometimes included efforts to form alliances with movements and countries abroad that were perceived to be hostile to the USA. The Black Panther Party, for example, forged alliances with a number of states with a radical political posture, including Algeria, Cuba, North Korea, and North Vietnam (Malloy 2017).

We know, of course, that Black internationalism in the USA did not begin with the Cold War. It goes back at least to the 1800s with the birth of pan-Africanism, beginning especially with the formative ideas of people like Martin R. Delaney (1812–1885), Alexander Crummell (1822–1898), and Edward Wilmot Blyden (1832–1912). From about 1937, Paul Robeson (1898–1976) – himself known for having studied Swahili at the School of Oriental and African Studies at the University of London – and his Council on African Affairs made concerted efforts to promote the idea of pan-Africanism among Americans of African descent. Later, leaders of what were to become independent African countries, figures like Kwame Nkrumah and Jomo Kenyatta, joined forces with their American and Caribbean counterparts – W. E. B. Du Bois, George Padmore, Ras MaKonnen, and others – in the activities of the pan-African movement in Europe. In time, as an ideology of liberation, the pan-African movement came to give Swahili some special appeal not only among African Americans, but also among continental Africans in countries like Ghana, Nigeria, and Egypt.

As the name suggests, pan-Africanism was a "cold war" ideology intended to forge a solidarity among people of African descent globally in their struggle for self-determination and collective self-reliance. In the racial context of the time, the term African and the term Black were seen as almost interchangeable. As a result, people of Arab and Amazigh origin in North Africa had no role in the initial phase of pan-Africanism precisely because they were not considered Black – or Africans of the blood. In the America of the 1960s and 1970s, however, there was the accompanying Black Power ideology, a moment that reflected the desire of African Americans to be respected and valued like other races and ethnicities in America, to unite and be self-reliant, and to fight against the racism and segregation that had been part of the social and politico-economic fabric of the country. In a sense, the Black Power movement was itself a type of war on various fronts – identitarian, cultural, economic, political, and, in the case of the Black Panther Party, military – all in a struggle against racism and racial injustice and inequality in the USA. As a consequence, the movement resulted not only in the establishment of African American businesses – restaurants, bookstores, schools, clinics, publishing houses, and so forth – for purposes of promoting the goal of self-reliance, but also militant organizations like the Black Panther Party, which were ready to take up arms to fight for liberation. Swahili came to gain in popularity among African Americans as a result of this new racial consciousness that emerged from the interplay between pan-Africanism and the Black Power movement.

The rise of independent African states in the 1960s also contributed to African American interest in Swahili. With the continuing rise of pan-African consciousness, many African Americans now made concerted efforts to visit the African continent of which they had long been made to feel ashamed. During these visits there were efforts to link the aims of Africa's independence with some of the activities of the Black Power movement that were taking place in America. It must be remembered that since the 1950s, links and relationships had already begun to develop between leaders of the Black Power movement and African leaders of anti-colonial political parties studying in the USA – leaders like Kwame Nkrumah, Nnamdi Azikiwe, and Sibusiso Vil-Nkomo, for example, who had studied at Lincoln University, one of the Historically Black Colleges and Universities in the USA.

The late Lyndon Harries, a leading scholar of Swahili, was astonished that African Americans elected Swahili as a symbol of their Africanity. He was surprised because, in his opinion, Swahili as an East African language had once been a medium of slavery, of feudal oppression, and of the sultanate of Zanzibar. In the USA, then,

> it would seem that the black community has made what at first sight seems a strange choice of this particular African language as a 'symbol of pride.' Since their forefathers came from west Africa a more logical choice would have been some West African language…[If] the black community in the States wishes to find an African language which represents best what has been most consistently the vehicle of Africa's aspirations and Africa's resistance against foreign domination, Swahili must come very low on the list. (Harries 1968, 146)

Debatable as Harries's claims are, he failed to take into account that language is a malleable tool that can have multiple functions at different times and in different contexts. If Swahili was once used in the East African slave trade, it was also an instrument of political mobilization against colonialism in Tanganyika and trade union action for independence in Kenya. After all, the Russian language of czarist feudalism also became the Russian of a communist revolution. And for the African American, in particular, Africa was not an ancestral land divided into regions and nations, but a single, composite womb of their origins. Just as importantly, Harries failed to take into account the significance of Tanzania as a source of the Swahili consciousness in the political imagination of African Americans of the 1960s and 1970s especially.

Of all the African countries that attained independence, none became so central in motivating African Americans to study Swahili as Tanzania. Tanzania was particularly attractive to African Americans for four reasons: (1) the prestige and moral integrity of Julius Nyerere himself as an African leader, enjoying a reputation among African Americans comparable to that of Kwame Nkrumah, the first President of Ghana; (2) the politics of Ujamaa, especially of one of its core principles of *kujitegemea* (self-reliance), which also featured prominently in the politics of the Black Power movement; (3) Tanzania's leadership in the pan-African movement, a leadership that culminated in its hosting of the 6th Pan-African Congress in 1974; and (4) Tanzania's leadership in supporting the liberation movements of African countries, especially Mozambique, Zimbabwe, Namibia, and South Africa, that were still under European colonialism or White domination.

All these features of Tanzania were in perfect sync with the politics of the Black Power movement, giving African Americans a new source of pride in their African origins. As Seth Markle explains:

> With African decolonization came the desire, yet the struggle, to connect to and understand Africa's new historical moment and where they [African Americans] fit in a world profoundly being shaped by the formation of new nation-states. Tanzania emerged as one dynamic force that seized the attention of black political activists, extending, deepening, and complicating their relationship with Africa and their conceptions of Pan-Africanism.

Between 1964 and 1974, a number of Caribbean and African American nationalists, leftists, and pan-Africanists traveled to and settled in Dar es Salaam to live and work in a nation that many believed was on the forefront of Africa's liberation struggle. (Markle 2017, 1–2)

As some leaders of the Black Radical Congress – an organization founded in 1998 with the aim of promoting a new brand of politics among African Americans – acknowledged many years later, Tanzania received and hosted them warmly in that important decade of struggle between 1964 and 1974 (Markle 2017, 179). And because Swahili was the primary medium in which Tanzania's revolutionary philosophy was framed and articulated, it was easy to see why it became embraced by African Americans in their quest to affirm their African identity in the racial politics of the USA within the wider global context of the Cold War. As Tanzania pressed on with Swahili as its national and official language, then, the "Black Power activists were pushing for the Kiswahili language to be taught in U.S. schools" (Markle 2017, 117). And from these African American efforts, the Swahili language quickly gained momentum as an important subject of study in the corridors of the American academy.

Ali Mazrui once coined the term "Tanzaphilia" to convey the extent to which Tanzania had become an intellectual magnet of a sort, fascinating and attracting scholars from Europe, the USA, and other parts of the world. In Mazrui's words:

> It is to the credit of Tanzania that she had managed to command the varied loyalties and affections of a wide of external admirers. From Gandhians to Maoists, humanitarians to ruthless revolutionaries–all these have been known to fall under the soothing spell of Tanzaphilia. (1967, 26)

This state of "Tanzaphilia" also had a major impact on African American consciousness, especially in their relationship to Africa. And this consciousness became an important stimulus for the rapid growth of Swahili Studies in the USA.

To African Americans, Swahili was not only an instrument of communication; it was also part of the reflection of their Africanity. Many African Americans wore West African clothes, boubous and dashikis, as a symbol of an African identity they had long been denied. Some converted to Islam as a path to re-Africanization. But from East Africa, what attracted African Americans most was its lingua franca, Swahili, making it an important pillar for projecting their African origins. For African Americans, as John Mugane puts it, "Swahili has been an inexhaustible resource of symbols of identity …" (Mugane 2015, 268). African American poets, singers, scholars, and others all attempted to drink from this linguistic fountain of East Africa. And on top of it all, an African American holiday, Kwanzaa, was established, with its seven principles firmly based on Swahili and anchored in African cultural traditions.

The African American embrace of Swahili had some academic implications in terms of the disciplinary home of the language in the American academy. Hitherto, the few American universities that taught Swahili at all, like Indiana University and the University of Illinois, tended to place it in departments of linguistics. Even though some of the students in these departments came to acquire great fluency in Swahili, the primary objective of its study was simply to have a comparative frame for enhancing their understanding of linguistics. Later, the promotion of Swahili to serve the state's purposes in the ideological Cold War against communism also tended to link the language with (Centers of) African Studies. The Black Power demand for Swahili, on the other hand, often consigned it to newly formed departments of Black Studies or African American Studies. And in some of these departments, Swahili or some other African language became a necessary subject in fulfilling the requirements for the relevant degree.

The Economic Cold War

The more recent competition and tensions between the USA and China have sometimes been described as the Second Cold War. This is the main theme of the book *U.S.-China Competition for Global Influence* by Ashley Tellis and her co-authors (Tellis et al. 2020) and several other publications that have appeared in the last ten years or so. Different from the first Cold War, from the conflict between the USA and the Soviet Union and their allies, the USA–China conflict is not based on ideological difference as such, but on economic and technological competition taking place in different parts of the world, including in East Africa. China has become an engine of globalization in its own right in competition with the USA.

By the early 1980s, post-Mao reforms were in full swing in China, transforming the country into a market economy by the end of the 1990s, culminating in its admission into the World Trade Organization in 2001 and its economy becoming more integrated into the world capitalist system. In the process, China's economy grew rapidly under the stimulus of global capitalism. These developments led to a shift in Chinese economic priorities in East Africa as elsewhere, increasingly investing in projects that would favor returns for the Chinese economy. This Chinese ideological-cum-economic shift led post-socialist China to be a major competitor of the USA in the global marketplace and a central cause of their economic Cold War.

Earlier we saw how the ideological Cold War gave Swahili a boost in both the USA and the Soviet Union. To what extent will the economic cold war between the USA and China affect the destiny of Swahili? So far it does not appear that the US government believes that knowledge of Swahili is necessary in outmaneuvering China in East Africa economically, even though some American colleges and universities have been encouraging the study of languages for special purposes, as in Swahili for Business and the like. In this regard, it is instructive that in 2008, the ICON Group International based in San Diego, California, produced a Webster's Swahili Thesaurus Edition of *The Prince*. The ICON Group International is regarded as the largest publisher of global market research and business intelligence in the world. Its products include comprehensive reports on world industries, transnational companies, specific geographical regions, global economic management, world trends, world cultures, and other specialized topics. Its central objective is to provide information to help in the planning and implementation of strategies for a global economy. It is essentially a research engine for neoliberalism.

In advancing its mission, the ICON Group International also produces material to foster multilingual competence globally. It seeks to help Americans studying other languages and citizens of other nations studying English, especially by providing bilingual thesaurus editions of "the classics" used for assigned reading in many language courses. The Webster's Swahili Thesaurus Edition of *The Prince*, for example, is intended not only for Swahili-speaking Africans enrolled in EFL and ESL programs, but also for American students studying Swahili for purposes of translation certification or the foreign service (Macchiavelli 2008, 1). So far, Swahili seems to be the only sub-Saharan African language to have made it to the ICON Group International's Webster Thesaurus series, though numerous African languages are included in the organization's bilingual crossword puzzles designed for the foreign language learner.

But the language that seems to be given greater prominence in the US academy in the American economic competition with China is the Chinese language itself. There is no doubt that some encouragement is given to American students to study the Chinese language, not only in colleges and universities, but also in elementary and high schools. According to one source:

> Chinese language courses are now available in primary and secondary schools in Washington D.C. and every U.S. state except South Dakota, ranks it the fourth most widely taught foreign language in the country's education system, according to a national survey released Thursday. (Tazama 2017)

Even though many of these American students are reported to be of Chinese origin, there has also been a dramatic rise of American students of non-Chinese origin enrolling in Chinese language courses (National K-12 Foreign Language). And in their project "One Million Strong," the former American President Barrack Obama and Chinese President Xi Jinping intended to give a major boost to the number of American students studying Chinese, the Mandarin variety in particular, at the elementary and high school level ("America's Languages").

On the other hand, this economic cold war may have greater linguistic implications for China than for the USA, for two reasons. America's main language is English, a language that is also widely used and serves as an official language in all three East African countries. To a large extent, then, leaders in the American corporate and business world feel little pressure to have knowledge of Swahili for purposes of communication and transaction with business leaders from East Africa. The major language of China, on the other hand, is not one that has much currency in East Africa or many other parts of the world outside China. As a result, China has developed three strategies to facilitate linguistic communication with East African nations and elsewhere in its bid to become a dominant economic superpower.

The first strategy aims at promoting the study of Chinese language and culture globally. This strategy has been entrusted to the worldwide network of Confucius Institutes. All three East African countries, for example, host Confucius Institutes at their national universities – University of Dar es Salaam, Makerere University, and the University of Nairobi. The institutes offer courses, certificates, and undergraduate degree programs in Chinese language and culture. On each of the Confucius Institute websites of the three East African universities, the economic and business imperative stands out quite clearly.[3]

The second strategy is to encourage more and more people in China to study English as an international language with all the cultural and ideological trappings that such a linguistic internationalism implies. The rise in the demand for English coincided with the end of the Cultural Revolution toward the close of the 1970s. This development became manifest with the "Open Door Policy" instituted by Deng Xiaoping in 1978, opening China to foreign businesses that sought to invest in the country. By the year 2000, China was cited as "a major English-learning society" where the number of English learners exceeded 200 million (Bolton and Graddol 2012, 7). And in spite of recent government attempts to curtail the force of English partly to reduce its influence as a source of Westernization, the language continues to experience tremendous demand.

The third approach is to stimulate within China the study of other languages of nations and regions that are deemed to be of economic and trade importance to China. With regard to the latter, Swahili was already a subject of study at institutions like Beijing Foreign Studies University

---

[3] See the Confucius Institute websites of the University of Nairobi: https://confucius.uonbi.ac.ke/, Makerere University: http://ci.mak.ac.ug/, and the University of Dar es Salaam: https://www.udsm.ac.tz/web/index.php/institutes/ci/admission (accessed on February 25, 2022).

and the Communication University of China, but now its space in China has expanded. In 2019, for example, Shanghai International Studies University introduced a Bachelor of Arts degree program in Swahili with the goal of cultivating a cadre of Chinese graduates with sufficient Swahili competence to represent and promote Chinese interests in East Africa (see "Tanzania" 2019). At the same time, the Confucius Institute of the University of Dar es Salaam began offering a special Swahili course intended specifically for "all Chinese persons living in Tanzania" with instruction provided by tutors who are themselves Chinese.[4] Meanwhile, in 2022, *The People's Daily*, the organ of the Communist Party of China, added Swahili to its list of foreign languages used to transmit world news.

Another important difference between the USA and China is that in East Africa, American businesses are usually the large corporate type that are led by directors of major companies. Chinese businesses in Africa, on the other hand, are not limited to those sponsored by the government and big corporations. There are many people of Chinese background who live in Africa and run a variety of small businesses. As Howard French has explained:

> By common estimate, Africa has received millions of…Chinese newcomers in the space of a mere decade, during which time they have rapidly penetrated every conceivable walk of life: farmers, entrepreneurs building small and medium-sized factories, and practitioners of the full range of trades, doctors, teachers, smugglers, prostitutes. (2014, 5)

Many of these businesses are of the kind that force Chinese entrepreneurs to interact with the average citizen, in the process developing proficiency in local African languages like Swahili. And the faster the Chinese Diaspora in Africa grows, the more likely it is that the Chinese government and institutions will promote the study of languages like Swahili.

In addition, just as the USA and Russia engaged in Swahili translation projects to promote their ideological platforms, there is evidence of Chinese interest in Chinese–Swahili translation projects, with emphasis

---

[4] See the website of the Confucius Institute of the University of Dar es Salaam: https://www.udsm. ac.tz/web/index.php/institutes/ci/events/welcome-to-the-kiswahili-course-with-chinese-tutors (Accessed February 26, 2022).

6 Swahili in the Context of Cold Wars 173

now on moving away from writings and imaginative works with overtly political content, to works that highlight cross-cultural convergence. One concrete example of this trend is *Hekaya za Kale za China* (Ancient tales of China), translated into Swahili by Huang Jiongxiang and produced by the Foreign Languages Press. The translation itself was based on a collection of allegorical tales, selected by Wei Jinzhi, from several centuries of classical Chinese writing, including *Yanzichunqiu, Liezi, Zhuangzi, and Hanfeizi*. Short, terse, satirical, and often humorous, these tales contain social messages and moral lessons that, in many ways, compare with African folktales. Many express some of the fundamental principles of Taoism: compassion, moderation, and humility, and the relativistic orientation of human society. Appearing in 1989, the Swahili translation coincided with China's pro-democracy movement that had given rise to the interrogation, by some, of communistic values and a quest for a new humanistic order. Part of the process involved a reexamination of possible lessons that modern China could draw from traditions of pre-communistic China. And as the translator writes on the back cover of the translation, "Angalau jamii ya kale ilitofautiana na jamii ya sasa, wasomaji bado wanaweza kupata mafunzo mengi baada ya kusoma hekaya hizio zenye maana" (Though the ancient society differs from the modern society, readers can still get many useful lessons after reading these meaningful tales).

Many of the stories in the collection have a relativist thrust that is probably intended to communicate post-communist China's policy orientation toward Africa. China has been going all out to do business with Africa without taking into account the human rights record of individual nations. It responds to its critics by invoking the relativist argument that China does not interfere with the internal affairs of any country, that every nation must pursue its own course of development, and that what is good for China in political orientation need not be good for Africa. Whether in the Sudan or Niger, China has thus maintained a "hands off" policy in the political arena based essentially on relativist rationalization. To its African economic "partners," then, the stories provide a window for understanding the relativist political framework within which China deals with them.

Conclusion

In sum, then, the Swahili language seems to have made some significant gains from the dynamics precipitated by the three cold wars. In East Africa, the ideological Cold War was important in stimulating the Ujamaa ideology of Tanzania and the accompanying strategy of promoting Swahili as the language of the common person in pursuit of the Ujamaa agenda. This development in Tanzania became an important factor in the promotion from above of the study of the language in the American academy and, to a lesser extent, the Soviet academy. More significant in terms of the popularity of the language in the USA, the socialist turn in Tanzania was an important stimulus, from below, of the African American quest for a linguistic identification with Mother Africa in the context of the racial cold war in the USA.

With regard to the economic cold war between China and the USA, so far China seems to be surpassing American efforts to overcome the state of monolingualism. As a result, Swahili seems to have made more gains under Chinese than American cultural investment. The reality on the ground points to a critical economic need for the study of foreign languages in the USA. In *Making Languages Our Business: Addressing Foreign Language Demand Among US Employers*, a report by the American Council on the Teaching of Foreign Languages (2019), for example, argues that the ability to communicate effectively in a language other than English has become critical not only in helping university graduates thrive in a global economy, but also in boosting their marketability in the workplace. In spite of such findings, however, much of the American public is under the sway of the belief that "Global Business Speaks English" (Neeley 2012).

The end of the ideological Cold War, in the meantime, contributed to the rise of a particular construction of Islam as the new global enemy of America and Europe. This understanding of the Muslim–Western divide has been part of what Samuel Huntington described as "a clash of civilizations" (1996). Has the relationship between the West and the Muslim world become yet another form of cold war? According to Buzan, "Washington is now embarked on a campaign to persuade itself, the

American people and the rest of the world that the 'global war on terrorism' (GWoT) will be a 'long war.' This 'long war' is explicitly compared to the Cold War as a similar sort of zero-sum, global-scale, generational struggle against anti-liberal ideological extremists who want to rule the world" (2006, 1101). If Buzan is right, then what are the implications of this GWoT for the Swahili language? This interplay between Swahili and the war on terrorism is the subject of our next chapter.

References

ACTFL (American Council for the Teaching of Foreign Languages). 2019. *Making Languages Our Business: Addressing Foreign Language Demand Among US Employers*. Alexandria, Virginia: American Council for the Teaching of Foreign Languages.
"America's Languages: Investing in Language Education for the 21st Century," Mradi wa Commission on Language Learning wa American Academy of Arts and Sciences. https://www.amacad.org/sites/default/files/publication/downloads/Commission-on-Language-Learning_Americas-Languages.pdf. Accessed May 21, 2021.
Attwood, William. 1967. *The Reds and the Blacks: A Personal Adventure*. New York: Harper and Row.
Bolton, Kingsley, and David Graddol. 2012. English in China Today. *English Today 111* 28 (3): 3–9.
Bursov, B. n.d. "Dibaji" (Foreword). In *Mama*, ed. M. Gorky, 3–5. Moscow: Progress Publishers.
Buzan, Barry. 2006. Will the 'global war on terrorism' be the new Cold War? *International Affairs* 82 (6): 1101–1118.
Clark, K. 1981. *The Soviet Novel: History as Ritual*. Chicago: University of Chicago Press.
Colony and Protectorate of Kenya. 1962. *Legislative Council Debates: Official Report, May 8–July 27, 1962*. Vol. 89, Second Session. Nairobi: Government Press.
Curtis, Edward E., IV. 2019. *Muslim American Politics and the Future of US Democracy*. New York: New York University Press.
French, Howard W. 2014. *China's Second Continent: How a Million Migrants Are Building a New Empire in Africa*. New York: Vintage Books.

Gromov, Mikail D. 2018. Swahili Literature in the Russian Language. *Swahili Forum* 25: 165–168.
Gromova, N.V. 2004. Tafsiri Mpya ya Fasihi ya Kirusi Katika Kiswahili. *Swahili Forum* 11: 121–125.
Harries, Lyndon. 1968. The Teaching of Swahili. *The Modern Language Journal* 52 (3): 146–148.
Herrington, O.A. 2015. Language of Their Own: Swahili and Its Influence. *Harvard Political Review.* http://harvardpolitics.com/books-arts/swahili-language-influence/. Accessed May 21, 2015.
Huntington, Samuel P. 1996. *The Clash of Civilizations and the Remaking of World Order.* New York: Simon and Schuster.
Ingle, S. 1993. *George Orwell: A Political Life.* Manchester, UK: Manchester University Press.
KU Libraries Exhibits. 2015. *Shamba la Wanyama [Animal Farm].* http://exhibits.lib.ku.edu/items/show/6039. Accessed December 19, 2015.
Lal, Priya. 2014. Maoism in Tanzania: Material Connections and Shared Imaginaries. In *Mao's Little Red Book: A Global History,* ed. Alexander C. Cook, 96–126. Cambridge, UK: Cambridge University Press.
Larkin, B.D. 1971. *China and Africa 1949–1970: The Foreign Policy of the People's Republic of China.* Berkeley: University of California Press.
Macchiavelli, Nicoló. 2008. *The Prince and Other Stories.* Webster's Swahili Thesaurus ed. San Diego: ICON Group International.
Malloy, Sean L. 2017. *Out of Oakland: Black Panther Party Internationalism During the Cold War.* Ithaca, NY: Cornell University Press.
Mamdani, Mahmood. 1983. *Imperialism and Fascism in Uganda.* London: Henemann.
Markle, Seth M. 2017. *A Motorcycle on Hell Run: Tanzania, Black Power, and the Uncertain Future of Umajumui wa Africa, 1964–1974.* East Lansing: Michigan State University Press.
Mazrui, Ali A. 1967. Tanzaphilia: A Diagnosis. *Transition (Kampala)* 31: 20–26.
———. 1975. *The Political Sociology of the English Language: An African Perspective.* The Hauge: Mouton.
Mugane, John. 2015. *The Story of Swahili.* Athens: Ohio University Press.
National K-12 Foreign Language Enrollment Survey, The. American Councils for International Education, 2017. [Hii ni ripoti ya utafiti uliofadhiliwa na The Language Flagship at the Defense Language and National Security Education Office.] https://www.americancouncils.org/sites/default/files/FLE-report-June17.pdf. Accessed May 21, 2021.

Neeley, Tsedal. 2012. Global Business Speaks English: Why You Need a Language Strategy Now. *Harvard Business Review* 90 (5): 116–124.

Odinga, O. 1967. *Not Yet Uhuru*. London: Heinemann.

Pansare, M.A. 2012. Target-oriented Study of Maxim Gorky's *Mother* in Marathi Polysystem. In *Collection of Papers Presented at the International Symposium Organized by the Russian State University of Humanities*, ed. N. Reinhold, 215–233. Moscow: Russian State University of the Humanities.

"Peace Corps." Website entry. John F. Kennedy Presidential Library and Museum. https://www.jfklibrary.org/learn/about-jfk/jfk-in-history/peace-corps. Accessed March 25, 2021.

Rasberry, Vaugh. 2016. *Race and the Totalitarian Century: Geopolitics in the Black Literary Imagination*. Cambridge, MA: Harvard University Press.

Roberts, George. 2021. *Revolutionary State-Making in Dar es Salaam: African Liberation and the Global Cold War, 1961–1974*. New York: Cambridge University Press.

Rubin, A.N. 2012. *Archives of Authority: Empire, Culture and the Cold War*. Princeton, NJ: Princeton University Press.

"Tanzania: Chinese University Embraces Kiswahili" iliyotoka katika *Daily News ya Tanzania*, 12 June, 2019. https://allafrica.com/stories/201906120583.html. Accessed March 6, 2021.

Tazama. 2017. Popularity of Chinese Language Learning Soaring Within the US Education System Survey. http://www.xinhuanet.com/english/2017-06/03/c_136336004.htm. Accessed May 21, 2021.

Tellis, Ashley J., A. Swailski, and M. Wills. 2020. *US-China Competition for Global Influence*. Washington, DC: The National Bureau of Asian Research.

Traore, F.A. 2013. Translating Culture: Literary Translations into Swahili by East African Translator. *Swahili Forum* 20: 19–30.

Uttaro, Ralph A. 1982. The Voices of America in International Radio Propaganda. *Law and Contemporary Problems* 45 (1): 103–122.

Venuti, Lawrence. 2004. Translation, Community, Utopia. In *The Translation Studies Reader*, 2nd ed., 469–500. London: Routledge.

Wilson, Amrit. 1989. *US Foreign Policy and Revolution: The Creation of Tanzania*. London: Pluto Press.

Winek, Mark D. 2009. Radio as a Tool of the State: Radio Moscow and the Early Cold War. *Comparative Humanities Review* 3: 99–113.

7

Swahili and the War on Terrorism

Alamin Mazrui

Following the 9/11 tragedy in the USA, President George W. Bush declared the attacks as an "act of war." In calling this criminal offensive a war, the Bush administration was seeking to provide a legitimating language for its intended exercise of extraordinary powers, both at the domestic and international level. These powers included invasion and occupation of foreign spaces, abduction and forced disappearances, holding suspects of terrorism at Guantanamo Bay without trial, use of torture, surveillance even of citizens of the USA, and so forth. The language of the "war on terrorism," in other words, became a dominant political paradigm in American foreign policy after September 11, 2001.

There is a sense, however, in which non-state terrorism could indeed be regarded as a kind of warfare, often resorted to by those who are at a great military disadvantage but have a cause they believe in. We saw this in the case of the Irish Republican Army in its bid to end British control of Ireland, Basque separatists yearning for their own independent nation from Spain, and Chechens (of Chechnya) seeking autonomy from Russia, among many other examples throughout the world. In earlier chapters we encountered war conditions in East Africa – the Maji Maji war in

Tanzania and the Mau Mau war in Kenya – in which the term "terrorist" was regularly employed to describe the African combatants seeking to end colonial rule.

What has made the Muslim dimension of terrorism as a form of war, in Kenya and elsewhere, particularly unique, however, is that terrorism has now become globalized. International airports throughout the world, serving as important nodes of a global network, for example, have been forced to seek ever more advanced methods and technologies to keep up with the growing sophistication and creativity of terrorist organizations. In the process, measures to combat terrorism have also required coordination of efforts across the globe. And it was through this American attempt to globalize the war on terrorism that Swahili-speaking East African nations, especially Kenya, became party to the war.

American influence on Kenya was clearly evident in the government's attempts to pass anti-terrorist legislation. The September 2001 bombing of the World Trade Center in New York City was the critical event, of course, that gave birth to the American Patriot Act, intended to be the primary legal weapon against terrorism in the USA. This tragic attack was also the source of American pressure on other countries to construct specific regional alliances that would support the American-led war against terrorism (especially from the Muslim "Other"). In Africa, these alliances have included the US East Africa Counterterrorism Initiative – intended to improve the police and judicial anti-terrorist capabilities of Kenya, Uganda, Tanzania, Djibouti, Eritrea, and Ethiopia.

Swahili and the War on Terrorism in East Africa

The Swahili language came to have a place in the war against terrorism partly because it is a language of a native-speaking community of the East African coastline, the Swahili people, for whom Islam has been an inalienable component of their ethnic identity. In the global context, the Swahili too became subject to the Western demonization of Islam because of real or potential Muslim opposition to Western hegemony. It is arguable that no civilization has more persistently challenged Western global hegemony than Islam. No culture in Africa or Asia has been more of a thorn in the side of Western imperialism than Muslim resistance. That is partly why, in the words of John E. Woods, a professor of Middle Eastern history at the University of Chicago, almost "immediately after the collapse of Communism, Islam emerged as the new evil force" (quoted by Brooke 1995) in the imagination of the American state. And because Islam is primarily an Afro-Asian religion, a faith whose followers are located mainly in Africa and Asia, there is also a racial undertone behind this Western aggressive posture toward Muslims. Deepa Kumar (2010), Edward Said (1997), Sherman Jackson (2011), and Sahar Aziz (2021) are among the many scholars who have explored precisely this interplay between racism and Islamophobia in the American imagination, a connection that became even more explicit, and its implication more draconian, when Donald Trump was in office as America's forty-fifth president.

Like many Muslims across the world, the Swahili have also been supportive of the Palestinian cause and have often expressed outrage over American unconditional support for Israel. One of the latest books to draw attention to the sufferings of Palestinians and the collective trauma they experience under Israeli occupation is *Kingdom of Olives and Ash*, a collection of essays by a group of internationally acclaimed authors, many of Jewish origin themselves, edited by Michael Chabon and Ayelet Waldman (2017). Of course, not all Palestinians are Muslim. It is likely that as many as 20 percent of Palestinians are Christian of various denominations. The Popular Front for the Liberation of Palestine, once the most militant Palestinian organization against the Israeli occupation, was founded and led by George Habash, himself a Christian. But because the majority of Palestinians are Muslim, and because Jerusalem is the location of one of the holiest Islamic sites, the Dome of the Rock, the question of Palestine continues to arouse strong Muslim indignation throughout the world, including among the Swahili-speaking people of East Africa.

In sum, then, the post-Cold War hostility of the American state toward much of the Muslim world – rooted as it is in the politics of oil, its unconditional support for Israel and tyrants in Muslim-majority nations while continuing to undermine the more independent-leaning Muslim nations, and its duplicity in its foreign policy posture that has contributed to the suffering of Muslims internationally – will continue to feed

Muslim angst and anger against America and, by extension, against its allies in the West and elsewhere. The Swahili, in particular, and East African Muslims more generally, have reacted to this set of global issues with the same degree of outrage as Muslims elsewhere in the world. And these circumstances help to explain the continued Muslim resistance against Western, especially American, hegemony, fringes of which have sometimes responded with terrorist violence.

In addition to this global context of Western reaction to Islam, there are local factors that trigger Muslim-related terrorism and that make the Swahili particularly prone to recruitment by Islamist organizations. Some of these are still linked to America and Israel. Certain groups of Muslims in Saudi Arabia and Egypt are militantly opposed to the Saudi royalty and the regime of Aldel Fattah el-Sisi, respectively, because of their cozy relationship with America in spite of its unconditional support for Israel. Similarly, many Muslims in Kenya have been suspicious of their successive governments because they have been excessively obedient to the USA and too keen to forge closer ties with Israel. In spite of some ups and downs in Kenya–US government relations over the years, Kenya has generally been a strong ally of the USA. It should come as no surprise, then, that Kenya became a target of Muslim-related terrorist attacks against American and Israeli interests in the country. The attacks in Kenya were at times symbolic of the convergence of anti-Americanism and anti-Zionism.

But Swahili and Muslim grievances against the Kenyan government go well beyond its relationship with the USA. It is fair to say that religion as a point of contention in postcolonial Kenya did not become a burning question until President Daniel arap Moi came to power in 1978. In terms of political orientation, the previous fifteen years or so of Jomo Kenyatta's presidency were more ethnocratic than sectarian. This does not mean that the ethnic-centered actions of the Kenyatta regime did not have religious implications; sometimes they did. A good example was the establishment, beginning in 1970, of the Lake Kenyatta Harambee Settlement Scheme in Mpeketoni in what was then a predominantly Swahili district of Lamu on the northern coast of Kenya. By 1975, over 3000 Gikuyu families had been settled and allocated land in the area, with a provision for yet more to come. This was the era of a Gikuyu ethnic oligarchy, and the settlement scheme quickly acquired an ethnic face, pitting Gikuyu settlers against Swahili locals over the issue of land ownership.

However, when religion was later added into the mix of calculations in Kenya's body politic, what started as an ethnic issue over land matters also assumed religious overtones in later generations precisely because the offspring of the Gikuyu settlers continued to be predominantly Christian while the Swahili are predominantly Muslim. It is against this backdrop that we need to understand the tragic 2014 Al-Shabaab attack on Mpeketoni, killing over sixty residents, mostly Christians of Gikuyu ethnic origin. Some reports say that language was critical here in determining the religious identity of the victims: Those who were unable to pronounce "There is no deity but Allah" as it is pronounced by Muslims in the Arabic language were likely to be shot dead. Under a new dispensation that had come to conflate sectarian politics with preexisting ethnic politics, terrorists were able to capitalize on the context of an existing land grievance, highlighting an important interplay between terrorism and the economics of marginalization.

Of course, given Kenya's colonial history, Christianity always had an underlying structural presence in the affairs of the state. As Bishop Henry Okullu once put it, Kenya, Tanzania, and Uganda are in fact "secular only in the sense that their constitutions do not specially state that they are based on Christian Laws" (1992, 26). Under Moi, however, the interplay between Christianity and the state became overt. Part of the reason for the sectarian turn in Kenya had to do with the place of Christianity in Moi's own vision of governance, which, in his view, "is set upon the solid rock of history and heritage and fired by the eternal concepts of a living Christian faith" (Moi 1986, 21–22) and "singularly embeds the kernel of the principles of Christian life into the national philosophy" (Moi 1986, 31). Any semblance of a secular state now disappeared, resulting in systematic imbalances that allowed the management of national public affairs to be especially biased against Muslims and members of other religious minorities. Chande (2000), Kresse (2009), Bradbury and Kleinman (2010), Prestholdt (2011), Goldsmith (2011), and others have all discussed these religious-based imbalances in Kenya in various degrees of detail. These have included discrimination in matters of citizenship and national belonging, unequal access to educational opportunities, disparities in civil service appointments in favor of non-Muslims even in Muslim-majority constituencies, and the burning question of land ownership and dispossession.

Muslims were somewhat hopeful that finally their grievances might be resolved during the tenure of President Mwai Kibaki (2002–2013) in spite of his greater collaboration with the USA in matters of combatting terrorism. Indeed in 2007, Kibaki even proceeded to establish the eleven-member "Presidential Special Action Committee to Address Specific Concerns of the Muslim Community in Regard to Alleged Harassment and/or Discrimination in the Application of the Law," chaired by Abdullahi M. H. Sharawe. The report, finally released on March 31, 2008, reaffirmed many of the complaints about Muslim marginalization, violation in matters of security and land rights, and discrimination in the areas of citizenship, education, and access to justice. The report even concluded that it confirmed "most of the complaints raised by the Muslim community and, therefore, recommends that the Government urgently address the issues in order to restore public confidence, fully integrate the Muslim community in the mainstream development so as to build national cohesion" (Republic of Kenya 2008, xix). Like many other reports submitted to the government, however, little came out of this committee's report in terms of implementation of the core recommendations.

It is significant that the politicization of religion in Kenya since the early days of Moi's presidency has coincided with the rise of Christian Evangelism globally that has been feeding the Kenyan scene in direct ways. John Chesworth (2006) provides a good description of this interplay between the politics of pluralism in Kenya and Christian Evangelist activism globally. The debate over the Kadhi Courts, the constitutionally established courts restricted to matters of Muslim personal law, for example, became one concrete constitutional arena in which American Christian Evangelical groups attempted to intervene (Kelley 2012). The more recent sectarian manifestations of Kenyan politics, in other words, are not without international linkages, and Kenyan Muslim reactions to them must be understood within this broader, global context.

On the other hand, this history also became the basis of a peculiar tradition of political "Othering" of the Swahili in a way that often questioned their right of belonging to Kenya. Of course, by insisting on the uniqueness of their culture, heritage, and outlook – with some identifying with an Arab descent often for quasi-religious reasons – the Swahili themselves became inadvertently complicit in the attempted denial of their citizenship. Whatever the case, reducing the citizenship status of the Swahili, to either noncitizen or lesser citizen, conveniently served the kleptocratic interests of those in power and as a legitimating ideology for the collective dispossession of the Swahili people (Mazrui and Shariff 1994). The unfolding of this postcolonial Swahili reality is what later came to stimulate forms of resistance articulated in either religious or regional terms.

When Kenyans especially think of Muslims in East Africa, the image that often comes to mind is that of the Swahili people of the coast. This community is generally "assumed to be far more radicalized than current information suggests. As a target of anti-terror legislation and actions by the Kenyan government (funded by Western countries), one would surely expect a deep hatred for the political system and the West. This hatred undeniably exists to some extent. It has created a coastal society that feels as if it is 'second class' to Bantu Africans" (Aronson 2013, 29–30). Over the last couple of decades, the image has naturally been reinforced by the fact that the coast was the stronghold of both the Islamic Party of Kenya (IPK) and the Mombasa Republican Council (MRC). The IPK was a political party with a strong Swahili-Muslim base that sought to compete in Kenya's electoral politics but was denied registration, while the MRC was a separatist organization that advocated for the "independence" of the coast from the rest of Kenya. The evolution of the cosmopolitan Swahili coastal community gave it a fundamentally different if complex precolonial and colonial history from the rest of Kenya, which had major ramifications for its postcolonial experience. That history was the basis upon which the community unsuccessfully sought coastal autonomy in the early 1960s, a move that contributed to tensions, often racialized, between the Swahili and upcountry Africans who came to assume the reins of power at independence.

There is a need to bear in mind that initially terrorism in Kenya was not targeted against Kenyans at all. The intended targets were Israel and the USA, even though in every instance the majority of those killed turned out to be Kenyan. One of the earliest terrorist attacks in Kenya took place on December 31, 1980, when a bomb was planted and then exploded at the iconic Norfolk Hotel, Nairobi, killing around twenty and injuring over eighty people. At that time the hotel was owned and controlled by a Jewish firm, the Block Hotels. The suspected culprit was a Moroccan citizen, Qaddura Mohammed Abdel al-Hamid, presumably a Palestinian sympathizer even though both the Palestinian Liberation Organization (PLO) and the Popular Front for the Liberation of Palestine (PFLP) denied any association with al-Hamid. It was believed that al-Hamid's action was partly in retaliation against Kenya's logistical support for Israel in the so-called Entebbe raid of July 1976 in which commandos of the Israeli Defense Forces launched a mission to rescue Israelis held hostage by the Popular Front for the Liberation of Palestine at Uganda's Entebbe International Airport. This development intensified cooperation between the Kenyan police and Israeli intelligence, the Mossad.

Another Israel-targeted terrorist assault came on November 28, 2002. This was a twin attack: bombing of the Paradise Hotel in Mombasa, owned by Israeli nationals, and the attempted downing of an Israeli charter plane with surface-to-air missiles. The attack on the hotel left about thirteen dead and over eighty injured. Kenyans were caught in the crossfire; in order to kill a few Israelis, three times as many Kenyans were killed. This attack led to the arrest of the controversial Kenyan clergyman Sheikh Muhammad Aboud Rogo and some twenty others who were charged with several counts of murder related to the attack on the Paradise Hotel. Though Rogo was eventually cleared of the charges in 2005, he was assassinated by unknown gunmen who, in the opinion of several human rights groups, were members of Kenya's Anti-Terrorism Police Unit.

The first anti-American terrorist attack on Kenyan soil came in 1998. This was more clearly the work of operatives associated with Al-Qaeda, and came about two years after Osama bin Laden had declared his war against the USA, claiming that "[t]he occupying American army is the principal and the main cause of the situation. Therefore, efforts should be concentrated on destroying, fighting, and killing the enemy until, by the grace of Allah, it is completely defeated" (quoted by Rubin and Rubin 2002, 139). Bin Laden was, of course, referring to the establishment of American military bases in the Muslim holy land following the Gulf War of 1990–1991. The bomb attacks of August 7, 1998, were targeted against American embassies both in Nairobi and Dar es Salaam. They were intended to hit America in areas where it was vulnerable and where it least expected it, though the majority of the dead and injured were again by far Kenyans and Tanzanians. However, those hundreds of lives lost in Kenya and Tanzania in terrorist attacks directed at America seemed to have left "little impression…on the American conscience" (Hoffman 2014, 210), even though the tragedy did foster closer ties in the security domain between Kenya and the USA (which hitherto had been less supportive of the then President Daniel arap Moi allegedly because of his horrendous human rights record).

To reiterate, then, though the majority of the victims were always Kenyan, these earlier Muslim-associated terrorist attacks were not targeted at Kenyans as such. Kenyans died in the crossfire. Kenyans did not become targets of Muslim-based terrorism until Kenya decided to serve as a proxy in American intervention in Somalia. By then, American President George W. Bush was of the conviction that controlling the situation in Somalia was critical in America's war against terrorism (Mogire and Agade 2011). First, there was Kenya's role in the illegal rendition of many Somalis fleeing the outbreak of war caused by the American-supported Ethiopian invasion of Somalia to eliminate the newly formed government of the Islamic Courts Union. More significant perhaps was Kenya's acceptance of its expected role as America's closest ally in its war on terrorism in the Horn of Africa (Davis 2007). Kenya became

> an important example of a 'partner' state that has now become imbricated in the business of war. The combination of political, economic and military support from the US has emboldened the Kenyan state to engage in its own 'war on terror' at home and abroad. In October 2011, the Kenya Defense Forces (KDF) invaded southern Somalia with the declared intention of addressing the threat posed by Al-Shabaab. (Al-Bulushi 2020, 41)

This military invasion was launched under the name *Operation Linda Nchi* (Operation Defend the Country/Homeland), which has continued to maintain a military presence in the country. In the process, Kenyan forces are reported to have indiscriminately bombed and shelled "populated areas, killing and wounding civilians and livestock" (Human Rights Watch 2013). By all indications, this Kenyan offensive marked a critical juncture in the relationship between Kenya and Al-Shabaab. Due to Kenya opting to become America's shield against terrorism, more Kenyans have become a target of what started as anti-American terrorist attacks.

The mixed code English-Swahili phrase "Operation Linda Nchi" is indicative of the message that the Kenyan state sought to convey. With the English term "operation" it was able to reassure its American partner that it has set in motion a full-scale military campaign against the Somali-based Al-Shabaab. It was an offensive of a magnitude not seen since the Shifta War of the 1960s when Kenya was fighting against ethnic-Somali secessionist forces in what was then known as the Northern Frontier District (NFD). The term embodies all of its suggested militaristic meanings – practical, strategic, exerting power. With a ring similar to America's "Homeland Security," the Swahili Linda Nchi (Defend the Country/Homeland), on the other hand, was intended for local consumption. The message was that Kenya was not invading Somalia – with the likelihood that many of its own citizens would die in the process – to placate the American government, but to protect its own nation and citizens from an external enemy. Locally, then, Linda Nchi was a particular framing of the legitimating principle of the invasion.

As indicated in Chap. 3, Swahili had been cultivated to serve as the language of the armed forces in East Africa since the colonial period. The multiethnic composition of the military continued to give Swahili a central role and even consolidated the place of the language in the forces well into the postcolonial period. Operation Linda Nchi, then, was an invading Kenyan force that had Swahili as its official language in its lower ranks. The soldiers of Operation Linda Nchi were now patrolling the streets of Somalia, interacting in Swahili with a predominantly Somali-speaking population that had minimal proficiency in Swahili. The question thus arose as to whether the presence of the forces of Operation

Linda Nchi in Somalia would help or harm the fortunes of the Swahili in that country. Would the interaction between the Swahili-speaking Kenyan soldiers and Somali-speaking communities in public places help the spread of the language? Or would the Somali communities turn their backs on Swahili because of its association with an invading force?

Of course, a dialect of Swahili, Chimiini, had long been prevalent in the southern Somalia region of Brava. Though different from the Swahili that was likely spoken by the forces of Operation Linda Nchi, Chimiini and its speakers might have facilitated communication between the Kenyan forces and the local Somali communities. However, the condition of insecurity resulting from the Somali civil war that grew out of resistance to the military regime headed by Mohamed Siad Barre in the 1980s had a direct impact on the Brava population. Many speakers of Chimiini and many other Somalis left the region to join the ranks of immigrants in the UK, the USA, and other spaces of the world. As Brava continues to become depopulated, the future of its variety of Swahili has become increasingly uncertain. According to Brent Henderson (2011, 14):

> Though spoken in Brava for a millennium, the horrors of the ongoing civil war in Somali have caused nearly all speakers of the language to become refugees now living in large international cities like Atlanta, London, and Mombasa. As a result, the unique language and culture of the Bravanese is quickly disappearing.

Under these conditions, will Operation Linda Nchi eventually lead to a Kenyan variety of Swahili moving in to fill the potential vacuum left by the emigration of Chimiini-speaking people, or will it give rise to anti-Swahili sentiments in the country?

It is significant that most of the Brava and other Somali immigrants passed through and stayed for years among Swahili-speaking communities in Kenya as a transit point for their planned emigration to the West. In the process, many acquired some proficiency in Swahili, a development that stimulated a continuing interest in the language even after their relocation to the West. In addition, many ended up living in Kenya for good, with successive generations having Swahili as a first or additional language. Language shift from Chimiini, either into Kimivita, the dialect of Mombasa, or a variety of Standard Swahili, is also increasingly marking the linguistic practices of the children of Chimiini-speaking immigrants in Kenya, opening a whole new possible area of sociolinguistic research.[1]

The Somali-speaking population on the Kenyan side of the border between Kenya and Somalia has, of course, come to acquire sufficient command of Swahili as an additional language, especially in the urban areas. This linguistic development is partly the result of the outcome of the Shifta War (1963–1967) that broke out soon after Kenya gained its independence from British colonial rule. As mentioned earlier, the Shifta War was triggered by a secessionist attempt by ethnic Somali-speaking people who constituted the largest native majority of the region of Kenya that was then called the Northern Frontier District (NFD). Calling themselves the Northern Frontier District Liberation Movement (NFDLM), and supported by the bordering state of Somalia, the insurgents also had an irredentist agenda, seeking to unite with fellow Somalis toward a Greater Somalia. By the end of 1967, the NFDLM had been vanquished by Kenya's armed forces, though small-scale "Shifta banditry," as the Kenyan government preferred to call it, continued for years after the war.

The defeat of the NFDLM had two consequences related to the Swahili language. On the one hand, the language continued to make inroads into the Kenyan Somali population partly as a result of its own momentum in the marketplace and partly due to policies that made Swahili a compulsory subject in schools and, later, a co-official language of the nation. This degree of "Swahilization" of Somalis of this region would not have been possible if NFDLM had achieved its irredentist goal. In time, even as an additional language, Swahili helped in bringing the Somali people of the then Northern Frontier District into greater contact with other Kenyans, fostering a sense of Kenyanness within their ranks. On the other hand, partly because of the memory of the Shifta War, successive Kenyan regimes continued to regard Kenyan Somalis as second-class citizens, a political situation that made them especially vulnerable to Al-Shabaab recruitment efforts. And those among them who do get recruited by

---

[1] We are grateful to Professor Peter Githinji for this observation.

Al-Shabaab have easier access to their targets of terrorist attacks in Kenya partly because of their knowledge of the Swahili language.

But the future of Swahili in Somalia itself remains an open question. It is possible that the language has made some gains partly because Al-Shabaab has increasingly found it useful for its activities in the region. Since Operation Linda Nchi, Kenya has experienced several Al-Shabaab-engineered attacks, large and small, including those horrendous acts of terrorism at the Westgate Mall on September 21, 2013, Mpeketoni on June 15, 2014, and Garissa University on April 2, 2015. In virtually all these instances, knowledge of Swahili is likely to have helped the Al-Shabaab operatives in infiltrating their targeted sites. Of course, Al-Shabaab had made clear its intentions of "revenge" from the very beginning of Kenya's invasion. And these intentions were confirmed when, immediately after the Westgate Mall attack, Ahmed Godane, then Al-Shabaab's leader in Somalia, released a statement saying:

> The attack at Westgate Mall was to torment the Kenyan leaders who've impulsively invaded [Somalia]. It was a retribution against the Western states that supported the Kenyan invasion and are spilling the blood of innocent Muslims in order to pave the way for their mineral companies… There is no way you could possibly endure a prolonged war in Somalia and you cannot also withstand a war of attrition inside your own country. … So make your choice today and withdraw all your forces [or] an abundance of blood will be spilt in your country. (quoted by McConnell 2013)

Kenya's geographical proximity to Somalia, its relatively porous borders, and the existence within its borders of a marginalized and aggrieved constituency of citizens of Somali and Muslim background among whom terrorists could both "pass" and recruit potential sympathizers have made the danger of Al-Shabaab a visceral reality.

Al-Shabaab's grievance against the Kenyan state and Swahili feelings of systemic marginalization within their East African nations combined to make the two communities potential bedfellows in their struggles against the Kenyan state and its American backers. The possibility of this Al-Shabaab–Swahili alliance also contributed to giving the Swahili language a role in the war on terrorism. In particular, Al-Qaeda has used

Swahili to recruit East Africans into its ranks. In the Pumwani Riyadha Mosque in Nairobi, for example, pamphlets of articles and speeches of Anwar al-'Awlaqi, the Yemeni-American member of Al-Qaeda who was killed in Yemen by a US drone attack in 2011, all translated into Swahili, were regularly circulated (Nzes 2012, 13). Al-Shabaab has also regularly turned to Swahili as a tool to recruit potential youth into the organization from the Swahili-speaking East African nations in spite of the fact that it is based in a Somali- rather than a Swahili-speaking region. A recruitment video in the Somali language, for example,

> was subtitled in both English and Swahili, suggesting that its target audiences are potential recruits from abroad. Ali Rage, al-Shabaab's spokesman, closed the video by specifically inviting East African foreign fighters to join the Somali insurgency, finishing his comments by saying, 'to our people/family in East Africa we say "welcome to Somalia,"' *hakuna matata* (there are no worries, using a famous Swahili phrase). Swahili speakers have also been subsequently featured in a number of other official al-Shabab videos, including the movement's video celebrating the formalization of its affiliation with al-Qa'ida central, which was released in April 2012, and a video released in February documenting a battle between insurgents and Kenyan backed militias. (Anzalone 2012, 10)

Even when used symbolically, then, Swahili terms like *hakuna matata* are intended to be a signal to potential recruits from East Africa that Al-Shabaab regards them as members of their in-group, their community.

The use of Swahili, side by side with Somali, English, and Arabic, has often allowed Al-Shabaab to operate on social media platforms without being easily noticed. A recent study by the Institute for Strategic Dialogue, for example, showed how Facebook repeatedly failed to intercept narratives of organizations that openly advocate violent extremism. The study found that "Facebook posts that openly supported IS or the Somalia-based al-Shabab—even ones carrying al-Shabab branding and calling for violence in languages including Swahili, Somali and Arabic—were allowed to be widely shared" (Anna 2022, 1). Clearly, America's excessive reliance on the English language has limited its capacity to detect and combat extremist groups like ISIS.

It is not only the association between the Swahili-speaking people of Kenya and Al-Shabaab of Somalia in the context of terrorism and counterterrorism that has had Swahili linguistic implications. Since 2017, there has been the specter of yet another, seemingly independent organization, also calling itself Al-Shabaab, that has been operating in the Cabo Delgado region of Mozambique. Sharing a border with Tanzania, this is a Muslim-majority region with ethnic links in Tanzania connected by the Swahili language and faith in Islam. Like the Muslims of coastal Kenya, the Muslim community in Cabo Delgado has long felt marginalized and disenfranchised: "Over the years the ruling Frelimo party has privileged the Christian population in the country and the capital Maputo, overlooking the Muslim dominated Cabo Delgado coastal regions of Northern provinces" (van Rentergem 2022, 1–2). At the same time, French extractive investments in the region's natural gas fields are seen to have benefited others at the expense of the local constituencies. The region was ripe for a terrorist matchstick.

There is also a Kenyan connection to the Mozambican Al-Shabaab since "a large majority of the leaders of the movement belong to a sect installed in the region in 2014 and identify themselves as the followers of the Kenyan Imam and preacher Aboud Mohamed Rogo, who was killed in 2012 in Kenya" (El Ouassif and Kitenge 2021, 8). The group is also said to work closely with Islamist groups inspired by or linked to the global Islamic State in the Democratic Republic of the Congo and Tanzania, at a time when thousands of Rwandan troops, with Swahili as one of their official languages, have been dispatched to "conduct counterterrorism operations in Cabo Delgado" (van Rentergem 2022, 4). The activities of the Al-Shabaab of Mozambique, then, not only threaten to have a spillover effect into Tanzania and other countries, but also to have significant economic and political ramifications for the wider Eastern African region. They may also have cultural and (Swahili) linguistic implications which may be unfolding in ways that are yet uncertain.[2]

Naturally, the increasing use of Swahili by extremist elements and in the war against terrorism challenged the language to express concepts that were relatively new in its universe of meanings. The language was

[2] We are again grateful to Professor Peter Githinji for his suggestions on the Mozambican situation.

now forced to imagine terms like terrorism, suicide bombing, explosives, extremism, fundamentalism, and so forth, in a language that the average citizen could understand. Once used to mean "bandit" primarily, the Swahili *gaidi* underwent semantic expansion to become the dominant term for "terrorist." Several Swahili words and phrases were now repackaged semantically to address the reality of terrorism and counterterrorism. These have included, for example, *siasa kali* (from intense politics to mean "radicalism"), *siasa isiyo kadiri* (from politics without moderation to mean "extremism"), *bomu la kujitoa mhanga* (from a bomb of self-sacrifice to mean "suicide bomb"), and of course *vita dhidi ya ugaidi* (war on terrorism), among many others (Adika Kevogo and Kevogo 2014, 183).

Caught in the midst of this linguistic situation were of course Muslim-owned radio stations such as IQRA FM (established 2000); Radio Rahma (established 2004); and Radio Salaam (established 2006), among others that sought to balance the perspectives of their listenership on terrorism with those of the state. IQRA FM, for example, does not use the term "Islamists," preferring "rebels" instead. Nor does it use terms like "extremist" or "jihadist," describing such individuals as people with *fikra tofauti* (an alternative view). It avoids the term "terrorist organizations" and refers to such bodies by their names as Al-Shabaab, ISIS, or Boko Haram. In other words, IQRA FM adopts a discourse that helps in buttressing the religion from the Islamophobic generalizations and essentialisms that one finds in mainstream media outlets. At the same time, IQRA FM solicits the participation of officers from the Kenya Defence Forces and other security bodies, thereby creating a space of open conversation, all in the Swahili language, between the state and its Muslim citizens toward a new understanding of Islam and its community of faith.

US Policy and Foreign Language Education After 9/11

The aftermath of the September 11, 2001, tragic attacks on the USA was a historical moment that revealed how linguistically unprepared the country was to deal effectively with the new enemy at hand. Americans were especially ill prepared to undertake the urgent tasks of communication, translation, and interpretation across languages and cultures that were so necessary for decoding messages at many critical levels in a context of war and peace. The situation seemed so dire that a special US Senate hearing on the matter was conducted in 2012, resulting in a major report entitled *A National Security Crisis: Foreign Language Capabilities in the Federal Government* (Committee 2012). The sudden surge of court trials against suspected terrorists created an urgent need for translation services, with the US government sometimes hiring individuals who were ill equipped for the task. Consider the following examples provided by a reporter of the *Los Angeles Times*:

> A prosecution in New York unraveled after the government admitted that key evidence – a document that supposedly described one of the defendants as a senior terrorist leader – had been incorrectly translated by an Army language specialist. A prosecutor in Detroit, unable to find a linguist through the FBI, found someone else to prepare a summary of more than 100 audiotapes used in a terrorism trial. The translator turned out to be a federal informant with a history of drug dealing – and to have terrorist ties. And translators at the military prison for suspected terrorists at Guantanamo Bay, Cuba, have been prosecuted for crimes, including mishandling sensitive documents. Now some of the translation work done for military tribunals at the prison is being reviewed for evidence that it might have been slanted to favor prosecutors. (Schmitt 2005, A-24)

The zone of mistranslation, therefore, deliberate or inadvertent, increased to a new high in the aftermath of 9/11.

In the meantime, the US government established, in February 2003, the National Virtual Translation Center, though the idea was first proposed in Section 907 of the USA Patriot Act of 2001. The Center is charged with the responsibility of providing translations of foreign intelligence for all sections of the US Intelligence machinery. Its operation relies on a computer-connected network of over 100 translators of over forty different global languages, aided by state-of-the-art translation technology. The virtual cadre of translators has been security-cleared to help in the "war against terrorism" from the comfort of their homes and offices, wherever they may be. The Center is even reported to have hired "one expert who lives on a boat near San Francisco" (Schmitt 2005, A-24).

As much as the US government had turned to translation to help in the prosecution cases of alleged terrorism, it had sometimes criminalized translation for the defense. A widely publicized case, of course, was that of Mohammed Yousry, an Egyptian graduate student at New York University who, with the approval of the government, was appointed the official translator for the defense in the case of Sheikh Omar Abdul Rahman, who was charged with masterminding the first bombing of the World Trade Center on October 26, 1993. Apparently, the FBI shadowed and wiretapped Yousry, eventually charging and convicting him of supporting terrorism on extremely flimsy evidence. Critics considered the conviction of Yousry as a terrible travesty of justice, a dangerous precedent of criminalizing the translator for doing what (s)he has been officially appointed to do. What Yousry's case revealed, above all, was how translators began to be regarded as people with split allegiance between two language communities, "as both enemy and friend…as potential traitors or double agents" (Apter 2006, 4).

Whatever the case, this ambiguous relationship of the US government with translation – enlisting it as an ally while criminalizing it as a foe – is part of the wider picture of linguistic incompetence that the USA suddenly realized could have a crippling effect on its society. As a result, as "America's monolingualism was publicly criticized as part of renewed calls for shared information, mutual understanding across cultural and religious divides, and multilateral cooperation, translation moved to the fore as an issue of major political and cultural significance" (Apter 2006, 3). Expectedly, this concern with translation also had an effect on American policy on foreign language study in the American academy.

The specter of the unconventional war embodied by terrorism was in several spaces of the Muslim world led to the new realization that, in fact, Pax-Americana needs the languages of the "Other" to prevent it from plunging into a crisis of legitimacy. This realization, in turn, led to a new emphasis on Area Studies and foreign (including African) language study in the American academy. This change of academic course is well captured by the International Studies in Higher Education Bill (HR 3077) that was passed by the US Congress on October 21, 2003 (though later revised). According to the summary of the bill:

America's international interests and national security concerns have taken on new importance in the post-9/11 era. Whether in business and industry, education, politics, trade and commerce, or national and international security, America's interests are tied to ... a group of programs at colleges and universities which work to advance knowledge of world regions, encourage the study of foreign languages, and train Americans to have the international expertise and understanding to fulfill pressing national security needs.

The fulfillment of these "pressing national security needs" has included "gunboat democracy" with the self-censoring American mass media as an important ideological arsenal. In time the academic emphasis shifted from the study of languages once connected with Cold War politics to languages of the Muslim world, especially Arabic. There is even evidence that the USA cut its services to Eastern Europe – the former Communist Bloc – because American emphasis of broadcasting funding has been diverted to the Muslim world (*Clandestine Radio Watch 147*, November 30, 2003).

The design of the International Studies in Higher Education Bill (before its revision) relied on the views of several American scholars, but none more prominently than Stanley Kurtz, a research fellow at Stanford University's Hoover Institution on War, Revolution, and Peace. On June 19, 2003, Kurtz presented a statement of testimony on Area Studies before the US House of Representatives' Subcommittee on Select Education. The primary problem of Area Studies in the American academy, according to Kurtz, is its domination by advocates of postcolonial theory – singling out for attack the late Edward Said and his "followers" – whose core premise, allegedly, is that "it is immoral for a scholar to put his knowledge of foreign languages and cultures at the service of American power." For Kurtz, then, foreign language study in the USA had to be canalized to serve the interests, not of national security, but of American (imperial?) power.

In his testimony, Kurtz was particularly incensed against African Studies Programs in American universities that had boycotted funding from another US federal government program, the National Security Education Program (NSEP). Noting how knowledge of Arabic among members of the American intelligence service might have averted the tragedy of September 11, Kurtz considers this boycott of NSEP by African Studies Programs in the USA as a blatant act of treachery that undermines the power and foreign policy concerns of the USA.

The National Security Education Program (NSEP) provides grants to American institutions of higher learning to promote the study of foreign languages and cultures. Yet, from its inception, NSEP has been lodged in the military and intelligence services of the USA. Its own publicity material indicates that the program's "policies and directions are provided by the Secretary of Defense in consultation with the thirteen members National Security Education Board" drawn disproportionately from representatives of federal agencies (including the CIA). When African Studies Centers decided to boycott NSEP funds, therefore, it was out of the fear that the type of clandestine work experienced in Africa during the Cold War probably continues in the post-Cold War dispensation and most certainly in the aftermath of September 11, 2001.

America's post-9/11 concern with issues of language and translation was by no means limited to Arabic and the Middle East. It extended to its wider zone of combat against terrorism. The National Foreign Language Center at the University of Maryland is among institutions receiving US government funding to enhance instruction in "critical" languages for reasons of "security." This expanded zone of language study and translation has included East Africa, bringing the importance of Swahili into focus. The US National Security Education Program (NSEP), for example, has instituted the African Flagship Languages project intended to enhance acquisition and superior proficiency among American students in "critical African languages." The only language that interested institutions must offer in order to qualify for African Flagship Languages grants is, in fact, Swahili.

In sum, then, the study of language came to be seen as part and parcel of the military training necessary for war combat in various spaces in the world. This American militaristic understanding of foreign language training, of language as a weapon of war, is nowhere clearer than in the US Department of Defense's Directive Number 1315.17 of April 28, 2005. According to article 3 of the directive, it is the policy of the Department of Defense that "[t]o achieve national security objectives and success in current and future operations, including the War of Terrorism, the U.S. Armed Forces shall be prepared to conduct military operations in a variety of conditions around the world. The Combatant Commands shall have the requisite war fighting capabilities to achieve success on the non-linear battlefields of the future. These critical war fighting capabilities include foreign language proficiency and detailed knowledge of the regions of the world gained through in-depth study and personal experience" (Department of Defense 2005, 2). It is this logic that came to promote Swahili as the language of American combat in the East African context.

The US Swahili Initiative to Win Hearts and Minds

In time, however, the utility of Swahili in the East African war situation was seen not only in terms of defeating the enemy, but also of winning over the enemy. As Zake Gbotokuma explains:

> The tragic events of Sept. 11 and the global war in terrorism have raised key questions about, and shown the major problems with, American monolingualism. Hunting down terrorists requires more than smart bombs, drones and interpreters. It also requires cultural understanding, communication and public diplomacy, all of which require world language skills, most of which must be integral parts of the curriculum and world-ready education. (2017, 3)

Toward this end, the US government decided to complement the legalistic and security machinery against terrorism with cultural projects that rely on the local lingua franca, Swahili. In particular, the US Embassy in Kenya decided to launch a Swahili journalistic project, *Maisha Amerika, Uislamu Amerika* (Life in America, Islam in America), in a desperate bid to capture the "hearts and minds" of East African Muslims. The inaugural issue of the magazine appeared in January 2002, a few months after the September 11, 2001, attacks in the USA. Many of its essays are Swahili translations of selected news and interpretive items from the *Washington*

File, a product of the Office of International Information Programs of the US Department of State providing official texts of the US government, policy statements, features, and byline articles. Its primary objective seems to be the projection of the USA as a friend of Islam and Muslims within its borders, but also of the Muslim community worldwide.

In addition to translated essays from the *Washington File*, the journal carries a few items written originally in Swahili. These include letters to the editor, Swahili poems, periodic announcements (e.g., of Fulbright scholarships), and periodic competitive essays by high school students on topics predetermined by the Embassy. For example, the essay topic for 2004 was "Kijana Mwislamu wa Kenya anaweza kumweleza nini mwenzake Amerika kuhusu Uislamu Kenya?" (What can a Kenyan Muslim student tell an American student about Islam in Kenya?) (Issue 14, June 2004). All these appear at the end of the journal. A glaring exception is the Swahili poem entitled "Amerika" and composed by Abzein Alawy, essentially singing the praises of the USA, and which opens Issue 13 of May 2004. Interesting as these Swahili compositions are in their own right, however, our focus here will be on the *Washington File* items translated from English.

A number of the essays depict an American Muslim community enjoying the respect of the US government and American society at large. The freedom of expression in the USA has enabled Muslims to establish a successful television channel of their own (No. 20, June 2005) and a Muslim women's journal, *Aziza* (No. 4, April 2002), as well as to televise a successful Arab American show (No. 19, April 2005). In American schools, Muslim students get the opportunity to teach tenets of their faith and culture to their fellow non-Muslim students (No. 20, June 2005), with some aiming to serve as good civilian ambassadors on behalf of the USA (No. 22, March 2006). America is shown to be a tolerant multireligious society: Translated excerpts from Diana L. Eck's 1997 book *A New Religious America* (No. 1, January 2002) and an article by Jeffrey L. Shelter and others that appeared in the *US News and World Report* of May 6, 2002 (No. 5, May 2005), highlight not only the increasingly multireligious composition of American society fostered by recent migrations, but also how this state of diversity thrives on American constitutional provisions of religious rights and freedoms. This image is then buttressed by reports of Muslim visitors to the USA who discover the "truth" about Muslims in the USA, presumably contrary to the false images of a suppressed Muslim minority perpetrated by Al-Qaeda's propaganda machinery.[3] At the same time, the US government does not tolerate any discrimination against people of Muslim and Arab origin.[4] And due to the great respect that the US government has for the religion of Islam, several issues of the periodical report White House events hosting Muslims during Ramadhan and Eid festivities.

The question of American leadership in stimulating democratic transformations in non-European nations is inscribed in almost every issue. Issue No. 15 of August 2004 explicitly lays out, step-by-step, the building blocks for a constitution necessary for establishing democracy in a young nation. The central foreign policy mission of the Bush administration is described as one of promoting democracy and defending freedoms (No. 14, June 2004). Ali Mazrui's interview with the *Washington File* is given special prominence in its Swahili translation in Issue No. 14 of June 2004 partly because he is the most prominent East African scholar with Swahili roots. Long considered a critic of US foreign policy, Mazrui is now quoted as welcoming Bush's "Forward Strategy of Freedom" intended to push democracy in the Arab world, which had been explicated in Issue No. 13 of May 2004. Ultimately, the periodical makes an implicit suggestion that the promotion of an American-style democracy in East Africa would allow the Muslim minorities in the region to enjoy the same rights, freedoms, and privileges that Muslim and other minorities are enjoying in the USA.

Interspersed among these public relations essays are articles on other recurrent themes. There is coverage of America's war on terrorism, which far from being anti-Muslim is framed in a language that gives it the appearance of a Muslim-sensitive and Muslim-friendly project, sometimes with American servicemen providing help to local Muslim communities (e.g., No. 15, August 2004). This is accompanied by updates on

---

[3] See, for example, issues No. 19 of April 2005, No. 21 of 2005, No. 22 of June 2005, and No. 23 of July 2006.

[4] Issue No. 7 of October 2002, for example, carries a story of Muslims applauding the government for suspending a government agent for anti-Muslim remarks, and another of how the Marriott was penalized for discrimination against Arabs.

Afghanistan and Iraq, especially the success of America's reconstructive efforts. Another theme is America's contribution to the fight against the AIDS epidemic, especially within a faith-based framework that seems to enjoy the support of Muslims. Through these types of essay a discourse has been created that even if they do not share the same values, America and Muslims in East Africa at least have common interests and concerns.

The intended audience of East Africans is, of course, both Muslim and Black. At times, therefore, the journal is concerned with projecting an American national image that is inclusive not only of people of other faiths (especially Islam), but also of people of other races (especially Black people). Both Muslim Americans (e.g., Issue 12 of February 2004) and African Americans (e.g., Issue 14 of June 2004), for example, are seen exercising their democratic rights through the ballot box. Both groups are said to have made great gains as electoral constituencies, having developed sufficient confidence in the fairness of the system over the years to turn up in numbers, almost proportional to the White voter turnout, to vote for their preferred political candidates. At the very end of the report on Muslim American voters is a picture of Black Muslim marines saying their prayers on an American naval ship (Issue 12 of February 2004). Democracy is working in America, and both Black people and Muslims are among its great beneficiaries – the one factor that explains their enduring patriotism, ready to die to "defend" America in its war on terrorism.

Interestingly, the prevailing tendency in East Africa to link Arabs and Muslims – and many make no difference between the two – with African enslavement had led to a similar translation attempt by the local Muslim community to (re)claim Islam for Africa. There is, for example, the translation of *Slavery: Islamic and Western Perspectives*, a book authored by Allamah Sayyid Sa'eed Akhtar Rizvi and produced deliberately to coincide with the United Nations Conference on Racism that took place in Durban, South Africa, in August 2001. Translated into Swahili by Salma Shou under the title *Utumwa: Mtazamo wa Kiislamu na wa Nchi za Magharibi* (Rizvi 2005), this translation essentially argues in the same tradition as Sheikh Muhammad Kasim's *Utumwa katika Uislamu na Dini Nyinginezo* (Slavery in Islam and other religions) and seeks to project slavery under Islam as more humane and less commercialized.

More relevant for our purposes, however, is a translation designed to expose East Africans to the life of yet another Diaspora African, one not from the West but from the East. We refer here to the life of Bilal, the emancipated slave of African descent who became one of the early companions of the Prophet Muhammad. The Swahili translation, also by Salman Shou, is entitled *Bilal wa Afrika* (Bilal of Africa) and is based on an English translation, *Bilal of Africa*, of a Persian original by Husayn Malika Ashtiyani (2005). In a sense, the book not only rescues Islam from charges of African enslavement but claims for Islam a foundational African heritage. Whether from the West or the East, therefore, the African Diaspora is sometimes inscribed, through translation, into local discourses of race, domination, and liberation.

Across the border, in Tanzania, the US Embassy also launched its own translation project of essays from the *Washington File*. But while the US Embassy in Kenya produced a quarterly publication, the Embassy in Tanzania maintained online coverage of selected essays on its website, http://tanzania.usembassy.gov/kiswahili_wash_file.html. Again, the selected topics were very similar to those of Kenya: The Swahili *Washington File* articles for 2007, for example, underscore the importance of Africa in the fight against terrorism; America's democratic intentions worldwide; the tripling of the US foreign aid package to Africa under the Bush administration; and its efforts to combat AIDS that reached a historical high point. Partly because women in Africa stand to gain the most from a more open political dispensation, and because women often turn out to vote in great numbers, women and women's organizations are an important "catchment" constituency for the USA. As a result, several essays in both the Tanzanian online *Washington File* Swahili articles and the Kenyan printed journal were devoted to projecting the USA as not only protective of the multiracial population of Muslim women in the USA, but also as a committed advocate of women's rights and freedoms globally. Some issues of *Maisha Amerika/Uislamu Amerika*, in fact, bear cover pictures of Muslim women in hijab (see, e.g., Issues 12 and 13 of 2004). In spite of the fact that the US government continues to have close relations with the regime in Saudi Arabia that has been one of the worst offenders against women today, and in spite of the severe deterioration of the condition and status of women precipitated directly by Bush's war in

Iraq, the selective Swahili translations of the *Washington File* continued to create the image of a principled USA in favor of women's empowerment worldwide.

The title of the journal carries its own story, "Life in America, Islam in America" – creating the impression that the journal is essentially about Muslims in America, and that the Islamic way of life is part of the accepted fabric of American life. The Library of Congress Online Catalog describes the journal's mission as that of highlighting the day-to-day life of Muslims in America. From the title, the innocent reader will naturally expect to find much to learn about the state and conditions of Muslims in the USA. In this (s)he will be greatly disappointed. Several issues of the journal contain not a single item on Muslims in the USA, and those that do will have no more than an average of 10 percent of their content devoted to this theme.

In fact, Muslim life in America is much more a subject of visual translation than linguistic translation. Within its pages, there are very few pictures, but every issue has a picture on its cover page. It is these cover images that suddenly give Islam's presumed oddity and exceptionality in the USA an aura of normative existence. We see Muslims in congregational prayer in New York (Issue 14, June 2004) or preparing for prayer in Lehigh Valley, Pennsylvania (Issue 7, October 2002). There are American Muslim students attending a meeting of the Islamic Society of North America (February 2002 issue) and Muslim and non-Muslim students in a public high school in New Jersey working together in preparation for a class project (Issue 4, April 2002). African American Muslims in the military recurs as an important theme, with the covers of Issue 5 of May 2002 and Issue 21 of October 2005 carrying the picture of the Muslim chaplain of the US Army.

Of particular prominence in this frame of visual translation and representation is the question of Muslim women. Globally, Muslim anger against the West has been predicated in part on the hegemonic imposition of Western cultural values and lifestyles. As expected, the display of the female body has been at the center of Muslim protest, leading many Muslim communities throughout the world to reclaim and sometimes reinvent the *hijab* as a symbol of resistance to what is seen as Western cultural imperialism. It is not surprising therefore that cover pages of several issues of the journal bear images of Muslim women in hijab. Issue 7 of October 2002 depicts a *"hijab* woman" being sworn in at a citizenship ceremony in Texas. As Muslim students in hijab attend the Al-Ghazaly Elementary School in Jersey City, New Jersey (Issue 13, May 2004), their hijab-clad sisters sit at the computer terminals of the US Embassy in Kenya (Issue 23, July 2006), perhaps exploring opportunities to migrate to the USA. And as a *"hijab* woman" in San Francisco explains the importance of Ramadhan to American students (Issue 12, February 2004), Karen Hughes of the US Department of Foreign Affairs is congratulating Ingrid Mattson (in hijab, of course), the Canadian Muslim of White background who was then the president of the Islamic Society of North America (Issue 22, March 2006). In the final analysis, then, if Muslim conservatives in East Africa (and elsewhere) have regarded the female body as a core element of their militant contestation with the West, *Maisha Amerika/Uislamu Amerika* seeks to represent it as a site of potential cooperation: The hijab is as American as it is East African, so the visual claim goes.

Emily Apter has presented a fascinating analysis of how the issue of translation assumed great importance in the aftermath of the September 11 tragedy in the USA. In the wake of the military invasion of Iraq, mistranslation, in particular, became "a concrete particular of the art of war, crucial to strategy and tactics, part and parcel of the way in which images and bodies are read ..." (Apter 2006, 15). Taking war in its wider sense (as in the declared war against terrorism) and with the world as a whole as its zone of operation, then, the Swahili translation project of the US Embassy in Nairobi clearly became an integral part of the US cultural arsenal in East Africa against an elusive enemy.

Local Reactions to the American Initiative

There are definitely people in the Kenya Muslim community who, having read some of the issues of the magazine, developed a new appreciation for the USA. Some interviewees felt that the US government was making greater efforts to reach out to them and understand them than their own Kenyan government. These saw the magazine as yet another attempt by the USA to enter into constructive dialogue with Muslims. Amina Farah, a secretary for the Nairobi City Council, was particularly impressed by the image of the Muslim woman projected by the magazine: "I get the impression that the Muslim woman in hijab *hawi* [is not] disrespected in America – *si kama hapa kwetu* (not like here at home). *Unajua, kama una hijab hapa* (You know, if you have on hijab here), people think you are backward, *huna elimu* (you are uneducated). *Mara nyingi tunadiscriminatiwa katika kazi* (We are often discriminated against at work). *Si kama Amerika* (Not as in America)" (Personal interview, February 27, 2008). Clearly, then, the magazine made some successes in creating a positive impression of the USA, especially in its treatment of its Muslim population after 9/11.

These positive responses are partly triggered by popular Muslim perceptions, as indicated earlier, that Muslims in Kenya have long been treated like second-class citizens. As Ali Mazrui once argued with regard to Muslims of the Kenya coast:

> As someone who comes from the Kenya coast, I have seen over the years the wealth of the coast passing from Coastal hands of the 'upcountry [Christian] citizens' with tribal connections in the central government in Nairobi. Under both President Jomo Kenyatta and President Daniel arap Moi the coast has been, quite literally, looted by non-coastal Kenyans. Who owns the best land at the coast? Who runs the best hotels? Who controls the tourist industry at the coast? Who enjoys the best jobs? Even a relatively superficial scrutiny will soon reveal the overwhelming domination of non-coastal names. (Mazrui 1993, 3–4)

In Kenya, Muslims have felt marginalized economically and politically, and have experienced unequal access to educational opportunities and to government means of mass communication. This local condition is one that the American Embassy seems to have understood and to have used, indirectly and in some cases successfully, to project a different image of Muslims in the USA.

On the other hand, like the East African response to the early Swahili translation of European literary classics, much of the East African Muslim response to *Maisha Amerika/Uislamu Amerika* was predominantly resistance through rejection. A particularly scathing attack against the magazine came from Sheikh Mohamed Idris during a lecture at Sakina Mosque on March 28, 2008. Sheikh Idris wanted to warn his audience against what appeared as friendly American overtures toward the coastal Muslims of Kenya. He revealed that the American Embassy in Nairobi had been busy trying to reach out to Muslim leaders supposedly to foster dialogue with them toward a better understanding and healthier relationship between the American government and Muslim peoples of Africa. Sheikh Idris was very suspicious of this American initiative, calling it "kukumbatiwa na satu" (a python's embrace), not an act of love but of homicide through strangulation, and a certain kiss of death, "kama kuumwa na nyoka, auma akivivia" (like the bite of a snake), biting and blowing [so that one does not feel the pain] at the same time.

Ironically the above is the same Sheikh Idris who was fatally gunned down in Mombasa in the early morning hours of June 10, 2014, allegedly by Muslim extremist youth linked to Al-Shabaab. At the time of his assassination, he was the chairperson of the Council of Imams and Preachers of Mombasa, a body that had been repeatedly threatened by an unknown body of Muslim youth in Mombasa for opposing its militant agenda. For years, however, Sheikh Idris was regarded as a radical cleric who inadvertently turned the mosque he was heading, the Sakina Mosque in Mombasa, into a hotbed of Islamic radicalism. His own views at that time were also anti-imperialist and reflected a strong opposition to American interventionism in the Muslim world. The metaphors he uses of the serpent and the snake captured his own position at the time of how the role of America in Muslim world affairs was gradually suffocating and poisoning the Muslim organism.

Sheikh Idris then singled out the magazine, *Maisha Amerika/Uislamu Amerika*, describing it as a patchwork of lies intended to hoodwink "us" into believing that the US government loves Muslims:

Twajua namna ndugu zetu Islamu wapatavyo taabu huko tokomezoni, huko Amerika. Wewe ukiingia tu ... maadamu una jina la Kiislamu utasumbuliwa kwa hili na hili. Munfahamu? Wengine wangapi wanshikwa bwana, wafungiwa ... walilolifanya halijulikani. Naam. Munfahamu? Huwaje basi leo wakaja humu makwetu wakitudanganya ... ati watutakia mema, ati wataka kutusaidia. Huja wakatuenezea hicho kigazeti chao ... mushakiona sio? ... porojo tupu, wataka tutezea kiini mato. Munfahamu? Ukikisoma utafikiri ndugu zetu waishi kwenye nti ya manna-wa-ssalwa. Sisi si wapumbavu bwana! Munfahamu? Ala! Si wapumbavu hata kidogo! Kama wataka mema si kuwafanyia haki hao ndugu zetu walioko huko, bwana. Jambo la kusikitisha—tena yasikitisha sana–wanwateka ndugu zetu wengine wakiwatumia kutuwekea sumu hii. Kigazeti hichi nsumu, bwana. Naam. Kikulacho ki nguoni mwako bwana! Munfahamu?

We know how our Muslim brothers and sisters are suffering there in the wilderness, there in America. The moment you step ... as long as you have a Muslim name you will be harassed for this and that. Do you understand? How many of them have been arrested, imprisoned ... the offence they committed is unknown. Yes. Do you understand? So how is it today that they come to our homes deceiving us ... pretending they wish well for us, pretending they wish to assist us. They come distributing their little magazine ... you have seen it, haven't you ... just nonsense, wishing to do magic tricks. Do you understand? When you read you would think our brother and sisters are living in a land of milk-and- honey. We are not so stupid, man! You understand? Gee, not stupid at all! If they wish us well, why don't they act justly to our brothers and sisters who are there, man. The sad thing is–and it is very sad indeed–they have attracted some of our own people, using them to implant this poison. This little magazine is poison, man! Yes. What bites you is in your clothes, man! You understand?

The position of Sheikh Idris on the persecution of Muslims in the USA is one that was and continues to be popular in East Africa. Each time Alamin Mazrui has gone to Kenya over the last decade or so, for example, this has been a recurrent subject of discussion with relatives and friends, who often wonder how life is for Muslim people like him in the USA. It is partly these views that the magazine was established to change. Yet, from the words of Sheikh Idris, the appearance of the magazine had only intensified Muslim suspicion of American intentions. He referred to the magazine as *kigazeti* (little magazine), using a diminutive form, not to refer to its size – as the size of the publication was by no means small by Swahili standards – but to underrate the value and significance of its content. This reading conforms with another designation that the Sheikh invoked – that of *porojo* (nonsense). On the other hand, as insignificant as it may be deemed to have been, the *kigazeti* ironically was seen to be potentially poisonous for the Muslim body politic. And the greatest danger of this poison was its ability to create disunity among Muslims, with some captured to work for the American agenda rather than for the welfare of the Muslim community. "Kikulacho kinguoni mwako" is a Swahili saying suggesting that sometimes those who can cause you greatest harm are precisely those who are closest to you – your siblings and relatives, your brothers and sisters in Islam – who, in this case, had supposedly aligned themselves with American interests rather than with the welfare of their own people.

Elsewhere in his address Sheikh Idrisa counseled his congregation to boycott the magazine:

> *Najua kwamba wengine wenu hamjakisikia kamwe kigazeti hichi. Lakini mkikiskia msikisome bwana. Najua Mtume wetu sallallahu alayhi wassallamu antwambia 'twalabal'ilmu walau kaana fi sswin.' Lakini yaliyomo humu si ilmu bwana; ni porojo ya sumu tu. Na ni muhimu sana wafahamu kwamba hata wakaifitaje nia yao idhahiri kwetu – hatutaki kushirikiana nao, hatutaaaaki! Ni madhambi kamwe! Munfahamu?*

> I know some of you have not even heard of this little magazine. But if you do hear of it, do not bother to read it. I know our Prophet may peace and blessings of Allah be on him has told us 'Search for knowledge even if it be in China.' But what is in here is not education at all; it is just poisonous nonsense. And it is very important that they understand no matter how much they try to hide it, their intention is manifest to us… We do not want to cooperate with them; we do not want to do so at all! It is even a sin [to cooperate with them]. You understand?

Realizing that Islam encourages the faithful to take a keen interest in education of various kinds wherever they can find it, Sheikh Idris tried to delegitimize the *kigazeti* as providing content that falls outside the scope of what could be considered of educational value. He then proceeded to discourage his audience from reading the *kigazeti*, for to do so becomes sinful precisely because of its divisive potential.

There were also instances in which the publication was read very closely, not because of any enlightenment that the readers were seeking, but with a view to understanding the kind of textual selections that the

USA made in its bid to penetrate and influence the East African Muslim mind. This tendency was particularly prominent among followers of the Khilafah group of political Islam that had emerged in the region partly as a consequence of the post-Cold War, neoliberal phase of globalization. This group had a few young but very studious members, primarily operating in Kenya at that time, who were opposed to "democracy" and believed in the supremacy of the Islamic political system to which, in their opinion, it was the duty of every Muslim to aspire. They even discouraged Muslims from voting during elections. The members of this group studied the publication closely for two reasons, one defensive and the other offensive. The defensive motive had to do with how best to prepare local Muslims to resist American cultural and intellectual infiltration; the offensive motive was based on the expectation that understanding the American insurgency mind revealed in the magazine would help in devising strategies of counter-penetrating the USA with the Islamic message.

In sum, then, the analysis here demonstrates how the US foreign language "policy," the launching of the magazine *Maisha Amerika/Uislamu Amerika*, and the selection of its texts and visuals enact particular significations that answer to the condition of war (on terrorism). On average, the local response to this US media initiative in Swahili was a hostile one, often amounting to a rejection of its alleged aims and mission. In a sense, the kind of response that the magazine elicited locally corresponds to the same condition of war that led to its establishment in the first place. To the extent to which the translation project was a component of the arsenal of war (on terrorism), it became a weapon that, galvanized to maximum effect, took for granted the idea that mistranslation is part of a legitimate strategy in a time of war. And if a state of war is partly a manifestation of irreconcilable differences, it embeds a condition of non-translatability, a condition in which we can often expect translation failure. The rejection of the magazine was demonstrative of that failure in the Swahili translation project of the US Embassy in Kenya. Under the circumstances, its death was a foregone conclusion.

References

Adika Kevogo, Stanley, and Alex Umbima Kevogo. 2014. Swahili Military Terminology: A Case of an Evolving Non-Institutionalized Language Standard. *Research on Humanities and Social Sciences* 4 (21): 176–193.
Al-Bulushi, Samar. 2020. Making Sense of the East African Warscape. *Africa and the Middle East: Beyond the Divides* 40: 41–44.
Anna, Cara 2022. Study: Facebook Fails to Catch East Africa Extremist Content. *AP News*, June 15, 2022. https://apnews.com/article/islamic-state-group-2022-midterm-elections-technology-politics-religion-1031f90a8956eb3feb6c6fb5283003f9.
Anzalone, Christopher. 2012. Kenya Muslim Youth Center and Al-Shabab's East African Recruitment. *CTC Sentinel* 5 (10): 9–13.
Apter, Emily. 2006. *The Translation Zone: A New Comparative Literature*. Princeton, NJ: Princeton University Press.
Aronson, Samuel L. 2013. Kenya and the Global War on Terror: Neglecting History and Geopolitics in Approaches to Counterterrorism. *African Journal of Criminology and Justice Studies* 7 (1–2): 24–34.
Aziz, Sahar. 2021. *The Racial Muslim: When Racism Quashes Religious Freedom*. Los Angeles: University of California Press.
Bradbury, M., and M. Kleinman 2010. Winning Hearts and Minds? Examining the Relationship Between Aid and Security in Kenya. Medford, MA: Feinstein International Centre. http://fic.tufts.edu/assets/WinningHearts-in-Kenya.pdf.
Brooke, James. 1995. Attacks on U.S. Muslims Surge Even as Their Faith Takes Hold. *The New York Times*, August 28, 1995. Web.
Chabon, Michael, and Ayelet Waldman. 2017. *Kingdom of Olives and Ash: Writers Confront the Occupation*. New York: Harper Perennial.
Chande, Abdin. 2000. Radicalism and Reform in East Africa. In *The History of Islam in Africa*, ed. Nehemia Levtzion and Randall L. Pouwels, 349–369. Athens: Ohio University Press.
Chesworth, John. 2006. Fundamentalism and Outreach Strategies in East Africa: Christian Evangelism and Muslim Da'wa. In *Muslim-Christian Encounters in Africa*, ed. Benjamin F. Soares, 159–186. Leiden: Brill.
Davis, John. 2007. Introduction: Africa's Road to the War on Terror. In *Africa and the War on Terrorism*, ed. John Davis, 1–16. Burlington, VT: Ashgate.
Department of Defense. 2005. SUBJECT: Military Department Foreign Area Officer (FAO) Programs. Directive Number 1315.17, April 28, 2005.

El Ouassif, Ama, and Seleman Yusuph Kitenge. 2021. *Terrorist Insurgency in Northern Mozambique: Context, Analysis, and Spillover Effects on Tanzania.* Policy Paper. Rabat, Morocco: Policy Center for the New South.

Gbotokuma, Zekeh. 2017. World Language Skills Matter for U.S. National Security. *Baltimore Sun,* September 12, 2017.

Goldsmith, Paul. 2011. *The Mombasa Republican Council Conflict Assessment: Threats and Opportunities in Engagement.* Financed by USAID. Nairobi: Kenya Civil Society Strengthening Programme.

Henderson, Brent. 2011. *When an Endangered Language Goes Global: Documenting Chimiini.* Gainesville: University of Florida Center for African Studies Research Reports.

Hoffman, T. 2014. *Al-Qaeda Declares War: The African Embassy Bombings and America's Search for Justice.* Lebanon, NH: University Press of New England.

Human Rights Watch. 2013. World Report 2013: Kenya. https://www.hrw.org/world-report/2013/country-chapters/kenya.

Jackson, Sherman A. 2011. Muslims, Islam(s), Race and American Islamophobia. In *Islamophobia: The Challenge of Pluralism in the 21st Century,* ed. John Esposito and Ibrahim Kalin, 93–103. New York: Oxford University Press.

Kelley, Kevin. 2012. Kadhi Courts Focus of US Groups' Opposition to New Kenya Law. *Daily Nation* (Nairobi), July 12, 2012.

Kumar, Deepa. 2010. Framing Islam: The Resurgence of Orientalism During the Bush II Era. *Journal of Communication Inquiry* 34 (3): 254–277.

Kresse, Kai. 2009. Knowledge and Intellectual Practice in a Swahili Context: 'Wisdom' and the Social Dimensions of Knowledge. *Africa: Journal of the International African Institute* 79 (1): 148–167. Special issue on *Knowledge in Practice: Expertise and the Transmission of Knowledge,* edited by K. Kresse and T. Marchand.

Kurtz, S. 2003. Statement of Stanley Kurtz Before the Subcommittee on Select Education. Committee on Education and the Workforce, US House of Representatives. http://www.house.gov/ed_workforce/hearings/108th/sed/titlevi61903/kuttz.htm. May 20, 2006.

Mazrui, Ali A. 1993. The Black Intifadah? Religion and Rage at the Kenya Coast. *Journal of Asian and African Affairs* 4 (2): 87–93.

Mazrui, Alamin, and Ibrahim Shariff. 1994. *The Swahili: Idiom and Identity.* Trenton, NJ: Africa World Press.

McConnell, Tristan. 2013. Who Is Al Shabaab Leader Ahmed Godane? *The World,* October 1, 2013. https://theworld.org/stories/2013-10-01/who-al-shabaab-leader-ahmed-godane.

Mogire, Edward, and Kennedy Mkutu Agade. 2011. Counter-Terrorism in Kenya. *Journal of Contemporary African Studies* 29 (4): 473–491.

Moi, Damiel Arap. 1986. *Kenya African Nationalism: Nyayo Philosophy and Principles.* Nairobi: Macmillan.

Nzes, Fredric. 2012. Terrorist Attacks in Kenya Reveal Domestic Radicalization. *CTC Sentinel* 5 (10): 13–15.

Okullu, Bisho H. 1992. Church, State and Society in East Africa. In *Thirty Years of Independence in Africa: The Last Decade*, ed. Peter Anyang Nyong'o, 25–35. Nairobi: Academy Science Publisher.

Prestholdt, Jeremy. 2011. Kenya, the United States, and Counterterrorism. *Africa Today* 57 (4): 2–27.

Republic of Kenya. 2008. *Report of the Presidential Special Action Committee to Address Specific Concerns of the Muslim Community in Regard to Alleged Harassment and/or Discrimination in the Application/Enforcement of the Law.* Presented to His Excellency Hon. Mwai Kibaki on March 31, 2008.

Rizvi, Allamah Sayyid Sa'eed Akhtar. 2005. *Utumwa: Mtazamo wa Kiislam, u na wa Nchi za Magharibi.* Translated by Salma Shoul. Dar es Salaam: Al-Itrah Foundation.

Rubin, Barry, and Judith C. Rubin, eds. 2002. *Anti-American Terrorism and the Middle East: A Documentary Reader.* Oxford: Oxford University Press.

Said, Edward. 1997. *Covering Islam: How the Media and the Experts Determine How We See the Rest of the World.* New York: Vintage.

Schmitt, Richard B. 2005. Translation Capacity Still Spotty After 9/11. *Los Angeles Times*, A4, May 1, 2005.

van Rentergem, Tom. 2022. Al-Shabab in Mozambique: Taking Stock of an Insurgency Under Cover. *Egmont Policy Brief 281.* https://www.egmontinstitute.be/app/uploads/2022/06/PB-281-Tom-VR_Al-Shabab-in-Mozambique.pdf?type=pdf. Accessed October 20, 2022.

8

Conclusion

Alamin Mazrui

The relationship between war and language can be viewed from many angles, and the chapters in this book have attempted to provide one reading of a particular dimension of the war history of the Swahili language. We look at its roles and functions in conflict situations, its uses and abuses by different warring parties, and, as significantly, the impact of war on the destiny of the language. Beginning with the Maji Maji war against German rule in the first decade of the twentieth century and culminating in the ongoing war on terrorism in East Africa in the twenty-first century, Swahili's functions in theaters of war have been both organizational and inspirational and, through written and electronic media, it has sometimes been galvanized for propaganda purposes. It has served the interests of colonizers and imperial powers as much as those of African military and political combatants seeking liberation from both external and internal tyranny. Taken together, the war experiences of Swahili provide another affirmation that language is a malleable tool that can be used, configured and reconfigured, by different constituencies to serve different ends.

As many of the chapters here demonstrate, Swahili played a crucial role in and often made significant gains directly or indirectly from conditions of war, sometimes contributing to its geographic, demographic, and even lexical expansion. But what has been Swahili's role in postwar situations? As indicated in the Introduction, initially Swahili was linked with Islam and Muslim culture and identity. This lingua-religious association and the roles that Swahili-speaking Muslims might have played in specific contexts may have triggered East African conversion to Islam in the aftermath of the Maji Maji war, as indicated in Chap. 2, and following the triumph of the Rwandan Patriotic Front in Rwanda, as shown in Chap. 5.

In time, however, while Swahili continues to manifest some influences of Islam, it is no longer associated exclusively with Islam, Muslims, and Muslim culture. The language has undergone a complete metamorphosis in this regard. By the end of the European colonial period in East Africa, it had become fully sacralized, serving Muslim as well as Christian religious functions, in Muslim Friday sermons and Christian Sunday services, and was well on its way to seculiarization (Mazrui and Zirimu 1990). As it evolved over time, then, might Swahili as an interfaith medium have been one of the mitigating factors against a full-blown Christian-Muslim conflict in East Africa in spite of external extremist interventions from various sources? This certainly seems to be the argument of Fresto Mkenda, who maintains that the "East African context, especially as marked by Kiswahili, manifests relative facility for multiple religions. We saw a language that grew because of new encounters and was adjusted to accommodate diversity, giving the lie to pessimistic predictions of inevitable clash when different 'civilizations' meet" (2011, 9). It is widely understood, of course, that language can sometimes be a cause for conflict. If Mkenda is right in his analysis, however, Swahili is a case of a language that might have contributed to the prevention of conflict.

The period from the end of World War I until the end of colonialism in East Africa in the 1960s was dominated by British presence and especially British settlers in the Kenya Colony. Throughout this time, some British officers, missionaries, and settlers learned the Swahili language quite well. At the same time, a settler variety of Swahili emerged, as did one associated with the King's African Rifles. Swahili, in its reconstructed varieties, became an indispensable instrument of domination. As much as they relied on the language to maintain the colonial order, however, the British had condescending attitudes toward it, seeing it as the medium

8 Conclusion

of one of the less civilized portions of humanity. Decades later, however, the use of Swahili among descendants of British settlers seems to be less of an attempt to mark social distance from Africans and, in contrast, an attempt to signal an African dimension of their identity, some priding "themselves on their Kiswahili abilities and say[ing] it is their language of 'connections' to Afro-Kenyans" (McIntosh 2014, 1165). From a cultural weapon of war that was contested along racial lines between the White colonizer and the Black colonized, Swahili now became a potential space for redefining citizenship and belonging in transracial terms.

Some of the countries of the Great Lakes region discussed in Chap. 5 also provide examples of the role of Swahili in postwar reconstruction efforts. From the eve of Uganda's independence to the end of the Obote II period, Swahili was one of the features that marked a division between the predominantly Nilotic north and the predominantly Bantu south. The National Resistance Army's "bush war" and its subsequent victory were partly facilitated by a Bantu embrace of Swahili in spite of residual hostility toward the language by some members of the Baganda community. Swahili experienced a demographic expansion to the south without losing its foothold in the north. In effect, it became a language that carried the potential to reduce the gap in the north–south divide. It was partly this new position of Swahili in Uganda that made it possible for the government to eventually adopt it, in addition to English, as a co-official language of the country in July 2022.

Chapter 5 also traced similar developments of the Swahili language as an integrative agent in Rwanda and Burundi. If the rapid growth of Swahili in Rwanda can be attributed, in part, to the Rwandan Patriotic Front that was once dominated by Tutsi refugees from Uganda, it is Hutu returnees from Tanzanian refugee camps that helped the growth of the language in Burundi. In both countries, then, Swahili is helping in mitigating against some of the negative effects of "othering" arising from the colonial construction of the Hutu–Tutsi divide, and, especially in Rwanda, it has been an important medium for the transmission of narratives that seek to reimagine and reconstruct the nation. This same potential of Swahili to foster transethnic integration is also evident in the Congo, though to a lesser extent, as discussed in Chap. 5.

The question arises as to whether more recent political developments in places like Uganda and Rwanda may undermine the progress of Swahili in these countries. We may remember that the dictatorship of Milton Obote and Idi Amin Dada in Uganda was one of the factors that made Swahili, then associated with northern domination, unpopular among sections of Bantu-speaking communities in the south. Yoweri Museveni came to power under the banner of liberation and a new, united, and democratic Uganda, as did Paul Kagame in Rwanda. Museveni has been in office since 1986 and Kagame since 2000. Over the years, both leaders have turned increasingly dictatorial and ready to employ unlawful means to muzzle descent. How might this unfolding reality affect the destiny of Swahili in Uganda and Rwanda? Or has the language gained its own social momentum to a point where it is no longer associated with the regimes in power? Only time will tell.

South Sudan is one country where Swahili is slowly taking root even though the language did not feature in either its war of succession or its subsequent civil war that erupted in 2013 between forces loyal to President Salva Kiir Mayardit and those of his former deputy, Riek Machar. Many political leaders of the Sudanese People's Liberation Movement lived in Kenya and had their children educated in the Kenyan school system where Swahili was a mandatory subject. In the meantime, the post-independence civil war led to a sustained flow of Southern Sudanese refugees into Kenya, many of whom acquired some Swahili either informally at the marketplace or formally in a school environment. All these conditions helped give Swahili some visibility in South Sudan. As significant, perhaps, Swahili became important because of the role that Kenya played in facilitating discussions that led to the Comprehensive Peace Agreement of 2005 that prepared the way for the autonomy of South Sudan and in establishing a new government system in South Sudan. In time, many Kenyan citizens moved to and established businesses in South Sudan and several Kenyan firms started investing in the country. All these interchanges had the effect of increasing the presence of Swahili in South Sudan.

The growing consolidation of Swahili in each of these individual countries, however, was also due to the expansion of the East African Community resulting from additional members – including Rwanda,

Burundi, South Sudan, and the Congo – emerging from conditions of war. As also indicated in Chap. 5, with Swahili as an important linguistic attribute of the Community's identity, member states have been stimulated to demonstrate the will to promote the language within their own borders. As much as the EAC is helping promote the Swahili language, however, the Community itself might be more sustainable today because of postwar conditions that have emerged in the Great Lakes region. As a result of the wars, there has been an intense degree of cross-border interaction that has led to a certain amount of cultural and linguistic sharing, including the greater consolidation of Swahili as a lingua franca. But before we can fully understand the importance of Swahili for East African integration, we must assess the significance of culture as a whole for regional unification.

For a number of years, Kenya, Tanzania, and Uganda pursued the principles of economic cooperation and common market under the umbrella of the East African Community. This cooperative endeavor, however, began experiencing tensions not too long after its formation, partly because of the pull of national self-interest in a climate of deteriorating economic conditions. These tensions were later exacerbated by an increasing deterioration of political relations between Idi Amin's Uganda and Julius Nyerere's Tanzania, the two nations that later had a military confrontation. The Community finally collapsed in 1977 after Tanzania took the dramatic decision to close its borders with Kenya, complaining that capitalist Kenya was reaping more benefits. But, in fact, is it possible that the Community's instability and its final break-up had much deeper cultural roots?

In terms of what happened at this time in East Africa, it is worth interpreting the experience of Western European countries in a comparative perspective and deriving from this an understanding of the sequence of integration. There is first the fact of imposed hegemony, which, in the case of Europe, ranged from the Roman Empire to the more diffuse Holy Roman Empire and into Hitler's attempts to create a new German hegemony on the continent. Partly out of imposed hegemony and general interaction among European peoples, some cultural convergence took place, resulting in a broadly defined Western culture. Cultural integration in Europe's case was therefore the second major step toward general continental unification. It was out of this cultural convergence that Europeans regarded themselves as European and sought to give expression to this collective identity in a new modern economic community.

Our thesis here is that there had been inadequate cultural unification, in the sense of a shared universe of values and predispositions, a shared approach to the definition of interests, a shared book of rules of the game, and the limits of competition. The East African Community started with a larger structure of economic unification than the cultural foundation could support. But since 1977, a process of cultural convergence has been under way regardless of the collapse of the Community. In particular, there has been a maturing of national consciousness that has implied a greater similarity of outlook in spite of differences in ideological rhetoric. Kenyanism, Ugandanuism, and Tanzanian nationalism are much more real forces from the point of view of East African integration than the official ideologies that each of these countries seeks to pursue. Because of its role in transethnic communication, Swahili has been at the center of this growth of national consciousness in the individual countries.

National consciousness, however, has two stages – the stage of inner orientation with an obsession for protecting narrow national interests, and the stage of outer orientation when national interests are defined partly in transnational terms. For a long time, East Africa was in the agonies of the first stage. In the aftermath of the civil war in Uganda and the wars of the Great Lakes region, in general, however, an outer-oriented nationalism seems to have developed in tandem with the inner-oriented nationalism. The conditions of the various wars and their aftermath in all the countries that constitute the new East African Community have contributed to a tremendous increase and flux in human traffic in the region as a whole. The polarization that once existed among some of these nations due to forces of economic nationalism and within some of the countries between capitalist-leaning and socialist-leading parties seems to have capitulated to the dictates of economic and political liberalism. All these postwar developments have combined to foster convergence at the level of culture, especially in economic and political values, with Swahili as an important facilitator of the process.

The increasing state of cultural convergence in the greater Eastern African region is likely to make the new East African Community, reconstituted in 2000, more viable and more sustainable than the Community that collapsed in 1977. Through one of its primary institutions, the East African Kiswahili Commission, the Community seeks to widen the space and increase the potential for regional integration. And as the scope of integration continues to widen, broadening the space for economic exchange, both formal and informal, and leading to further cultural convergence, we may be entering an era of reduced civil and interstate wars among members of the East African Community. As lamentable as the wars of the Great Lakes region were, therefore, they may have contributed to the emergence of a new, outer-oriented reality that could result in a shrinkage of the space of war partly because the room for peaceful conflict resolution has been widened by the new dispensation of more shared political and economic values.

The East African Community faced a new challenge in 2022 when M23, the March 23 Congolese rebel group, launched a fresh attack, threatening to take much of the eastern part of the Democratic Republic of the Congo and possibly sparking wider regional tensions. This development prompted the East African Community to mobilize a large regional force to intervene in the DRC with peacekeeping and conflict resolution as its primary objective. In the process, the East African Community exercised authority over the regional military force while initiating and leading a political dialogue between the warring parties. While the outcome of the talks has been uncertain and the state of war in the country continues to unfold in yet unpredictable ways, the presence of a predominantly Swahili-speaking regional force and the role that the Community has been playing in the DRC are likely to help in the consolidation of Swahili.

At the global level, there are the continuing tensions between the USA and Russia that have recently been accentuated by the Russia-Ukraine War precipitated by the Russian invasion of Ukraine in February 2022. Several African countries resisted US pressure to condemn Russia and instead elected to remain neutral. The East African Community even released a statement calling for a ceasefire and encouraging both parties to seek an amicable settlement through existing international avenues of conflict resolution. This seeming neutrality of the East African Community is essentially to the benefit of Russia at a time when Russia feels increasingly isolated in the international arena. As a result, Russia has been engaged in new efforts to strengthen its diplomatic relations with several African countries. What is yet to be seen is whether this new Russian interest in Africa will lead to greater interest in understanding Africa through its own languages, including the EAC language, Swahili. Will the study of Swahili in Russian universities, for example, benefit in the aftermath of the Ukraine war?

In the meantime, the White House released a new policy statement in August 2022 on *U.S. Strategy Toward Sub-Saharan Africa*. While the document faults both Russian and Chinese approaches to and interests in Africa, it is clear that its primary goal is to undermine the Chinese presence and economic edge on the continent. This counter-China strategy was also behind the US-Africa Leaders Summit that took place in Washington DC in December 2022 followed by visits to various African countries by Jill Biden, the First Lady, Anthony Blinken, the Secretary of State, and US Vice-President Kamala Harris. All this comes at a time when trade between China and Africa has grown to over 254 billion dollars in 2021, while trade between the USA and Africa has declined dramatically, dropping from 142 billion dollars in 2008 to a mere 64 billion by 2021 (Zeleza 2022). In spite of this intensifying economic cold war between the USA and China, however, neither the US government nor the American corporate world seems stimulated yet to promote seriously the study of Swahili and other African languages in the US academy. This American response contrasts sharply with that of China where the study of Swahili appears to be expanding.

What is clear is that the government of the USA is often ready to invest in the study of Swahili and languages of other nations when the goal is the globalization of its politico-economic ideology – either to promote or defend that ideology, as was the case in its Cold War with the Soviet Union. However, the American state now seems persuaded by Francis Fukuyama's conclusion in *The End of History and the Last Man* that the world has experienced not only the end of the Cold War, but the triumph of "Western liberal democracy as a final form of human government" on a global scale (1992, 5). In other words, the grand ideological war is over. At the same time, given the predominance of the private sector in its economy, its faith in the globalizing power of its economic engine, and the global presence of the English language, the USA has felt little pressure to encourage its citizens to study other languages of the world, including Swahili.

As indicated in Chap. 7, however, the end of the ideological Cold War with the Soviet Union made room for yet another ideological conflict, the conflict between the West and Islam. One dimension of this conflict has taken the form of terrorism and the war on terrorism with Eastern Africa as one of its theaters of operation. The full implications of this war in the countries of Eastern Africa as they relate to the Swahili language specifically continue to unfold in uncertain ways. In the USA, in the meantime, the Department of State and the Department of Defense continue to provide some financial support for the study of languages deemed critical to the country's national security, especially in relation to the war on terrorism. Swahili continues to be the only language of Africa south of the Sahara that appears on the USA's list of critical languages.

Finally, in several chapters of the book we paid attention to the interplay between war and literature. We highlighted the inspirational function of Swahili songs as a genre of Swahili oral literature in the two world wars as well as in Uganda's "bush war" when the National Resistance Army was fighting the Obote II regime. But Swahili literature has also played an important role in recuperating war memories in postwar periods – as Boubacar Boris Diop does in French in the case of the Rwandan genocide of 1994 in his *Murambi: Le Livre des ossements* (Murambi: The Book of Bones). Furthermore, in cases like those of the Maji Maji war and Mau Mau war, Swahili literature has been an important platform for providing anti-hegemonic and counter-imperial narratives of war experiences. But even as the collective and transgenerational trauma of wars meanders on in the river of time, Swahili has demonstrated its tremendous potential to open up new literary and political spaces for reconstituting and reimagining African realities toward a new and better tomorrow.

References

Fukuyama, Francis. 1992. *The End of History and the Last Man*. New York and Toronto: Free Press and Maxwell McMillan Canada.

Mazrui, Ali A., and Pio Zirimu. 1990. Secularization of an Afro-Islamic Language: Church, State and Marketplace in the Spread of Kiswahili. *Journal of Islamic Studies* 1: 24–53.

McIntosh, Janet. 2014. Linguistic Atonement: Penitence and Privilege in White Kenyan Language Ideologies. *Anthropological Quarterly* 87 (4): 1165–1199.

Mkenda, Festo. 2011. Tensions, Threats, and a Nation's Weakest Link: Muslim-Christian Relations and the Future of Peace in Tanzania. https://www.academic.edu/7076562/Tension_Threats_and_a_Nation_s_Weakest_Link_Muslim_Christian_Relations_and_the_Future_of_Peace_in_Tanzania. Accessed October 1, 2022.

Zeleza, Paul Tiyambe. 2022. Africa's Trajectory in the 21st Century: From a Historic Pawn into a Player. Inaugural Keynote Address, Celebrate Africa, University of Pittsburgh, September 6, 2022.

Index

A

Abdallah, Mwalimu Hussein Bashir, 49
  Jihadi Kuu ya Maji Maji, 49
Abdulaziz, Mohamed, 17, 42
Achebe, Chinua, 21
  Things Fall Apart, 21
Acholi, 72, 74, 99, 120
African Americans, 164–168, 174, 202
African Diaspora, 24, 203
African elite, 10, 109
African "ethnic" languages, 58
African intelligentsia, 10
Africanity, 165, 167
African migrant workers, 10
African nationalism, 9, 19, 99, 108
Afrikaans, 15
Afro-Asian interaction, 4
Afro-Asiatic, 129
Afro-Islamic identity, 5
Ajami, 21, 41, 93, 95, 96
Akida, 38, 44–46
Al-Inkishafi, 84
Al-Qa'ida, 191, 192
Al-Shabaab, 25, 183, 187, 188, 190–194, 207
American Central Intelligence Agency, 151
American Patriot Act, 180
Anglicization, 132
Anglophone, 12, 15, 139
Animal Farm, 155–157, 162, 163
An-Najah, 95
Annan, Kofi, 161
Anti-Americanism, 182
Anti-Zionism, 182

Arabic, 2, 3, 5, 21, 30, 40–42, 45, 54, 60, 71, 77, 93–96, 106, 156, 183, 192, 197, 198
Arabic script, 30, 35, 41, 93
Arabo-Islamic, 5, 7, 96
Arusha Declaration, 43, 141, 148
Askari [soldier], 59, 69, 80
Athumani, Mwengo wa, 19
   Chuo cha Herekali/Utenzi wa Tambuka, 19
Attwood, William, 150
   The Reds and the Blacks, 150

B

Babu, Abdulrahman, 150
Baganda, 10, 74, 98, 108, 109, 119, 128, 217
Bangladesh Liberation War, 18
Banyamulenge, 138, 139
Barre, Mohamed Siad, 189
Belgian administration, 61
Belgian colonial administration, 62
Belgian Congo, 8, 22, 60, 62
Belgian Trusteeship, 128
Bembe, 139
Berlin Conference, 31
Bismarck, Otto von, 31, 32
Bizimungu, Pasteur, 131
Black internationalism, 163, 164
Black Panther Party, 163–165
Black Power movement, 24, 147, 163–166
Black Radical Congress, 167
Boko Haram, 194
British colonial rule, 104, 148, 190
British East Africa, 22, 59, 66, 68
British imperial history, 89

Buganda Kingdom, 108, 119
Al-Buhry, Hemed Abdallah, 19, 33, 34
   Utenzi wa Vita vya Wadachi Kutamalaki Mrima, 19, 33, 52
Bunia Swahili, 140
Burundi, 3, 6, 9, 60, 117, 118, 128–136, 141–144, 217, 219
Bush, George W. (President), 179, 187, 201, 203
Buttner, Reverend C., 30

C

Cham, Haji, 19
   Utenzi wa Vita vya Uhud, 19
Christian Evangelism, 184
Christianity, 8, 9, 30, 37, 39, 40, 92–95, 183
Christian missionaries, 8, 30, 71, 90, 98
Civil wars, 14, 18, 20, 23, 117, 125, 134, 151, 189, 218, 220
Cold War, 2, 24, 136, 147–175, 197, 198, 222
Collective identity, 132, 143, 220
Colonialism, 6, 11, 16, 20, 23, 29, 37, 39, 43, 44, 47, 49, 51, 60, 62, 90, 93, 95, 97, 99, 100, 103, 104, 108, 110, 112, 113, 117, 118, 151, 166, 216
Colonization, 8, 12
Common Man's Charter: First Steps for Uganda to Move to the Left, 151

Communist revolution, 166
Confucius Institutes, 171
Congo, Democratic Republic of, 3, 6, 8, 60, 117, 118, 133–144, 193, 221
Council of Imams and Preachers of Mombasa, 207
Council of Trent, 92–93
Cultural Revolution, 171
Czarist feudalism, 166

D

Dar es Salaam, 32, 39, 51, 66, 71, 99, 100, 102, 149, 167, 171, 172, 187
Decolonization, 129, 166
De-ethnicization, 97–99, 101, 103
Democracy, 39, 125, 129, 152, 153, 201, 202, 210, 222
Diaspora, 109, 130, 151, 172, 203
Dis-Arabization, 96, 112
Dis-Islamization, 92–97, 99, 112

E

Ebrahim, Hussein, 20, 45, 50
  Kinjeketile, 20, 45
Economic cold war, 147, 168–174, 222
Education for Self-Reliance, 148
El-Najah, 41
El-Sisi, Aldel Fattah, 182
El Usbueyah, 60
Endesheni mapambano (Onward with the struggle), 126
Ethnic rivalry, 13
European colonization, 8, 12

F

Fanon, Frantz, 112, 113
Faqihi, Mgeni bin, 19
  Utenzi wa Rasi'l Ghuli, 19
Fasseke, Balla, 16
First World War, 2, 6, 8, 18, 22, 57–86, 95, 149, 216
Francophone, 12, 15, 135
Front for National Salvation (FRONASA), 121, 125

G

German civilization, 7
German East Africa, 1, 6–8, 22, 29, 31, 33, 35, 36, 40–43, 46, 58, 59, 63, 66, 67, 72, 73, 95, 96, 128
German language, 6, 40, 44, 63, 65
German rule, 1, 6, 7, 19, 22, 29–54, 64, 66, 72, 215
Gikuyu, 74, 93, 104–108, 162n2, 182, 183
Gikuyu origin, 105
Goldenberg, David Asher, 152
  Swahili on the Prairie, 152
Gorky, Maxim, 158–162
Götzen, Adolf von, 36, 43

H

Habari za Dunia, 111
Habari za Mwezi, 40
Habari za Vita, 80
Habyarimana, Juvenal (President), 131, 138
Haji, Muyaka wa Mwinyi, 17, 58

Harries, Lyndon, 165, 166
Hausa the national language of Nigeria, 13
Hegemonic language, 11
Heine, Bernd, 10
  Kenyan pidgin Swahili, 10
Hindi, 13, 110
Huntington, Samuel, 174
Hutu, 128–134, 137, 138, 143, 144, 217
Hutu militia, 132
Hutu national movement, 130
Hutu-Tutsi dichotomy, 129

Ideological cold war, 24, 147–163, 168, 169, 174, 222
Ideology of indirect rule, 64
Idi Amin Dada, 23, 85, 120, 122, 151, 218
Idris, Sheikh Mohamed, 207–209
Igbo language of Nigeria, 18
Imperial languages, 12, 14, 74
Imperial power, 62, 66, 197, 215
Interahamwe, 137, 138
Internalized conflicts, 14
Islam, 5, 7, 8, 19, 30, 38, 41, 42, 49, 63, 71, 72, 93–95, 98, 99, 132, 156, 163, 168, 174, 180–182, 193, 194, 199–204, 209, 210, 216, 223
Islamic nationalism, 19
Islamic Party of Kenya (IPK), 185
Islamization, 98, 99, 132
Islamophobic, 194

Jamahddini, Karim, 37
  Utenzi wa Vita vya Maji Maji, 37
Jinping, Xi, 170
Juma, Bwana Heri Bin, 32
Jumbe, 36, 43, 44, 46

Kabila, Joseph, 140
Kabila, Laurent, 138–140
Kagame, Paul, 130, 131, 137, 138, 218
Kagera war of 1979, 23
Kaggia, Bildad, 150
Kareithi, Peter, 20, 107
  Kaburi bila Msalaba, 20, 107
Kasim, Sheikh Muhammad, 202
  Utumwa katika Uislamu na Dini Nyinginezo, 202
Kawegere, Fortunatus, 155–157
  Shamba la Wanyama, 155, 157
Kenya African National Union, 150
Kenya Defence Forces, 194
Kenya Kwetu, 80
Kenya Land and Freedom Army (KLFA), 157
Kenyatta, Jomo, 149, 158, 164, 182, 206
Kibaki, Mwai, 184
Kibao, Salim, 20, 104
  Utenzi wa Uhuru wa Kenya, 20, 104
Kibara, 75
Kikeya, 69, 70, 78
Kikongo, 8, 140
Kimathi, Dedan, 157, 158

King's African Rifles (KAR), 2, 22, 59, 66–70, 72–74, 76–78, 85, 89, 99, 113, 216
Kisangani Swahili, 140
Kiswahili cha Bara [Kenya Upcountry Swahili], 10
Kivu Swahili, 140
Krapf, Johann Ludwig, 30
Kubai, Fred, 103, 111
Kwetu, 109

L

Laden, Osama bin, 186, 187
League of Nations, 65
Leopold II, King, 60
Lingala, 62, 140, 142
Linguistic nationalism, 13, 14
Linguistic plurality, 64
Lodhi, Abdulaziz Y., 5
    Oriental Influences in Swahili, 5
Lord's Resistance Army, 138
Lumumba, Patrice, 136, 137
Lusophone, 12
Luwero war of 1989, 23

M

Maimai, 139
Maisha Amerika/Uislamu Amerika, 199, 203, 205–207, 210
Maji Maji war, 7, 19, 20, 22, 29, 35, 37–39, 42, 43, 45, 46, 49, 51, 54, 57, 179, 215, 216, 223
Mambo Leo, 80–82, 110
Mau Mau Emergency, 104, 108
Mau Mau war, 20, 104, 106, 107, 157, 180, 223

Mazrui, Ali, 35, 44, 64, 103, 119, 120, 137, 141, 154, 167, 185, 201, 206, 216
Mboya, Tom, 108, 149
Meinhof, Carl, 41, 42, 45
Mgumi, Zahidi, 17
Militant Nazism, 2
Mkwawa, Chief, 19
Mohamed, Elijah, 163
Moi, Daniel Arap, 182–184, 187, 206
Mombasa, 5, 16, 17, 32, 58, 71, 72, 99, 101, 102, 106, 186, 189, 190, 207
Mombasa Republican Council (MRC), 185
Monotheistic religions, 8, 94
Mosques, 34, 63, 84, 132, 207
Msimulizi, 40
Muhanika, Henry, 20, 122
    Utenzi wa Vita vya Kagera, 20, 122
Muscat, 17, 151
Museveni, Yoweri Kaguta, 23, 121, 125, 130, 131, 138, 218
Muslim, Farouk, 20, 106
    Mkuki wa Moto, 20, 106
Muslim-related terrorism, 182
Muslim-Western divide, 174
Mvita, 17
Mwafrika, 109, 110
Mwamuyinga, Mkwaniyika Munyigumba (Chief), 34
Mwangaza, 110
Mwaruka, Ramadhani, 49
    Utenzi wa Jamhuri ya Tanzania, 49

Mwengo, Abu Bakari, 19
  Utenzi wa Katirifu, 19
Mwengo, Shomari, 19
  Utenzi wa Mkwawa, 19
Mzee, Said, 20, 106
  Mkuki wa Moto, 20, 106

N

Nation of Islam, 163
National Resistance Army (NRA), 18, 20, 23, 118–128, 130, 131, 139, 217, 223
National Virtual Translation Center, 195
Ngwale, Kinjeketile, 20, 37, 47, 49
Nkrumah, Kwame, 164–166
Northern Frontier District (NFD), 188, 190
Northern Frontier District Liberation Movement (NFDLM), 190
Nyasaland, 72, 78
Nyerere, Julius Kambarage, 43, 54, 109, 121, 122, 124, 138, 141, 148, 153, 154, 156, 166, 219
Nyota ya Kirinyaga, 111–112
Nywinywila, 42, 54

O

Obama, Barrack, 170
Obote, Milton, 18, 20, 23, 119, 121, 124, 125, 127, 130, 151, 218
Oginga, Jaramogi Odinga, 150, 157
Operation Linda Nchi, 188–189, 191

P

Pan-Africanism, 164–166
Pax-Americana, 196
Peace Corps, 152
Peking Foreign Language Press, 150
  Cheche Moja Yaweza Kuanzisha Moto Mbugani, 150
People's Republic of China, 150, 151
Peters, Carl, 31
Politics of oil, 181
Popular Front for the Liberation of Palestine (PFLP), 181, 186
Portuguese, 5, 6, 16, 58, 59
Postcolonial Africa, 12, 14
Preponderant language, 11
Proletarianization, 101, 102
Propaganda, 16, 17, 24, 59, 60, 79, 105, 106, 110, 111, 147, 153–155, 157, 201, 215
Pwani na Bara, 40

R

Racial cold war, 147, 163–168, 174
Racism, 99, 100, 147, 164, 181
Radio Moscow, 110, 153, 158
Rafiki Yangu, 40
Rafiq, Yunus, 21
  Swahili Fighting Words (documentary film), 21
Rahman, Sheikh Omar Abdul, 196
Rebmann, Johannes, 30
Regional integration, 66, 137, 141–143, 221
Robert, Shaaban, 20, 82, 83, 149
  Utenzi wa Vita vya Uhuru, 82
Roehl, Karl, 95, 96

Index

Rogo, Sheikh Mohammad Aboud, 186, 193
Rwanda, 3, 6, 9, 58, 60, 117, 118, 128–136, 138, 139, 141–144, 216–218, 223
Rwandan community in Uganda, 130
Rwandan Muslims, 132
Rwandan refugees, 130, 131
Rwanda Patriotic Front (RPF), 23, 128–136, 139, 216, 217
Rwanda's swahilization, 132
Rwigyema, Fred, 131

S

Said, Badru, 158, 158n1
Salim, Abushiri bin, 32, 33
Sauti ya Mvita, 106
Sauti ya TANU, 109
Seko, Mobutu Sese, 18, 136, 137
Shaba Swahili, 61, 140
Shifta War, 20, 188, 190
Singh, Makhan, 103
Society for German colonization, 31
Somalia, 3, 23, 25, 141–143, 187–193
South Sudan, 2, 141–144, 218, 219
Soviet Union, 24, 147, 150, 152–155, 158–161, 158n1, 168, 169, 222
Soweto uprising of 1976, 15
Standard Swahili, 2, 7, 8, 66, 68, 71, 72, 75, 96, 97, 190
Steere, Bishop Edward, 30
Sudanese soldiers, 59
Sultan, Seyyid Said bin, 5
Sundjata, 16

Superpower rivalries, 148
Swahili Diaspora, 151
Swahili poetry, 19, 21, 83
 mashairi ya kulumbana (*malumbano*), 21
Swahili-Portuguese wars, 5
Swahilists, 25, 26

T

Tanganyika African National Union (TANU), 43, 54, 109, 110, 156
Tanzanian refugee camps, 142, 217
Tanzania People's Defence Force (TPDF), 121, 122
Tanzaphilia, 167
Terminological intelligibility, 25, 26
Terrorism, 1, 2, 24, 175, 179–210, 215, 223
Trade unionism in East Africa, 10
Trade union movement, 103
Tshiluba, 8, 140
Tshisekedi, Félix, 140
Tutsi, 128–131, 134, 138, 139, 143, 144, 217
Tutsi genocide, 131
Tutsi refugees, 130, 217

U

Uganda National Liberation Army (UNLA), 122, 125, 126
Uganda National Liberation Front (UNLF), 121, 122
Uganda People's Congress (UPC), 124–126, 151

Ujamaa, 9, 134, 148, 153, 154, 156, 163, 166, 174
Ujamaa: The Basis of African Socialism, 156
Union for Democracy and Social Progress, 140
United Nations (UN), 130, 134, 161
Upcountry Swahili, 10, 75
Urundi, 6

V

Vil-Nkomo, Sibusiso, 165
Voice of America, 24, 153

W

War against terrorism, 1, 24, 180, 187, 193, 195, 205

Washington File, 199–201, 203, 204
Wazalendo wa NRA, 126
Wei Jinzhi, 173
Western cultural values, 204
World War I, 2, 6, 8, 18, 22, 57–86, 95, 149, 216
World War II, 10, 18, 22, 57–86, 102, 109, 149, 153

Z

Zanzibar, 5, 29, 31–33, 45, 49, 50, 60, 62, 66, 71, 72, 75, 78, 96, 100, 142, 148, 150, 151, 155, 156, 158, 158n1, 165
Zanzibar revolution, 150, 151, 156
Zuhra, 109, 110

Printed in the United States
by Baker & Taylor Publisher Services